.8574

Economic Reform in
Poland: The Aftermath
of Martial Law 1981-1988

RUSSIAN AND EAST EUROPEAN STUDIES, VOLUME 1

Editors: Stephen K. Batalden, *Russian and East European Studies Consortium,*
Arizona State University

Thomas S. Noonan, *Russian and East European Studies Program,*
University of Minnesota

RUSSIAN AND EAST EUROPEAN STUDIES

Series Editors

Stephen K. Batalden
Thomas S. Noonan

Editorial Board

Russian and East European Studies is cosponsored by
the Arizona State University Russian and East European Studies Consortium and
the University of Minnesota Russian and East European Studies Program.

RUSSIAN AND EAST EUROPEAN STUDIES

Editors:

Stephen K. Batalden
Russian and East European Studies Consortium
Arizona State University

Thomas S. Noonan
Russian and East European Studies Program
University of Minnesota

Library of Congress Cataloging-in-Publication Data

Economic reform in Poland : the aftermath of marital law, 1981-1988 /
    edited by David M. Kemme and Institute for East-West Security
    Studies.
        p.   cm. — (Russian and East European studies ; v. 1)
    A selection of revised papers originally presented at a conference
held Oct. 1987 at Wichita State University, sponsored by the Wichita
State University Center for Management Development.
    Includes bibliographical references and index.
    ISBN 1-55938-288-0
    1.   Poland—Economic policy—1981- —Congresses.   2.   Poland—
Commercial policy—Congresses.   I.   Kemme, David M.   II.   Institute
for East-West Security Studies.   II.   Wichita State University,
Center for Management Development.   IV.   Series: Russian and East
European studies (Greenwich, Conn.) : v. 1.
HC340.3.E3   1991
338.9438′009′048—dc20   90-21774
                                                                          CIP

Copyright © 1991 JAI PRESS INC.
55 Old Post Road, No. 2
Greenwich, Connecticut
06836

JAI PRESS LTD.
118 Pentonville Road
London N1 9JN
England

ISBN NUMBER: 1-55938-288-0

Library of Congress Catalog Card Number: 90-21774

Manufactured in the United States of America

Economic Reform in Poland: The Aftermath of Martial Law 1981-1988

Edited by: **DAVID M. KEMME**

Department of Economics
Wichita State University

and

Institute for East-West
Security Studies
New York, NY

 **JAI PRESS INC.**

Greenwich, Connecticut   *London, England*

To Jan, Sara, and Lindsay
with love,
for their understanding and support

CONTENTS

LIST OF CONTRIBUTORS

Jean F. Boone

Congressional Research Service
Library of Congress
Washington, DC

Josef C. Brada

Department of Economics
Arizona State University
Tempe, AZ

Richard P. Chaykowski

School of Industrial Relations
Queen's University
Kingston, Ontario

Keith Crane

Plan Econ Inc.
Washington, DC

Zbigniew M. Fallenbuchl

Professor Emeritus of Economics
University of Windsor
Windsor, Canada

John P. Hardt

Congressional Research Service
Library of Congress
Washington, DC

Zbigniew Kamecki

Central School of Planning &
    Statistics
Warsaw, Poland

Bartlomiej Kaminski

Department of Government
University of Maryland
College Park, MD

David M. Kemme

Department of Economics
Wichita State University
Wichita, KS and
Institute for East-West
    Security Studies
New York, NY

Karol Lutkowski

Central School of Planning &
    Statistics
Warsaw, Poland

David Mason

Department of History, Political
    Science, and Geography
Butler University
Indianapolis, IN

Marian Ostrowski

Institute of National Economy
Warsaw, Poland

Ben Slay

Department of Economics
Bates College
Lewiston, ME

Jozef Soldaczuk

Institute of Foreign Trade,
    Economics, and Politics
Warsaw, Poland

Jan Svejnar

Department of Economics
University of Pittsburgh
Pittsburgh, PA

FOREWORD

This work is the first volume in the series, *Russian and East European Studies*. Jointly sponsored by the Arizona State University Russian and East European Studies Consortium and the University of Minnesota Russian and East European Studies Program, this series has been launched to give timely and effective publication to original research in the Slavic field. The series will feature the finest international research in Slavic and East European studies and particularly welcomes contributions from underrepresented areas occasionally overlooked by major commercial publishing outlets. Projected numbers in the series include works from a wide range of disciplines in the humanities and social sciences—from early Slavic history to modern Russian literature in translation, from East European family studies to the history of Soviet sport.

It is particularly timely that the series should begin with a work on economic reform in Poland. Professor Kemme's anthology critically assesses the limits of the economic policies of the 1980s, thereby providing needed perspective on the new economic initiatives currently under way in Poland. In a period of rapid economic change in Eastern Europe, the need for understanding the roots of contemporary economic problems is particularly acute. In one other respect, this anthology establishes an important precedent for the series. In drawing upon contributions from East European scholars, this volume establishes a pattern that will be encouraged in future numbers.

We wish to extend a word of appreciation. The series owes much to the support of Deans Gary Krahenbuhl and Fred Lukermann of the respective Colleges of Liberal Arts and Sciences at Arizona State University and the University of Minnesota.

Stephen K. Batalden
Thomas S. Noonan

PREFACE

The chapters of this book were taken from papers originally presented at a conference on economic reform in Poland at The Wichita State University in October of 1987. The focus of the conference was on the so-called "Second Stage of Reform" initiated in 1986. The papers provide an evaluation of the 1986 reform proposals in the context of the successes and failures of the "First Stage of Reform" initiated in 1981/1982. Since that time events have swept away the 1986 proposals for reasons conference participants predicted: the proposals did not allow true marketization nor expunge the state from directly controlling the economy.

The papers selected for publication in this book are those that explain the limitations of the earlier reform proposals and provide clear lessons for students of economic reform in socialist economics. The papers have been revised to reflect events since the conference to the extent relevant. As such the papers focus on the events, strategy, and proposals of the 1981-1988 period. The obstacles to reform in Poland evidenced in this period are now being addressed in the most radical reform in history. The 1990 reform program advanced by Minister of Finance Leszik Balcerowicz represents the most radical reform program of any postwar socialist state: an attempt to transform a socialist centrally planned economy into a market economy with a significant role for private enterprise. While the papers published in this book could not have predicted such events, they do provide a discussion of the earlier failings and the obstacles which still must be overcome even for the 1990 program to succeed.

The conference at The Wichita State University was attended by over 120 persons. Thirty of the leading scholars on Poland in economics, political science, and sociology from the United States, Poland, and Canada participated directly. The conference was sponsored by The Wichita State University Center for Management Development with funding from The Office of the Vice President of Academic Affairs, the Dean of the Barton School of Business and the Economics Department. Partial travel funding for the Polish participants was provided by IREX. I personally would like to thank several individuals at The Wichita State University, not only for financial support but also for expressing their personal support and encouragement. These are Gerald McDougall, then Chair of the Department of Economics and now Associate Vice President of Academic Affairs, Joyce A. Scott, Executive Vice President of Academic Affairs, Douglas Sharp, Dean of the Barton School of Business, Dong C. Cho, Chair of the Department of Economics and Peggy Yockey, Director of the Center for Management Development.

In addition, there were many individuals who assisted in preparing and administering the conference program and in preparing this manuscript for publication. Josef Alba, Arnaz Binsardisastrowardojo, Carol Sagerty, and Brenda Arnold provided assistance at the conference. Diana Blackmon, Anne Corriston, Anna Yamada, Kristi Bahrenburg, and Orin Kurland assisted in preparation of the manuscript. I would also like to thank Stephen K. Batalden and Thomas Noonan, the editors of the *Russian and East European Studies* series, Sean Tape and Melissa Jones for copyediting and JAI Press for their efforts in bringing this work to print.

David M. Kemme
January, 1991

OBSTACLES TO REFORM:

1981-1988

David M. Kemme

Poland in 1991 faces enormous political and economic difficulties. The first democratically elected government in Eastern Europe is now attempting to transform a predominately centrally planned economy into a market economy. There is no clear guide for the new government. The transition from central planning to markets has never been made before. It is clear though that the previous attempts to move in that direction—stated goals of the earlier Polish reform attempts—have failed. Nonetheless there are important lessons to be learned from these experiences, not only for the current Polish leadership, but also for the leadership in those countries in which the reform process is just beginning, for example, Czechoslovakia, the Soviet Union, and to a lesser extent, Bulgaria and Romania.

Reforming the economic system of a nation is no mean task. Reform affects every dimension of society—political, economic, sociological—and all must be considered. This book examines what was officially termed the "First Stage of Reform" in Poland, initiated in July of 1981 and implemented during the early martial law period beginning in December of 1981. Its successes and failures through 1988 provide the basis for the dramatic changes

1

now being implemented. This chapter provides first the background for a discussion of the "First Stage of Reforms" and then an overview of the chapters to follow. The chapters provide a detailed analysis of the reforms of this period—from the reform proposal's dependence upon the actual performance of the economy to the practical suggestions of step-by-step political re-engagement with the United States, now being completed. The contributors make clear that the reform proposals and their implementation continued to be grossly inadequate as a means of increasing economic efficiency, enhancing economic growth or achieving external balance. They should, of course, be read with an understanding of the context in which they were written. Both domestic and external political pressures were providing a strong impetus for rapid change, not only in Poland but throughout Eastern Europe.

Economic reform in Poland is not a new phenomenon, nor is it new to Eastern Europe. Yet Poland's postwar history, shaped by crises and ineffectual reform responses, is unique.[1] And, this pattern continued through the 1980s. Whether or not the dramatic changes envisaged by the Mazowiecki government will succeed or regress to the political and economic stalemate of every previous reform effort is an open question. Many of the fundamental issues raised in the chapters below, for instance, flaws of the first stage reforms, have been addressed by the Council of Ministers' economic reform program of October 1989, and a series of legislative and institutional changes designed to move the economy away from the centrally planned economy to a market economy.[2]

Serious debate on economic reform began in 1956-57 and resulted in the decollectivization of agriculture, the implementation of domestic price reforms and the institutionalization of workers' councils. While these reforms were the first comprehensive reforms among CMEA countries, the effects of the changes in planning and management techniques were modest. The reform in the economic system, modest as it was, was closely linked to political and social events, as were all the reforms that followed. In this case, workers' disturbances in Poznan and a confrontation with authorities legitimized workers' grievances, highlighted social discontent, and led to development of the reform program. These events were only the beginning of society's continuing challenge to the Polish United Workers' Party's exclusive claim to political power.

Political crises in 1968 and 1970 led to more significant economic reforms in 1971-1973 and, more important, to a new development strategy opening the economy to international markets. The economic successes of the mid-1970s were also coupled with an increase in political activism and a budding free trade-union movement. Despite economic growth the schism between the government and dissatisfied social groups grew. Conflict between the Catholic church and the government escalated as a result of revisions to the Polish Constitution. Implementation of price increases in 1976 resulted in a wave of strikes. A harsh government response resulted in the creation of KOR, the Committee for the Defense of Workers, and an alliance between discontented workers and intellectuals. Then, when external economic pressures—excessive debt payments—forced a curtailment of imports in 1977, the seeds of an economic crisis were sown. The growing dissatisfaction of the population, accompanied by a greater willingness to express that discontent via political action, did not bode well for the future.

Economic performance, measured by the gross domestic product, peaked in 1978 and then deteriorated significantly. Even the modest annual plans for 1979 and 1980 could not be met. The curtailment of imported inputs, upon which industry was acutely dependent, led to a fall in industrial production. Crop production declined 25-30% as a result of bad weather. The combination of these factors led in turn to significant declines in national income in 1980. Attempts to correct imbalances in the consumer goods sector via price increases for food led to an outburst of popular discontent and the formation of Solidarity in August 1980.

During the sixteen months from the creation of Solidarity to the declaration of martial law in December 1981, economic performance plummeted and the debate on political and economic reform raged. Following Solidarity's success, other groups including students, intellectuals, and peasants, organized to demand change. Within the Polish United Workers Party the debate to accommodate social change and the demands of the public led to calls for "horizontal linkages," between political organizations, usurping the political center, and calls for an "orthodox" solution, strengthening vertical linkages, of re-exerting control by the center. On December 13, 1981 an end was put to the Polish renewal as a "state of war" was declared by General Wojciech Jaruzelski.

The reform proposals, two basic laws and enabling legislation, passed by the Sejm in the fall of 1981 were partially suspended and modified in early 1982. This new collection of reform legislation has come to be known as the "First Stage" of reform. This book focuses on this package of reforms, its implementation—successes and failures—and the implications. While there has been dramatic change in the political system, the foundation of the economic system is only now being reconstructed. While the political and economic system evolves, the issues raised in the chapters below must still be addressed.

The book is divided into two major sections. Part I focuses on the domestic economy and the political and economic consequences of the reforms to date. Part II focuses on international influences and Poland's connections to both the West and the East.

Zbigniew Fallenbuchl examines the initial 1986-1990 Five Year Plan, the underlying strategy of the plan, its dependence on reform proposals, and the prospects for success. Economic success in the early 1990s depends critically upon the ability to increase economic efficiency. According to Fallenbuchl the pattern of growth must become more intensive, but this cannot be obtained without additional far-reaching reform, changes in the allocation of investment and a reduction in internal and external disequilibria—all problems yet to be resolved. The plan also called for these types of changes, but, as Fallenbuchl emphasizes, these changes had been recommended by the Polish government before and little along these lines was actually accomplished during the first stage of reform. The latest reform proposals of this period, advanced in 1987, contained some of these elements but Fallenbuchl still regarded them as insufficient.

Marian Ostrowski, however, notes that there had been significant changes in the economy which should not go unnoticed. There was agreement that the existing methods of organizing and managing the economy were not the best suited for the problems Poland faced. The preconditions for reform were slowly being met and the current state of the economy was (and is) an important element among these preconditions. After surveying the state of the economy Ostrowski concludes that society's awareness of economic interrelationships during 1985-1987 had reached unprecedented levels and the capacity for economic development now rests on the government's ability to create and adjust to investment opportunities resulting from radical economic reform.

The whole complex of relations between the socialist state and society lie at the crux of the reform failures. Bartlomiej Kaminski argues that the limited political capacities of the state to impose necessary adjustments and circumvent political constraints on economic policy-making resulted in the failure of the first stage of reforms and had already undermined the implementation of the second stage of reforms in 1987. The institutional legacies of state socialism had displayed substantive resistance to change. The economic reform measures originally introduced were sidetracked by bureaucratic obstacles in 1984-1987 and the state and economy remained fused as one. Enterprises were still financially dependent upon central planners. National income distributed through the state budget was actually higher in 1985 than in 1978. The overlay of financial instruments on the administrative hierarchy of central planning produced an array of conflicting signals. Direct administrative mechanisms had not been weakened and rather than simplifying the management of the economy the Polish government had complicated it. The reform measures simply did not produce a clear boundary between the economy and the state. The search for a means to increase economic efficiency without sacrificing the power of the state had failed, according to Kaminski.

We may gain further insight as to how Poland will adjust to the radical reforms suggested by Ostrowski and Kaminski from the work of Keith Crane. Crane provides an assessment of the reform in state-owned industry. He provides an overview of changes in the system of planning and management in a step-by-step description of the organization of industry and the economic agents involved. There is little doubt that there had been significant changes, from the economic center to the enterprise manager. What was unclear was whether or not these changes had a bottom line impact upon productivity and economic efficiency. According to Crane neither aggregate economic data nor extensive interviews with enterprise managers and government officials provide a favorable impression of the efficacy of the reform. Markets were not yet functioning properly and managers were faced with a plethora of constantly changing regulations. Microeconomic policy goals rather than efficiency took precedence. While Ostrowski argues that society's level of awareness of the need for radical change had increased, Crane argues that the primary reasons for the failure of the reform to increase efficiency was the Polish central authorities' unwillingness to bear the political costs of antagonizing powerful interest groups and the resulting loss of power.

One of the most important policy goals that had supplanted the drive for efficiency was maintaining internal equilibrium. Karol Lutkowski outlines the role of the monetary system in attaining that goal. Enterprises were given more flexibility in utilizing their financial results, that is, profits, and were relieved of the necessity to utilize bank credits for financing investments. Self-financing became a real possibility, but it was not made fully operational. Lutkowski argues that the reform was an open ended process with numerous problems yet to be resolved. The role of the rate of interest, for example, was yet to be addressed. The cost of credit did not constrain the demand for credit, because the granting of credits by the central bank was not based on creditworthiness or economic efficiency, but simply to accommodate planned purchases by enterprises. As a result, monetary policy was extremely inflationary, destroying any semblance of aggregate equilibrium. Like Ostrowski, Lutkowski argues that there had been significant accomplishments, but there is still a long difficult road ahead.

All of the aforementioned chapters address problems in the domestic area. We must not forget the interaction between domestic reform forces and the international pressures which provided the impetus for reform. The second half of the book addresses Poland's opportunities and constraints arising from direct and indirect links with the international community—both East and West. The system of foreign trade that links the international and domestic economy has been the focus of significant debate. Political alliances and tension among partners and adversaries have complicated otherwise straightforward reform suggestions.

The economic policy chosen by planners is only part of the solution. Maintenance of political and economic relations between the West and the East is a two way street. Jozef Sołdaczuk argues that the second half of the eighties was and the 1990s will continue to be characterized by a return to détente and more favorable conditions for economic cooperation and development. Improved relations between the Soviet Union and the United States have had a positive effect on Eastern Europe, and Poland in particular. Overall East-West trade turnover contracted during the 1980s, primarily as a result of internal economic difficulties in East European countries. To a lesser extent the contraction was a result of unfavorable terms of trade movements, an economic slowdown in Western economies, financial constraints for additional hard currency imports for East European countries, and other political factors. Given a relaxation of political tensions, lower world interest rates and reforms in the domestic economy designed to increase participation in world markets, greater opportunities for East-West cooperation will develop. Direct government-to-government agreements and renegotiated loans will enhance these opportunities. While many of these steps have been taken, no one foresaw the complete collapse of the Council for Mutual Economic Assistance and the resulting host of new trade issues that Poland now faces.

A major constraint to such development opportunities, though, is the current state of indebtedness of the Polish economy. At the end of 1986, this amounted to some $33.5 billion owed to the West (17.0% of the total to the Federal Republic of Germany, 9.2% to France, 8.1% to the U.S., 8.1% to Austria, 6.0% to the U.K., and 3.3% to Italy) and the equivalent of $6.5 billion in transferable rubles (primarily owed to the USSR). This has grown to nearly $40.0 billion owed to the West alone at the end of 1989. Zbigniew Kamecki examines the problems associated with servicing the debt and the constraints on the economy which it causes. Initially, the development policy of the 1970s provided a manageable inflow of Western capital. The resulting flow of imports and the lack of exports to pay for them quickly accelerated and by the mid-1970s the investment stream was too much to be absorbed. The capacities of domestic construction, transportation, and industrial enterprises were quickly exceeded. Investment results were not realized according to plan, creating a shortage of intermediate goods and further increasing the demand for imports.

The servicing cost of the debts was also accelerating as debt repayment schedules began to overlap and world interest rates crept upward. The average length of credits was six years in 1975 but only three years in 1981. The overall debt servicing requirements may not have been a problem if exports would have grown as expected. The government's export development and promotion program failed to generate the anticipated results. In the 1980s Poland made tremendous efforts at servicing the debt; the current account deficits declined and the overall servicing requirements were reduced somewhat. Nonetheless, Poland today finds itself unable to service the debt and in need of World Bank and IMF assistance. Ironically, although Poland is not fully servicing its debt, recently negotiated IMF stand-by credits of US$700 million are not being drawn upon. Poland is running a balance of payments surplus of over US$3 billion for the first three quarters of 1990.

It is important to note that within any foreign trade mechanism economic policy decisions may dramatically influence the direction and composition of trade and overall economic growth. The economic development policy initiated in the 1970s was followed with great interest by other less developed countries as a potential model worth emulating. The strategy of borrowing heavily to import Western technology to modernize the economy and build a strong export sector to later pay off the debt, however, was critically dependent on investing in industrial sectors that had export potential. Jan Svejnar and Richard Chaykowski argue that these sectors were, and still are, exportable services—light industry, forestry, the food industry, construction, agriculture, and wood and paper. These sectors, however, did not receive adequate investment and were not designated for export development. Those sectors which did receive extensive investment resources and were developed for export were primarily in the area of mechanical engineering and chemicals. The strategy chosen was a high risk strategy in that it emphasized for development sectors with high import requirements and relatively low value added. The failure of the development strategy should have been foreseen. The fact that the low import content, high value added sectors were still not being promoted was not a good sign.

In many ways, the reform of Poland's foreign trade system and development of foreign linkages paralleled earlier changes in Hungary. Ben Slay compares and contrasts modifications in the two foreign trade systems. While the reform programs of each country were initiated in quite different environments—a relatively open economy with domestic equilibrium for Hungary and a somewhat more closed economy and high levels of internal imbalance in Poland—both countries faced generally unfavorable terms of trade movements and high levels of hard currency debt. Many of the general principles of the Hungarian 1968 reforms can be found in the 1980-1981 reforms in Poland. Major institutional changes included a reorganization of the Ministry of Foreign Trade designed to loosen its control on foreign trade organizations (FTOs), increasing the number of FTOs and the competition between FTOs, and increasing the ability for enterprises to directly participate in foreign trade. In Poland, however, the Ministry had not effectively relaxed its control over FTOs and in 1987 additional steps were taken to provide greater competition among FTOs and lessen control by the Ministry. Even these measures were ineffective, however, and the reform legislation approved in December 1989 goes much further.

In both Poland and Hungary the reforms of the 1970s and early 1980s have also sought to use world prices to rationalize domestic prices and effect a transition away from direct foreign trade planning toward a system of financial instruments. The new economic mechanisms were intended to orient the economy toward production for export. In Poland the reforms also called for a more active exchange rate policy: a market for hard currency and the implementation of a system of hard currency retention accounts allowing enterprises to utilize hard currency earnings independent of central decision makers. While all of these changes are seen positively and provide a stimulus for export production, Slay concludes that the Polish foreign trade mechanism of 1988 remained largely unreformed in practice.

The political and economic ties are particularly complex. David Mason, Josef Brada, and Jean Boone and John Hardt examine the international political and economic dimension. Mason argues that the "new thinking" in the Soviet Union promises dramatic changes in the nature of Soviet-East European relations. "Socialist internationalism" previously used to justify direct interventions by the Soviet Union has been downplayed and replaced with a movement toward polycentralism. Glasnost' and perestroika are the result of challenges to the legitimacy of the Soviet regime, now more and more dependent on economic success and satisfaction

of consumer wants—a situation faced by Poland over a decade
earlier.

Significantly, the Soviets were admitting that the Soviet model
of central planning may not have been the most appropriate for
Eastern Europe. They began to encourage reform in order to
stimulate the faltering East European economies, insure political
stability, and test Soviet reforms in the East European context.
Thus, the changes in the Soviet Union have served to legitimize
the earlier reform process in Poland and provided the opportunity
for Warsaw to push forward. Of course the responses of all East
European countries are not the same. Poland and Hungary are
tending to lead the reform process, with Czechoslovakia close
behind. The fall of the Berlin Wall and sudden integration of the
GDR into the FRG was unpredictable and will have economic
consequences for some time to come. Only in Bulgaria and
Romania is there still hestitation and some resistance to change.

Brada continues the discussion of the impact upon Eastern
Europe of the Soviet reform discussion by focusing on
Czechoslovakia, Hungary, and Poland. Arguing that there is
sufficient diversity in terms of economic circumstance and reform
experience to allow some generalizations, Brada concluded that the
seeds of reform sown by Gorbachev are likely to fall on barren
ground in Czechoslovakia *unless* there are significant changes in
the political leadership. Neither the political nor economic forces
favored reform as strongly as in the Soviet Union—economic
reform would take place only as a result of political changes caused
by external pressures, not internal. In Hungary, talk of reform has
dominated economic and political life for years. According to
Brada, however, Hungary was not likely to press the Gorbachev
openings to their limit. He argued that there is a strong belief that
reform programs have become dysfunctional—hindering
economic development. Reforms have hindered the implementation of macroeconomic policy, and efforts to strengthen incentives
in a period of austerity have resulted in a more unequal income
distribution.

The case of Poland is more complex. Unlike Czechoslovakia at
that time, there certainly were domestic, political, and economic
pressures for reform. But, like Hungary, the economic crisis was
not solely the result of the system but the result of policy decisions.
The reform in Poland was complicated by the extreme domestic

disequilibrium. Brada argues that, similar to measures in Hungary, microeconomic reform measures in Poland were being implemented to address an essentially macroeconomic problem. Furthermore, self-financing, bankruptcy of enterprises— eliminating inefficient producers—and other efficiency enhancing measures had not been realized. The large monetary overhang, the existing rules of wage formation, and continuing government deficits were (and continue to be) the primary source of inflation. None of them were addressed in the reform programs of 1981-82 or 1986-87. Again, whether or not Poland's leaders address the macroeconomic problems depends upon their political will, but resolution of these problems is a prerequisite for the success of efficiency enhancing measures. Today external pressures—the International Monetary Fund and World Bank—are forcing the government to implement a program of reform and restructuring which may not have been acceptable otherwise. While the government has bravely implemented a purposeful austerity program, the total costs to society have not yet been fully felt.

Given the strong tendencies during this period for Poland to move closer to the Soviet Union what is the role of the United States and the international financial community? Boone and Hardt offer a careful analysis of the interaction of policy forces originating not only from the Polish state and society, but also the Soviet Union, the United States, and the international financial community. These major actors can contribute to fulfillment of a strategy for significant progress or lead to complete gridlock. They argue that in 1986-1987 a consensus emerged on the need for Poland to implement its reform blueprint, to move beyond reform rhetoric toward concrete actions. The admission of Poland to the IMF, new reform initiatives in the Soviet Union, Jaruzelski's renewed commitment to reform, and the U.S. initiation of the step-by-step reengagement with Poland, all set the stage for real reform. While each action alone was not sufficient, taken together they provided the basis for significant change.

In summary, we may argue that there were significant changes in society's perceptions, opinions, attitudes, or "feelings" toward reform and systemic change during the 1981-88 period. It was also clear that the 1981-82 and 1986-87 reform programs must be judged as failures. The stage was set for the government and party to introduce dramatic programs for reform. And, indeed, these dramatic changes are being introduced. However, because the fundamental obstacles to reform posed by the system of state socialism were not removed, these reforms, like those sweeping the rest of Eastern Europe were originally driven by external forces. It was Mikhail Gorbachev who served as the impetus for reform, and it was Western multilateral financial institutions which insisted upon meaningful economic change. In Poland these changes took the form of a reform program and appropriate legislation approved by the Polish Parliament in December of 1989 and the IMF restructuring package. The reform program presented by Minister of Finance Balcerowicz calls for dramatic moves to introduce markets and remove price controls, break up state monopolies and privatize state enterprises. In addition, the macroeconomic stabilization program was designed to halt the hyper-inflation and put an end to chronic shortages. To do so the program called for ending subsidies and cutting the government budget deficit, stabilizing the exchange rate, making the zloty convertible, and implementing a monetary policy designed to achieve positive real interest rates.

In addition to the stabilization program there was a series of critical legislative and institutional changes designed to enhance markets and private sector activities. The four laws which marked extraordinary breaks with the past are: (1) The Law on Economic Activity, which removed limits on the number of employees and restrictive licensing and registration requirements for privately owned firms; (2) the Law on Foreign Economic Activity, which greatly liberalized joint venture regulations; (3) the Law on Counteracting Monopolistic Practices, which created the Anti-Monopoly Office and empowered it to act against enterprises engaging in anti-competitive behavior; and (4) the recent Law on Privatization, which provides the basis for the privatization of socialized economic activity.

Both the macroeconomic policy and the institutional changes are expected to bring about a massive restructuring of the economy. Unemployment and large differences in incomes will appear for the first time in the post-World War II period. How society as a whole reacts to these changes is yet to be seen. Further, as most of the authors have argued, the successful implementation of these programs depends on the willingness of party officials and government bureaucrats to give up control over economic decision making at the enterprise level and releasing the forces of the market. These programs must be realized not only by the new government taking control in Warsaw, but also by the bureaucrats and managers remaining in charge. The authors of these chapters have proven remarkably prescient, touching on nearly every critical issue that Polish reformers of the past had failed to solve. The Balcerowicz strategy called for taking on reform in every dimension, simultaneously and without hesitation in order to overcome the bureaucratic inertia which had doomed the gradualist strategy of the earlier reform programs. If the program stays on course, the 1990s will indeed prove to be a decade of unprecedented socioeconomic change, not only in Poland but in all of Eastern Europe.

ACKNOWLEDGMENTS

I would like to thank Phil Hersch and Ben Slay for helpful comments on an earlier draft of this chapter.

NOTES

1.   For details of political crises, see Jack Bielasiak. "The Evolution of Crises in Poland." *Polish Politics: Edge of the Abyss.* New York: Praeger Publishers, 1984.
2.   Preliminary details of this program are given in the report for the Council of Ministers, "Outline of Economic Program for Poland," Warsaw, October 1989. Detailed legislation and specific proposals are still being fashioned at this time.

PART I

AN EVALUATION OF ECONOMIC PERFORMANCE AND REFORM IN THE 1981-1988 PERIOD

THE 1986-1990 FIVE YEAR PLAN:
STRATEGY AND REFORM DEPENDENCY

Zbigniew M. Fallenbuchl

I. INTRODUCTION

In accordance with the new law on socioeconomic planning, the government presented the first draft of the 1986-1990 Five Year Plan to the *Sejm* (Parliament) on May 10, 1985, in three variants. At the same time a "social consultation" on the plan proposal was invited. A very lively debate followed in the Sejm, in the official and unofficial press, in various consultative bodies, professional associations, labor unions, and political groups. The Sejm finally approved the plan on December 18, 1986, at the end of its first year. Yet the debate did not end and arguments that the plan should be modified were immediate (Jeziorański 1987, pp. 1, 4). Nonetheless, even with events in Poland, the economy was still guided by the broad outlines of this plan.

In the original three variants, different increases in the Produced Net Material Product (PNMP), net value of national product excluding services, and different rates of growth of per capita consumption depended on reduction in material intensity of production and the volume of investment.[1]

Variant I envisaged an increase in PNMP of 16.0% during the five-year period, or 3.0% annually, and an increase in the Distributed Net Material Product (DNMP), reduced by the value of export and increased by the value of import, of 14.0%, or 3.5% annually, and the average rate of growth of per capita consumption of 1.5%. It would have required a reduction in material intensity per unit of PNMP of 6.1% over the period and total investment outlays of 9,600 billion zloty, as compared with 7,900 billion invested in 1981-85. The annual investment would have been 3.9% and the share of investment in DNMP would have needed to be increased from 18.3% in 1985 to 20.0% in 1990.

Variant II envisaged an increase of 19.0% in PNMP, or 3.5% annually, of 17.2% in DNMP, or 3.2% annually, and an average rate of growth of per capita consumption of 1.8%. It would have required, however, a reduction in material intensity of 8.6% over the period and 10,000 billion zloty for investment (4.7% rate of growth and the share of investment in DNMP of 21.1%).

Variant III would have resulted in an increase of 21.5% of PNMP, or 4.0% annually, a 19.8% increase in DNMP, or 3.7% annually, and a rate of growth of per capita consumption of 2.0%. It would have required a reduction in material intensity of 10.3% over the period and 10,300 billion zloty for investment (5.4% annually and 22.0% share).

The main objective of the plan was to achieve balanced and sustained economic growth. Under severe internal and external constraints, achieving this growth required expanding international economic relations, modernizing and restructuring the economy, implementing an anti-inflationary policy, and improving the economic mechanism (Gorywoda 1985, p. 9).

The proposal was soon criticized as "three variants of the same strategy" (Jeziorański 1985, p. 2), and "variants which are not really variants" (Nasiłowski 1985, p. 2). The Sejm accepted the middle variant but continued to express concern about the strategy. When, at the end of 1985, the government introduced eleven amendments to the 1982 economic reform legislation, explaining that the corrections were necessary to fulfill the plan, the Sejm objected. Some of the corrections were accepted in a modified form, others were rejected. Taking into consideration serious constraints and the lack of internal and external balance, the question was which strategy would give better results: the economic reform attempting to introduce the self-regulating mechanism of controlled market or the return to the strict administrative controls of the traditional command system?

Officially, the first strategy had been accepted as the result of another lively debate. It was supported by the official decision of the Tenth Party Congress that took place in July 1986 and by "The Theses on the Second Stage of the Economic Reform," published by the Secretariat of the Committee on Economic Reform in April 1987.[2] Unofficially, the clash between the two basic approaches continued until the establishment of the Solidarity-dominated government of Tadeusz Mazowiecki.

II. INADEQUACIES OF THE 1986-1990 FIVE YEAR PLAN

In formulating the 1986-1990 Five Year Plan, the planners took into consideration the following constraints:

1. an unsatisfactory demographic situation and a shortage of labor;
2. a very limited supply of raw materials;
3. an unsatisfactory state of capital stock, a large part of which had become obsolete and should have already been replaced;
4. a large volume of unfinished investment projects that had been started during the 1970s and had been selected for continuation even though they were material- and fuel-intensive;
5. a shortage of water and rapidly deteriorating ecological conditions;
6. heavy foreign indebtedness and the difficulty of obtaining new credits.

Most of these constraints were not absolute, but were system-related. While their impact has been reduced by a more far-reaching economic reform, their very existence created obstacles to the introduction of reform. In this way, as has been argued elsewhere (Fallenbuchl 1986a, pp. 135-160), the success of the 1986-1990 Five Year Plan was endangered by the operation of several vicious circles, and the reform debate still must address these problems.

Because of the demographic trends and the policy of granting early and generous retirements, introduced as the result of erroneous fears of unemployment at the early stages of the crisis, there was an apparent shortage of labor. The shortage of labor, however, could have been solved. The solution required granting real autonomy to enterprises in the determination of wages and real self-financing. The enterprises would then be forced to depend on their own profits or fully repayable credits at a high rate of interest, without expecting subsidies, exemptions, and special privileges. This, however, did not appear to be a safe policy to the central administration which, by instinct, tried to solve the shortages of labor by direct administrative measures. These measures included mandatory allocation of labor and wage controls to curb the inflationary spiral, making labor relatively inexpensive. As a result, it was difficult to introduce an economic reform that could have solved the problem of the labor shortage.

The second constraint was that the acute shortage of fuels and raw materials existed because of the systemic limitations on their efficient use, the lack of modern technologies, the lack of a fuel- and material-intensive structure of the economy, and the inability to expand. These constraints could have been removed by developing profitable exports, which would have secured the sufficient supply of fuels and materials from import.

The supply of materials from domestic sources, which represented about 80.0% of total supply, was expected to increase by 11.0% during the five year period. The supply of materials from import was expected to increase by 8-9%, including an increase of 5.0% in the import of fuels. About half of the rate of growth of 19.0% had to be achieved by reduced use of fuels and raw materials. The Planning Commission prepared a list of projects that provided 50.0% of the required saving of fuels and 30.0% of the required saving of other raw materials. The rest of saving was to be induced at the enterprise level by the instruments of the economic system.[3]

It is difficult to expect any improvement in saving fuel and raw materials with low prices of such important commodities as coal, large subsidies, the cost-plus formula used for determining most prices, administrative decisions as to what are "the necessary costs," and no effective economic pressure. In this situation the central authorities are tempted to introduce a greater degree of controls.

The general program of saving fuels and raw materials introduced in 1983, however, had limited success and was able to eliminate only the most obvious inefficiencies (Jeziorański 1986, p. 2).[4] For this reason, the modification of the price system and the financial mechanism was stressed by the Consultative Economic Council as a necessary condition for the better utilization of inputs because "their more economical use cannot be achieved by the preparation of various programs and counting on direct administrative measures."[5]

The supply of fuels and raw materials from imports was limited by Poland's ability to expand the export of manufactured goods. The possibility of exporting raw materials and simple intermediate goods was restricted on both the supply and demand sides. Faced with the balance-of-payments disequilibrium and growing foreign indebtedness, the authorities found it extremely difficult to liberalize trade and exchange controls. Yet without such liberalization it was impossible to make the foreign trade mechanism more flexible, to make it respond quickly to changes in foreign demand, and to compete successfully in world markets. Strict administrative controls could force increases in the export of relatively homogeneous primary and simple intermediate goods but not of manufactured goods. But, the more controls the less successful the expansion of exports. Again a vicious circle operated here, preventing an improvement in the situation.

Still another vicious circle appeared in the investment field. The level of national income was low and, therefore, the economy had a limited capacity to generate savings and investment. Further, it was impossible to increase national income without changing the industrial structure by replacing used-up capital and introducing modern technologies. Because of the shortage of investable funds the authorities attempted to centralize their allocation. To curb inflation they tried to limit financial resources at the disposal of the enterprises. The enterprises were unable to replace the used-up capital assets in those sectors that should have been expanded, effect their modernization, reduce labor-, fuel-, and material-intensity of production processes, or adjust their productive capacities better to the requirements of export markets (Karpinski 1985, pp. 1, 6; Górski and Zienkowski 1985, p. 8; Glikman 1986, p. 7; and Wilczyńska 1987, p. 7).

In all these fields the difficulties made the introduction of economic reform a risky process. Yet without far-reaching economic reform it would be unlikely that these difficulties would be eliminated and the plan successfully implemented. It was precisely because of the shortages of labor, fuels, raw materials, and capital that the extensive pattern of development could not give satisfactory results. The introduction of a more intensive pattern was not possible without economic reform. This point of view was shared by the Consultative Economic Council, which indicated that the economy still operated under an internally inconsistent system and that the reform had not been able to create the self-regulating mechanisms that were necessary for the success of the plan.[6]

III. PLANNED INVESTMENT AND RESTRUCTURING THE ECONOMY

In formulating the plan some major decisions had to be made in connection with the allocation of investments. They reflected the main strategy of the plan.

Total investment outlays in the national economy were expected to be 10,000 billion zloty during the period 1986-90, or 4.6% above the outlays (at constant prices) invested in 1981-85, but 5.2% lower than in 1971-75, and 29.0% lower than in 1976-80. The allocation for the material production sphere was to increase from 67.0% in 1985 to 72.0% in 1990. This policy led to the continuous underfinancing of housing, health services, education, science and technology, and other services, and adversely affected the efficiency of directly productive investments in the material sphere. This was often the case, not only in Poland but also in other Soviet-type economies.[7]

Industry's share in total investment was expected to increase from 30.0% in 1985, to 38.0% in 1990 (Wilczyńska 1987). As a result of the priority allocation of investment for the expansion of industry, industry's share in PNMP was expected to increase only slightly from 11.7% to 12.0%. The share of agriculture was to decline from 15.7% to 14.0%, and the share of the rest of material production, which includes transportation and telecommunications, was to decline from 22.7% to 22.0%.

The scarcity of investable funds was further aggravated by the continuation of many investments that had been started during the investment drive of the 1970s. Although in 1981 about 1,600 investment projects under construction were stopped, many unfinished investment projects were continued.[8] They often embodied highly capital-, fuel-, and material-intensive processes. Their continuation reduced the planners' freedom to maneuver with respect to modernization, replacement of used-up capital, and the ability to affect structural changes (Górnicka 1986, pp. 1, 4). The completion of these investments required 4,200 billion zloty. Of this, 3,100 billion, or 30.0% of total outlays, were allocated for this purpose in the 1986-1990 plan. Of 1,100 billion zloty to be centrally allocated during the plan period, 796.7 billion zloty, or 72.0%, were to be spent on the continuation of previously started projects. The greatest concentration of continuation took place during the first two years of the plan, when about 85.0% of total investment outlays in the socialist economy was allocated for this purpose.

The decision to allocate such high proportions of total investment outlays for the continuation of investments made it impossible to stop the process of decapitalization, defined as a decrease in the net value of capital stock. According to the calculations made by the Planning Commission, the proportion of used-up capital assets in the socialist economy increased from 34.3% to 37.0% between 1980 and 1985. The proportion of used-up machinery and equipment in the socialist economy increased from 48.5% to 59.0%. In industry the corresponding figures increased from 38.4% to 43.0% for total capital stock and from 49.2% to 60.0% for machinery and equipment. In construction the increase was 36.9% to 40.0% for total capital stock and 50.3% to 69.0% for machinery and equipment. In practice, much of the machinery and equipment are used until the end of their physical life. Frequent breakdowns and lengthy repairs cause work stoppages, while malfunctioning creates losses through wasted fuel, energy materials, and labor. These losses are quite substantial for the economy as a whole. No improvement could be expected during the 1986-90 period because of the plan's insufficient allocation of funds for the replacement of used-up equipment (Wilczyńska 1987).

The allocation of investment funds that ignores the problems created by nonreplacement does not seem to be consistent with the expectation that a very high proportion of the planned increase in output will result from reduced fuel- and material-intensity of production, increased labor productivity, and a better utilization of existing equipment. This expectation simply cannot be fulfilled with the increasing proportion of run-down, inefficient, and malfunctioning machines and equipment. No modern economy can function in this way.

The second important decision that was made by the planners concerned the decision to allocate funds either for the expansion of the production of fuel and power or for their more economical use throughout the economy. According to recent calculations the cost of extracting an additional ton of hard coal was 3 to 3.5 times higher than the cost of economizing one ton in the economy (Glikman 1986, p. 7).

For the fuel and energy industry the 1986-90 plan allocated 56.7% of the outlays on the continued centrally allocated investment projects. These projects included seven mines of hard coal, two mines of lignite, the gas pipe from the USSR, four conventional electric power stations, and one nuclear power station. The plan also allocated 76.8% of the centrally allocated investment outlays to new projects to be started during the plan period. These investments included one hard coal mine, one lignite mine, and two conventional electric power stations. Some 117.5 billion zloty were allocated during the 1986-90 plan to increase the output of coal by 14 million tons per year. Several analysts suggested that, with the annual domestic consumption of 125 million tons of coal and very high fuel-intensity production, the same 14 million tons of coal could have been obtained considerably less expensively by introducing various coal saving devices throughout the economy (Jeziorański 1986, p. 4).

There were also problems with decisions concerning the allocation of investments among individual industries. After the fuel and energy industry, a top priority was given to the engineering industry. Of total industry investments, 19.6% were allocated to the engineering industry, compared with 36% for the fuel and power generation industry, 9.7% to the chemical industry, 7.8% to the metallurgy industry, 4.5% to light industry, 3.6% to the wood processing and paper industry, and 12.1% to the food processing industry. The share for the engineering industry was expected to increase from 23.6% to 25.6% by 1990. The share for the chemical industry, which still seemed excessively small, was to increase from only 8.2% to 8.6%, while the shares for other sectors of industry were to decline: food processing from 23.5% to 22.0%, fuel and power generation from 14.5% to 13.6%, and the metallurgy industry from 9.4% to 8.6%. Despite a very large initial share of investment expenditures, allocations for the fuel and power generation industry were to decrease from 14.5% to 13.6% (Wilczyńska 1987).

Considering that it was difficult to expand the export of primary commodities and that an increased share of exportables had to be produced by the manufacturing industry, the decision to give such a high priority to the engineering industry could have been reasonable if this expansion had been geared to export possibilities. The officially provided reason was, however, that "the development of the engineering industry will determine the pace and the scale of the modernization of the economy."[9] This was again an autarkic approach, planning for a basically closed economy.

The total value of machines and equipment supplied to the domestic economy during the 1986-90 period was to be 3,350 billion zloty, including domestically produced machines and equipment worth 2,500 billion zloty. Machines and equipment valued at 400 billion zloty were to come from other socialist countries with a total of 450 billion coming from nonsocialist countries. In other words, 75.0% of all machines and equipment were to be supplied from domestic production. In contrast, the value of the machines and equipment imported from nonsocialist countries represented only 13.0% of the total supply.

For this reason the following comment of a Polish analyst should be carefully noted:

> In light of these figures it is possible to have doubts whether foreign trade will secure for the Polish economy a sufficient inflow of technological innovations. A significant part of them will have their origin in the socialist countries in which the technological level lags behind advanced capitalist countries (Wilczyńska 1987).

If the "Comprehensive Program of Cooperation in Science and Technology Up to the Year 2000," adopted by the CMEA in

December 1985, and the subsequently signed bilateral agreements with all CMEA countries had been successful in the long run—and they were not—the effects would not have been felt during that Five-Year-Plan period.

The very high proportion of machines that were domestically produced contrasted with the small proportion of machines that were imported from the most advanced countries undoubtedly slowed down technological progress, which had suffered very badly during the economic crisis. The adverse effect of the excessive dependence on domestically produced machines and equipment was augmented by the very poor state of the scientific and technological infrastructure. This group lost personnel, worked with unsatisfactory, obsolete equipment, and since the early 1980s experienced a shortage of foreign journals, books, and personal contacts. Although research and development (R&D) expenditures were to double between 1985 and 1990, reaching 3.0% of DNMP, it was not easy to remove serious backlogs which were created when these expenditures declined from 2.0% of DNMP in 1979 to 0.8% in 1982 and to 0.9% in 1983 and 1984. At constant prices, outlays on R&D increased continuously during the first half of the 1970s. Then the first decline occurred in 1976, followed by an increase in 1977. Subsequently, outlays declined from year to year in 1978-82. Positive rates appeared again in 1983-85 but the level in 1985 represented only 77.0% of the 1971 level and 52.0% of the 1975 level. The value of actually introduced projects from among the completed R & D projects in 1985 was only 29.0% of the 1979 level and 63.0% of the 1975 level.[10] These figures illustrate well the adverse impact of the crisis of the early 1980s on the R&D sector.

After the collapse of Gierek's "new development strategy," a negative reaction to the transfer of technology appeared, and the balance-of-payments difficulties strengthened this attitude. The sudden acceleration of technology transfer in the early 1970s was excessive only in relation to the limited short-term capacity of the economy to absorb it. The actual volume of technology transfer was still below the long-run optimum (Fallenbuchl 1986a). The total number of foreign licenses purchased declined from 316 in 1971-75 to 136 in 1976-80, including only 30 from the first period and 8 from the second, from socialist countries. As the result of the crisis the number of foreign licenses purchased declined to 6, including 4 from nonsocialist countries in 1981-85.[11] In 1985 the number of active licenses declined to about one third of the number of licenses active in the years 1975-79. Although the share of production based on foreign licenses in the total value of production had never exceeded 5.0%, the level reached in 1980, it dropped to 1.2% in 1985. The proportion of export production based on licenses declined from its highest level of 5.5% in 1977 to 1.6% in 1985.[12]

Without a sharp acceleration in technology transfer in the embodied and disembodied form, including purchases of licenses, technical assistance and training arrangements, industrial cooperation, and, above all, joint ventures and Western direct investments, prospects for technological progress were grim. But these were necessary conditions for effecting a switch to a more intensive pattern of development and reaching fulfillment of the targets of the 1986-90 plan under the existing constraints.

IV. RESULTS

The main targets of the plan and their implementation during the first three years of the plan period are presented in Table 1. In 1988 the PNMP was still about 1.0% below its 1978 level, or 8.0% below on the per capita basis, and the DNMP was 6.0% below its 1978 level, or about 13.0% below on the per capita basis. The crisis had, therefore, transformed itself into a prolonged stagnation. Moreover, the official statistics are now often criticized in Poland. They have an upward bias because of the unrealistically low rates of depreciation that are used, incomplete elimination of the impact of price increases during a period of high inflation, and inability of the administratively determined prices to reflect deterioration in the quality of products that had been very noticeable since the late 1970s.

Recovery in industry was not uniform. Table 2 presents the annual rates of growth of "sold industrial production" at constant prices, which is not regarded as a reliable measure at a time of strong inflation, shortages, and price distortions. In 1986 all rates of growth were positive. They ranged, however, from 2.2% in fuel, electric power and metallurgy to 7.1% in the engineering industry.

Table 1.   Net Material Product
(Average Annual Rates of Growth)

	1971-75	1976-80	1981-85	Plan 1986-90	1986-88
Produced Net Material					
Product	9.8	1.2	-0.8	3.0-3.5	3.8
Industry	10.8	2.6	-1.1	3.7-4.6	4.4
Agriculture	1.0	-2.6	3.4	1.1-1.5	1.0
Distributed New Material					
Product	11.6	-0.2	-1.6	2.6-3.2	3.8
Consumption	8.7	4.5	-0.8	2.3-2.9	3.8*
Accumulation	18.1	-11.8	-4.0	3.6-4.2	1.5*
Consumption for Personal					
Incomes—Per Capita	7.5	3.4	-2.5	1.8	3.4
Investment in Fixed Capital	19.6	-9.2	-4.8	5.9	5.9**

Notes: * 1986-1987
             ** 1986

Sources: G.U.S., *Rocznik statystyczny* (Statistical Yearbook), Warsaw 1987, pp. 87, 92.
             Economic Commission for Europe, *Economic Survey of Europe in 1988-89*, New
             York: United Nations 1989, pp. 235, 236.

In 1987 the metallurgy industry experienced a decline while other industries had rates of growth ranging from 0.9% in food processing to 7.1% in the engineering industry. In 1988 there was a decline by 0.1% in fuel and electrical power while other industries had postive rates of growth from 1.8% to 10.0%. However, a serious decline occurred in industrial production in 1989. Only the mineral, wood and paper, and light industries had positive rates of growth. Other industries experienced declines ranging from 1.0% in the chemical industry to 7.0% in the metallurgy industry.

The decline in industrial production in 1989 is explained by shortages of domestic and imported raw materials and intermediate goods, as well as, to a smaller extent, of labor (Misiak 1989, p. 11).

Probably because of the unsatisfactory nature of the index of sold production, the leading Polish economic weekly usually supplemented the index with the rates of growth of eleven selected industrial commodities calculated in physical units. On the whole, the results in 1984-88 and especially during the first nine months of 1989 were unsatisfactory (see Table 3).

Table 2. Selected Indicators 1979-1989

	1979	1980	1981	1982	1983	1984	1985	1986	1987	1988	1989 (estimate)
Industrial sold production	1.9	-1.0	-3.6	-1.7	6.4	5.3	3.8	4.2	3.3	5.4	-3.0
Fuel and electric power industry	0.9	-2.0	-11.7	6.4	4.7	3.1	1.4	2.2	1.8	-0.1	-5.0
Metallurgy industry	0.9	0.3	-17.3	-3.3	7.2	3.4	-0.2	2.2	-1.0	2.1	-7.0
Engineering industry	4.9	-0.9	-12.8	-2.0	7.5	7.6	6.5	7.1	7.1		-3.0
Chemical industry	3.2	1.5	-10.8	-1.3	8.3	5.7	2.6	3.7	5.2		-1.0
Mineral industry	-1.9	-0.2	-14.8	-0.4	6.3	4.3	-1.8	4.0	1.9	7-10	3.0
Wood and paper industry	-3.9	2.4	-9.8	-1.8	9.4	4.9	4.0	5.0	3.6		1.5
Light industry	-0.4	-1.3	-13.0	-6.1	3.6	7.5	5.8	2.4	2.9		1.5
Food processing industry	2.2	-2.2	-16.0	-1.9	6.0	3.7	4.0	3.7	0.9	1.8	-5.0
Purchases of animals for meat	5.0	-4.4	-25.8	0.4	-1.1	1.6	12.2	13.3	-0.8	-0.6	-10.1*
Purchases of milk	0.0	0.3	-0.5	0.6	15.0	7.3	-3.3	-4.6	1.1	2.6	5.9*
Output of socialist construction firms	-5.9	-10.9	-21.3	-6.1	5.0	7.7	4.2	2.2	-2.0	2.1	-3.3*

Note: * January-September

Sources: G.U.S., *Rocznik statystyczny przemysłu* (Statistical Yearbook of Industry), Warsaw 1987, pp. 42-43.
S.G.P.S., *Gospodarka światowa i gospodarka polski w 1987 roku* (The World Economy and the Polish Economy in 1987), Warsaw 1988, p. 38.
S.G.P.S., *Poland 1988/89*, Warsaw 1989, p. 2.
Życie gospodarcze 5, 1989, p. 11.

Table 3.   Output of Selected Commodities in Physical Units
(Rates of Growth)

Commodity	1984	1985	1986	1987	1988	1989 Jan.-Sept.
Hard coal (million tons)	0.3	0.0	0.2	0.5	0.0	-5.8
Electrical power (billion kWh)	7.1	2.2	1.9	4.0	-1.3	1.8
Crude steel (thousand tons)	1.8	-2.5	6.3	0.0	-1.6	-8.5
Agricultural tractors (thousands)	5.9	0.3	4.7	-3.6	-1.6	-10.9
Passenger cars (thousands)	3.6	1.7	2.5	1.2	0.0	-4.1
Washing machines (thousands)	3.4	1.1	4.6	0.8	-2.3	2.6
T.V. receivers (thousands)	3.1	4.1	3.1	2.8	16.8	5.8
Nitrogen fertilizers (thousand tons)	2.1	-8.5	5.3	6.8	5.1	2.3
Synthetic materials (thousand tons)	10.7	-1.1	4.6	2.6	12.4	-0.8
Cement (thousand tons)	3.0	-10.0	5.6	1.6	5.6	0.5
Boots and shoes (million pairs)	3.7	0.1	-0.5	3.4	3.3	-3.3

Sources: *Życie gospodarcze*, No. 5, 1986, p. 15; No. 6, 1987, p. 11; No. 35, 1987, p. 15; No. 5, 1989, p. 11; No. 43, 1989, p. 15.

In 1984 the rates of growth of all eleven commodities were positive and recovery progressed at a relatively high pace. In 1985 the situation deteriorated. The output of four commodities declined, and that of two others remained stationary, while the remaining rates were positive but were low. There was again an improvement in 1986 and 1987 when only one rate of growth was negative in each year. But in January-September 1989, in comparison with the same period one year earlier, six rates of growth were negative and two among the positive rates were less than 2.0%. The pattern of growth of all eleven commodities fluctuated from year to year, and every year there were considerable discrepancies among the rates. This was a picture of hesitant rather than solid growth.

As a result of the uneven pattern of growth within industry in 1986, it became impossible to meet the plan for the increase in the supply of manufactured consumption goods for the domestic market. While the plan envisaged that this production would grow at a rate exceeding the rate of growth of total industry, the relationship between the two rates was reversed. Shortages in the market were aggravated and inflation, which was expected to be somewhat mitigated by increases in the supply of goods for consumers, became even greater (Misiak 1987c, p. 10).

Agriculture had a good year in 1986, although there was a reduction in state purchases of milk, the result of a decline in the number of cows (see Table 2). State purchases of meat increased rapidly but they were induced by the farmers' decision to reduce the size of livestock. In 1987, 1988, and in the first nine months of 1989, purchases of livestock for meat declined while purchases of milk declined in 1986 but increased in the subsequent years.

Major difficulties appeared in construction. The output of socialist construction firms declined in 1987 and, again, during the first nine months of 1989 (see Table 2). Year after year there were delays in the completion of investment projects. The production capacity of the building industry was obsolete, technology relatively simple, and capital stock to a very great extent used up, requiring replacement (Misiak 1987b).

V. INTERNAL DISEQUILIBRIA

The success of the 1986-90 plan also depended considerably on the ability of the planners to cope with the internal and external disequilibria. Neither had been eliminated and no radical improvement could be expected within the remaining years of the plan period.

There were forces on both the supply and the demand sides that were responsible for the depth and persistence of the internal disequilibria. The aggregate supply was still below its 1978 level, although the population grew about 7.0% since then. Many factors caused bottlenecks and shortages that prevented full use of existing productive capacities. They were the uneven recovery; the limited import of materials, components, spare parts, and machines; and the rigidities and inefficiency of the present hybrid "manipulative system."[13] Various sectoral disequilibria persisted and the effective aggregate supply was, therefore, smaller than it would otherwise have been.

The full capacity of the economy was still below the 1978 level, growing very slowly at an uneven pace. To avoid the appearance of an inflationary gap aggregate demand would have to have been drastically adjusted downward to the level of capacity and move upward slowly. For various reasons, above all the lack of determination and political insecurity of the government, no such adjustment in aggregate demand took place at the time when aggregate supply collapsed in 1979-82. The serious inflationary gap that had been inherited from Gierek's "new development policy" was allowed to grow further.

The index of price movements does not measure the extent of inflation in an economy where a very large proportion of all prices are administratively determined or controlled and there are heavy subsidies. Increases in prices are often introduced as prices of "new products" and are not reflected in the price index. Many goods are unavailable at the official prices, or are available only in limited quantities. Often they have to be purchased in the second economy, that is, the black market (Wiśniewski 1984), or as the result of a privileged position, special efforts, connections, or in exchange for favors.

Movements in the price index are mainly determined by administrative adjustments in prices. These movements often reflect changes in the prices paid by the government agencies for the purchase of agricultural produce, or administratively effected changes in the rate of exchange. Taking the 1978 level of prices as 100, the price level at the end of 1986 was 561. Actual price increases exceeded those envisaged in the annual plans with the increase in 1986 higher than in the two preceding years: 18.0% as compared with 15.0% in both 1984 and 1985 (see Table 4). In the subsequent years prices of goods and services were rising quickly. They accelerated to 26.0% in 1987, 60.0% in 1988, and 220.0% during the first nine months of 1989. The objective to bring down the rate of growth of officially recorded prices to a one digit increase before the end of the plan was, of course, unobtainable.

A number of factors pushed aggregate demand upwards. They include, first of all, the excess of exports over imports, which is necessary if the foreign debt is to be serviced. Second, deficits in the central state budget contribute to excess aggregate demand. Yet deficits in the central state budget are difficult to curtail when there is a dramatic crisis in health services, a shortage of schools, serious losses in the scientific and technological infrastructure, a desperate need for daycare, facilities for preschoolers and elderly people, a need for a minimal level of cultural activities, an increasing number of public administration employees despite the reduction in the number of ministries, and a need for a certain level of security and national defense.

Table 4. Nominal Incomes, Expenditures, Savings, and Prices

	1980	1981	1982	1983	1984 Plan	1984	1985 Plan	1985	1986 Plan	1986	1987 Plan	1987	1988 Plan	1988	1989 Plan	1989 Jan.-Sept.
Nominal incomes	10	27	64	24	13.8	19.5	17.0	23.0	12.8	20.3	18.8	27.3	48.7	83.2	65.7	164.7
Wages	11	26	46	26	16.9	17.9	19.0	19.0	14.3	21.1	14.7	21.8	42.2	72.6	58.5	169.1
Social payments	15	37	139	19	12.3	17.9	11.6	13.6	25.6	23.9	31.1	29.9	59.4	78.3	67.6	142.3
Incomes from individual agriculture	9	39	66	6	6.1	9.7	7.2	19.1	6.8	19.5	14.4	19.8	48.2	94.4	41.7	137.1
Expenditures on goods and services	9	17	67	31	16.4	22	17.5	18.5	17.1	23.3	21.7	30.3	49.6	68.2	73.9	150.1
Savings (deposits and cash balances)	13	38	37	21	-19.0	16	7.9	30.5	56.6	-8.2	-17.3	-7.8	34.5	440.0	11.8	261.7
Cash balances	24	38	51	20	-9.8	14.8	11.9	23.0	-20.3	-19.7	13.4	-5.3	118.4	860.0	-4.7	301.2
Price index (goods and services)	9.4	21.1	104.5	21.4	N/A	14.8	13.0	15.0	13.0	18	N/A	26.0	N/A	60.0	N/A	220.0

Note: N/A = not available

Sources: Życie gospodarcze, No. 5, 1986, p. 15; No. 6, 1986, p. 11; No. 6, 1987, p. 11; No. 35, 1987, p. 15; No. 5, 1989, p. 11; No. 43, 1989, p. 15.

Expanding investment outlays also impact aggregate demand. The previously started projects and the large portion of new investments allocated to the fuel and power generation industry and other sectors with a lengthy gestation period also increase aggregate demand. The expected increase in aggregate supply will not appear, in many cases, before the end of the 1986-1990 plan period.

Finally, there are increases in nominal incomes that exceed improvements in productivity. The government was not able to control the increases despite considerable administrative efforts. Assuming the 1982 level of nominal incomes to be 100, the level of nominal incomes reached 224 at the end of 1986. Actual increases exceeded those envisaged in the annual plans and their pace was very uneven. After a large increase in 1982, increases in nominal wages declined in 1983, and again in 1984, then increased by 23.9% in 1985, 20.3% in 1986, 27.3% in 1987, 83.2% in 1988, and 164.7% in the first nine months of 1989 (see Table 4).

Expenditures on goods and services have not increased at the same rate as nominal incomes, despite the fact that prices, deposits, and cash balances have increased every year, except in 1986 and 1987 (see Table 4). It is difficult to expect an improvement in the consumers' market with the large and increasing inflationary "overhang."

It was equally difficult to cope with the external disequilibrium. The positive balance in trade effected in hard currencies, the so-called second payment region, was not sufficient to meet debt servicing needs. A large proportion of the hard-currency trade was with China, Yugoslavia, Brazil, and other countries on a clearing basis and did not increase the amount of available hard currency. It did induce some import of consumption goods, which, although useful because of shortages in the domestic market, was not as essential as some materials or components necessary for the expansion of industrial production. A part of the surplus originated in trade with the less-developed countries where the export of machines and equipment took place on a credit basis.

The growing difficulty in expanding the export of primary commodities, on the supply as well as the demand sides, made the expansion of export in this direction difficult. An example of this was the limited capacity of the manufacturing industry to offer modern, high quality products and the lack of sufficient reform in the foreign trade mechanism (Fallenbuchl 1986). The hard-currency debt increased from $29.3 billion in 1985 to $38.9 billion in 1988.

Although the actual excess of import over export in trade with CMEA countries was smaller every year than the amount envisaged in the annual plans, debt in rubles was growing. It increased from 5.6 billion rubles in 1985 to 6.8 billion rubles in 1988.

VI. CONCLUSIONS

It seems, therefore, that the 1986-90 plan depended on the ability to increase the efficiency of the economy. The pattern of growth had to become considerably more intensive. It is difficult, however, to see how this could possibly have been achieved without more significant far-reaching reform, a modification of the allocation of investment, and a reduction in the internal and external disequilibria. While the new government must consolidate its political power it must also enact new, more radical reform proposals and economic policy decisions which are not likely to be popular with Solidarity's traditional supporters. The movement toward a new economic system with necessary short run austerity programs is fraught with dangers yet to be identified, and the prospects for success are uncertain.

NOTES

1. For a detailed description see "Warianty Koncepcji Narodowego Planu Społeczno-Gospodarczego na lata 1986-1990" (Variants of the Proposal of the National Socioeconomic Plan for the Years 1986-1990), *Rzeczpospolita* (June 25, 1985); and M. Gorywoda, "Warianty Koncepcji Narodowego Planu Społeczno-Gospadarczego na lata 1986-1990 (NPSG)" (Variants of the Proposal of the National Socioeconomic Plan) *Życie gospodarcze* 20 (1985): p. 9.
2. "Tezy w sprawie II etapu reformy gospodarczej" (Theses on the Second Stage of the Economic Reform). *Reforma gospodarcza* 102 (April 17, 1987).
3. As outlined in "Konsultacyjna Rada Gospodarcza o NPSG 1986-1990: Uwagi do projektu" (The Consultative Economic Council on the National Socioeconomic Plan for 1986-1990: Comments on the Proposal). *Życie gospodarcze* 24 (1986): p. 9.
4. See "Rządowy program oszczędnościowy" (The Government Program of Saving Resources). *Życie gospodarcze* 13 (1983): p. 9.
5. See "Konsultacyjna," p. 7.

6. See "Konsultacyjna," pp. 1, 7 and also Fallenbuchl (1985) for a further analysis of the program of economic reform.

7. For a discussion of this point, see Fallenbuchl (1965), p. 7.

8. For details see "Ruszyć strukturę" (To Move the Structure). *Życie gospodarcze* 32 (1985): p. 7.

9. "NPSG w komisjach sejmowych" (The National Socio-economic Plan in the Parliamentary Committees). *Życie gospodarcze* 47 (1986): p. 11.

10. See G.U.S., *Rocznik statystyczny* (Statistical Yearbook) (Warsaw, 1980): pp. 68, 391, 458; (1981): p. 509; (1985): p. 410; (1986): pp. 87, 105, 452.

11. G.U.S., *Rocznik statystyczny* (Statistical Yearbook) (Warsaw, 1986): p. 456.

12. G.U.S., *Rocznik statystyczny* (Statistical Yearbook) (Warsaw, 1981): p. 514; (1986): p. 456.

13. See Fallenbuchl (1986a).

REFERENCES

Albinowski, S. "Pytanie za 300 miliardów" (A Question Worth 300 Billion). *Życie gospodarcze* 47 (1986).

Fallenbuchl, Z. "Some Structural Aspects of the Soviet-type Investment Policy." *Soviet Studies* 16,4 (1965).

————. "Poland: Internal Economic Development." In *The Economies of Eastern Europe and Their Foreign Economic Relations*, edited by P. Joseph. Brussels: NATO Conference Directorate, 1986a.

————. "Foreign Trade Reform in Poland." Paper presented at the AAASS Meetings in New Orleans, November 1986b.

————. "The Present State of Economic Reform in Poland." In *Creditworthiness: Can Poland Regain It?*, edited by P. Marer and W. Siwinski. London: Allen & Unwin, 1987a.

————. "The Polish Economy in the Year 2000: Need and Outlook for Systemic Reforms, Recovery and Growth Strategies (Western View)." The Carl Beck Papers in Russian and East European Studies, University of Pittsburgh, February 1987.

Glikman, P. "Dekapitalizacja" (Decapitalization). *Życie gospodarcze* 32 (1986).

Górnicka, T. "Inwestycje 1986-90: węzeł gordyjski planu" (Investments of 1986-90: Gordian Knot of the Plan). *Życie gospodarcze* 45 (1986).

Górski, J., and L. Zienkowski. "Spojrzenie w przeszłość i w przyszłość" (A Glance at the Past and into the Future). *Życie gospodarcze* 41 (1985).

Gorywoda, M. "Warianty Koncepcji NPSG" (Variants of the Proposal of the National Socio-economic Plan). *Życie gospodarcze* 20 (1985).

Głowny Urząd Statystyczny. *Rocznik statystyczny* (Statistical Yearbook). (Warsaw, 1980).

————. *Rocznik statystyczny* (Statistical Yearbook). (Warsaw, 1981).

————. *Rocznik statystyczny* (Statistical Yearbook). (Warsaw, 1985).

————. *Rocznik statystyczny* (Statistical Yearbook). (Warsaw, 1986).

Jeziorański, T. "Warianty Koncepcji Narodowego Planu Społeczno-Gospodarczego na lata 1986-1990" (Variants of the Proposal of the National Socioeconomic Plan for the Years 1986-1990). *Rzeczpospolita* (June 25, 1985).

_____. "Trzy odmiany jednej koncepcji" (Three Variants of the Same Concept). *Życie gospodarcze* 102 (April 17, 1987).

_____. "Czy plan pięcioletni wymaga zmian" (Does the Five Year Plan Require Modifications?). *Życie gospodarcze* 35 (1987).

_____. "Program oszczędnościowy" (The Saving Program). *Życie gospodarcze* 15 (1986).

Karpiński, A. "Co zrobić z inwestycjami" (What to do with Investments). *Życie gospodarcze* 1 (1985).

"Konsultacyjna Rada Gospodarcza o NSPG 1986-90: Uwagi do projektu" (The Consultative Economic Council on the National Socioeconomic Plan for 1986-90: Comments on the Proposal). *Życie gospodarcze* 24 (1986).

Misiak, M. "Co przyniesie 4 kwartał" (What Results Can Be Expected in the Fourth Quarter). *Życie gospodarcze* 46 (1989).

_____. "Gospodarka po I półroczu: potrzeba determinacji" (The Economy After the First Half of the Year: More Determination Is Needed). *Życie gospodarcze* 30 (1987a).

_____. "Gospodarka po 7 miesiącach: chmurno" (The Economy After 7 Months: A Clouded Picture). *Życie gosdpodarcze* 35 (1987b).

_____. "Na minus i na plus" (Minuses and Pluses). *Życie gospodarcze* 12 (1987c).

Nasiłowski, M. "Niewariantowe warianty" (Variants That Are Not Really Variants). *Życie gospodarcze* 20 (1985).

"NSPG w komisjach sejmowych" (The National Socioeconomic Plan in the Parliamentary Committees). *Życie gospodarcze* 47 (1986).

"Ruszyć strukturę" (To Move the Structure). *Życie gospodarcze* 45 (1986).

"Rządowy program oszczędnościowy" (The Government Program of Saving Resources). *Życie gospodarcze* 13 (1983).

Szeliga, Z. "Założenia planu 5-letniego" (The Determinants of the Five Year Plan). *Życie gospodarcze* 20 (1985).

"Tezy w sprawie II etapu reformy gospodarczej" (Theses on the Second Stage of Economic Reform). *Reforma gospodarcza* 17 (April 1987).

"Warianty Koncepcji Narodowego Planu Spoleczno-Gospodarczego na lata 1986-1990" (Variants of the Proposal of the National Socio-economic Plan for the Years 1986-1990). *Rzeczpospolita* 25 (June 1985).

Wilczyńska, D. "Dekapitalizacja a zmiany strukturalne" (Decapitalization and Structural Changes). *Życie gospodarcze* 4 (1987).

Wiśniewski, M. "Gospodarka i jej cień" (The Economy and Its Shadow). *Życie gospodarcze* 30 (1987).

ECONOMIC DEVELOPMENT AND THE ECONOMIC REFORM IN POLAND

Marian Ostrowski

I. INTRODUCTION

Both the economy and society of Poland are experiencing a deep and far-reaching transformation. This reconstruction is neither smooth nor painless. A common belief of the Polish people is that the former way of running the economy and organizing society has become irrelevant. This is often stressed by representatives of differing political orientations. For example, Professor J. Szczepański, a sociologist, claims that popular consciousness has surpassed existing structures. Reality had failed to match this consciousness. Therefore, there was a common will to change reality accordingly.[1] Although this is a sociologist's view, even General W. Jaruzelski expressed a similar thesis: "We had to pay dearly for postponing the necessary changes, withdrawing from processes already initiated, conservativism, and corroding the mechanism of the development of economy and democracy."[2]

Obviously, merely identifying or comparing assessments and opinions will neither lead to identical solutions, nor to equally well-defined proposals.[3] The questions of what, how, and when

39

to transform have become a basic dilemma of the socioeconomic transformation of Poland, a dilemma that exists in other countries as well.

It is evident that in reference to the reform, the questions of what, how, when, and by which social forces, are interdependent. Conditions for the success of the economic reform are based on the recognition of this interdependence. The most frequently proposed approach to the preconditions of economic reform presents the following three sets of problems:

1. Social support.
2. The political will of the authorities' and politicians' determination to carry out the reform, including self-restraint from exercising power.
3. Socioeconomic knowledge of what should be done.

Discussion of the conditions to be fulfilled for the success of the reform must consider the role of the real economic situation and its influence on those conditions for success, such as social support and the unique combination of courage and caution required from political decision makers. In Poland it is difficult to overestimate the influence of the state of the economy on the shape and course of the reform. An outline of economic conditions, the dilemma of agriculture and the basic principles of phase two of the reform are presented below.

II.   ECONOMIC CONDITIONS: 1982—1988

Poland's economy experienced positive growth from 1982-1987, as indicated in Table 1. The lower rate of national income (NMP) growth in 1987 resulted mainly from the poor performance of agriculture and construction. Adverse weather conditions in comparison to the previous year explain the lower agricultural output. They cannot, however, explain the decline in value added in construction (see Table 2).

Despite some successes, certain problems became more and more severe. First of all, debt repayment increased intra-industrial inbalances and shortages of material inputs. Bottlenecks, shortages

Table 1.   Rate of Real National Income (NMP) Growth
for 1982-1987

	1982	1983	1984	1985	1986	1987
Net Material Product, Produced	-5.5	6.0	5.6	3.4	4.9	1.9
Net Material Product, Consumed	-10.5	5.6	5.0	3.8	5.0	1.8

Sources: Rocznik statystyczny 1986, 1988. Warsaw: G.U.S., 1986, 1988.

Table 2.   Value-Added Rate of Growth in Industry,
Agriculture, and Construction, 1982-1987

	1982	1983	1984	1985	1986	1987*
Value added in:						
Industry	-4.5	5.8	5.4	4.0	4.5	4.7
Agriculture	4.9	5.1	5.3	0.1	6.3	-6.0
Construction	-8.4	7.7	8.1	4.3	3.9	3.7

Note: * 1982-1986 in 1982 zlotys, 1987 estimated in 1984 zlotys.
Sources: Rocznik statystyczny. Warsaw: G.U.S., 1986, *Mały rocznik statystyczny.* Warsaw:
G.U.S., 1987, Planning Commission data.

and their effects on investment, material inputs, and consumer
goods markets were intensifying. Numerous studies indicate that
the shortage of labor was considered by enterprises as the most
important constraint to their growth. In 1988 this picture changed:
a shortage of material inputs replaced the shortage of labor as the
main growth obstacle.

Further elaboration on the problems of Polish debt and the
consequences of its servicing may be found in later chapters by
Soldaczuk and Kamecki. It is clear that the cost of debt servicing
has impeded Poland's development potential. A positive trade
balance was achieved primarily through deep cuts in imports. As
readily available reserves are exhausted, the lack of progress in
easing the burden of debt servicing will constrain future
development possibilities. A considerable increase in hard-
currency private savings, which has taken place, represents only
a short-term solution.

Table 3. An Average Consumer Price Index (1982-1987)

1982	1983	1984	1985	1986	1987
104.5	121.4	114.8	115.0	117.5	125.3

Sources: *Rocznik statystyczny 1986, 1988.* Warsaw: G.U.S., 1986, 1988.

Table 4. Ratio of Money Supply to Total
Annual Consumers Expenditures

1982	1983	1984	1985	1986
0.51	0.43	0.41	0.45	0.50

Source: Herer, W. and Sadowski, W.: *Zagrożenia wynikające ze zmiany stopnia niezrównoważenia gospodarki.* Warsaw, Poland: Institute of National Economy, 1987.

Table 5. Estimates of the Accumulated Inflationary Gap
(billions of zlotys)

	1982	1983	1984	1985	1986	1987
Estimate made by:						
Economic Advisory Council	443[1]	535[1]	570-582[1] 615[2]	—	—	—
National Bank of Poland	493.5[3]	559.4[3]	615.0[3]	738.1[3]	900[4]	1120[4]
G.W. Kolodko	493.5[5]	559.1[5]	615.0[5]	750[6]	—	—
M. Mieszczankoswki	510[7]	650[7]	750[7]	1000[7]	—	—

Sources: [1] *O spożyciu, dochodach i równowadze rynkowej* (Warsaw, Poland: KAW, Konsultacyjna Rada Gospodarcza 1985).

[2] "Gospodarka w latach 1981-85: Raport KRG." *Życie gospodarcze* 16 (1986).

[3] *Analiza nawisu inflacyjnego w 1985 roku,* Materiały i Studia 29. (Warsaw: Narodowy Bank Polski, Zespół Ekspertów Naukowych, 1986).

[4] *Bilans przychodów pieniężnych i wydatków pieniężnych ludności. Sprawozdanie z wykonania za 1986 rok* (Warsaw: NBP, 1987).

[5] Planned by the NBP.

[6] Kołodko, G.W. *Polska w świecie inflacji* (Warsaw, Poland: KiW, 1987).

[7] Kołodko, G.W. "Na jaką inflację jesteśmy skazani." *Życie gospodarcze* 33 (1985).

The growth in the consumer price index (Table 3) is also a harmful phenomenon from both social and political points of view, posing a great threat to the reform. A fear of a strong inflationary spiral is a real menace.

It is worth adding that the consumer price index itself does not reflect the scale of disequilibrium prevailing in the consumer goods market. This results from the existence of two kinds of prices: directly fixed prices and those indirectly regulated by the government. Thus, a complementary index may be helpful in evaluating domestic disequilibrium. The ratio of money supply to total expenditures may serve such a purpose and is reported in Table 4. Although such an index cannot be interpreted precisely, it may reveal an approximate scale of tension in the marketplace. Other estimates of the inflationary gap are reported in Table 5 and provide a similar picture of domestic disequilibrium.

The success of the reform depends on the progress in restoring equilibrium. Success in this area should be regarded both as evidence of and a precondition for reform efficiency.

III. DILEMMAS OF AGRICULTURAL DEVELOPMENT

During 1986, Poland's agricultural policy was determined, to a large extent, by the concept of self-reliance and security.[4] This concept was developed and put forward as one of the fundamental principles of the economic policy. It was perceived more as a general recommendation for the economic policy than as an operational guideline for planning.

The focus on self-reliance and security was meant to strengthen a popular conviction that "we can feed ourselves" and give the economic policy a general orientation rather than define in detail the substance and preconditions of that policy. In its narrow meaning this concept has gained an increasing position in social consciousness, and as such it has played a positive role. It has not been precisely defined, however.

The policy of food self-reliance should be considered against the background of circumstances in which it was put into operation. Its adoption was less a free choice and more a result of the pressures imposed by the internal and external situation at the beginning of the eighties. The principal goals of this policy were to ensure food security of the country and reduce Poland's trade deficit as much as possible. Both goals have been achieved to a large extent. Foreign trade in agricultural and food products became balanced without a drop in per capita food consumption.[5]

The predominant opinion with regard to the future development of Polish agriculture rejected the view that agriculture lacks development opportunities. It also rejected the notions that agriculture was efficient, that the farm structure was appropriate, and that an increase in external inputs would solve all problems.

The agricultural sector needs not only additional machinery and equipment, but also more efficient use of them. The agricultural sector has to be transformed in such a way that its increasing inputs are allocated to the most efficient users. The entire agricultural sector should be modernized, and certain structural changes should be quickly undertaken. Modern agricultural infrastructures, including water supplies, transportation, and communications, are necessary to make further agricultural development possible at all. The development of market relations within the framework of a balanced market is seen as the only promising form of interrelations between agriculture and industry.

These guidelines constitute the backbone of the new development strategy for Poland's agriculture in the long run. Market forces are expected to play a greater role in the determination of incomes. The controversial discussion on the so-called income parity, which is the root of many social conflicts, could disappear as a result. The pressure on agricultural prices is more likely to diminish when there is a relevant agricultural structure with well-developed, healthy market relations between agriculture and its environment, rather than the inefficient structures and administrative constraints presently imposed on the market.

IV.   THE ECONOMIC REFORM PROGRAM: PHASE TWO

On October 2, 1987 the program of implementation of the second phase of the economic reform was presented by the Polish Government to the Economic Reform Committee for evaluation and assessment. The program itself was based on conclusions derived from broad public discussion on the previously released "Theses on Phase Two of the Economic Reform."

The program outlined a schedule of steps to be undertaken over the next two years. These steps embraced further changes in the way the economy operated, reorganizing the central administration and industrial structures, and shaping the tools of socioeconomic policy. In accordance with the conclusions from public discussions, the program proposed:

1. regaining economic equilibrium by the improvement in conditions for supply growth;
2. regaining economic equilibrium by stabilizing the currency, restructuring prices and incomes, and shaping other economic parameters;
3. reconstruction of the management system at a macro-level.

While some elements and details of the second phase of the economic reform were vague, special attention to integrate an economic policy with so-called systemic solutions proved to be a basic line adopted by this program.

The program openly acknowledged that the original expectations to introduce the economic reform in its ultimate shape in just two or three years had not been met. It may be added that the reform implementation process failed to abandon the traditional way of running the economy. And a new threat emerged: the incoherence of the system, where corporate independence was restrained by the remaining elements of central direct management and regimentation.

Causes of this phenomenon are fiercely discussed. One must not ignore the distortion in economic equilibrium linked to external imbalance and policy adopted to protect the standard of living of economically handicapped groups in society.

Such an environment seriously affects the ability to invest. Moreover, the traditional structure of investment outlays appeared to remain intact. The lack of required structural change in the industrial sector offered no help to efforts aimed at stabilizing the consumer goods market.

The second phase of reform also tried to deal with the political and social sphere. It stressed the strengthening of self-government at the local and corporate level, improving the state's leverage over traditional industrial and regional interest groups, and having equality in various forms of ownership (i.e., maintaining equal and stable conditions for their growth). The program envisaged the following:

1.   A substantial change in the institutional structure and the range of power exercised by the central economic authorities. This would be supplemented by the creation of new expansion possibilities for new establishments of various forms of ownership and sectors of the economy.

2.   Substantial progress in 1989 in regaining internal economic equilibrium, invigorating the market mechanism, and stimulating exports.

3.   Persistent output stimulation and strict control measures on demand in order to reduce the inflation rate to one-digit figures, and halting an increase in foreign debt by the beginning of the next decade.

Two points, in particular, should be emphasized as far as the expected results of phase two of the economic reform are concerned. First, the program gave a time priority to the reorganization of the central economic authorities, whereas the 1981 version of the reform and earlier similar projects had included this task as the last step in the reform process. Thus, the reform of the central economic agencies came to be seen as a precondition for and the first indication of a reforming process, rather than its result. Second, the obstacles in restoring equilibrium were fully taken into account, that is, the consumer goods market received greater attention.

According to the experts, after putting aside all efforts to increase outputs, there are two ways to balance this market segment. Balance can be achieved either in a one-step drastic operation involving a substantial price increase and the simultaneous recompensation of its effects on staple foods and services for consumers, or by extending such an operation over two, three, or more years.

The supporters of these solutions were deeply polarized, and the government was unlikely to avoid a public discussion, whatever form this discussion would take. In the 1987 perspective, it was difficult to foresee which of the two variants of balancing the market, both unpopular, would eventually be put forward. Unlike the situation during the fifties and sixties, decisive steps could no longer be postponed. The prevailing orthodoxy of the past gave priority to efforts aimed at achieving a "tolerable" level of economic equilibrium, rather than to the economic reforms. Such an approach to ties between reforms and equilibrium became completely outdated.

Virtually all proposals articulated during discussions on phase two of the economic reform were included in the three sets of problems above. Thus, in the case of balancing the economy through output stimulation, the following particular problems emerged. First there must be a search for entrepreneurship and innovative behavior in all sectors of the economy, regardless of their forms of ownership. A basic prerequisite for such guidance, however, the creation of a capital market or at least a quasi-market, was not discussed to an extent that resulted in any promising and concrete steps. Second, ways to achieve greater openness of Poland's economy must be found and this process must be made irreversible.

Reconstruction of price and income structures, currency stabilization, and effective control over the rise in nominal incomes is as difficult as regaining the overall equilibrium. It is a common belief that all previous methods of central involvement in this field proved to be ineffective.

Finally, the role of reconstruction of the management system of the economy is focusing on the reorganization of the central economic agencies. The most critical part of this task, defining the range of government intervention in the economy and methods of exercising these powers, must go beyond the limits of general statements and simple analogies. This is no surprise. Such projects belong to the spheres of politics and human relations, and this is the softest point of the actual reform program. Therefore, its results are hardly predictable.

V. SUMMARY

The interrelations between real economic development; its social perception, expressed through social consciousness; and the way various social groups act and react have reached an unprecedented degree of intensity. The parameters of this complex equation are not and cannot be fully recognized in the present state of disequilibrium. Those who are obliged to outline a plan of action have to assume that there is no easy way to induce positive feedback between all parameters of this equation. The capacity of Poland's economy and similar economies of this size to develop will depend on the rapid creation of adjustment and investment capabilities which result from radical reforms.

NOTES AND REFERENCES

1. *Tygodnik Kulturalny* (Cultural Weekly), 39 (1987).
2. W. Jaruzelski. "Ku nowym horyzontom" (Toward New Horizons). *Kommunist* 11 (1987).
3. Professor J. Szczepański generally but indirectly presented the following contrasting approaches. See *Życie gospodarcze* 39 (September 27, 1987):

> The Polish reformers usually called for great deeds deriving from ethical renewal ... Dreaming about the ethical grandeur, the great people are still present as a precondition for the power of Poland ... Whereas the matter is to reconsider whether a way to the power of our country lies in great deeds of poets' dreams or in ordinary wisdom. Therefore, may the ordinary people achieve their small goals independently and in the best possible manner. And may their power rise from their earthly-mindedness. Our daily bread but not the angel's virtues is the answer.

4. "Samowystarczalność, Bezpieczeństwo Żywościwe" (Self sufficiency, Food-supply Security). *Gospodarka planowa* 12 (1987).
5. Ibid.

ECONOMIC REFORM AND DIRECTIVE CAPACITY OF THE POLISH STATE IN THE 1980s

Bartlomiej Kaminski

I. INTRODUCTION

Neither the reform measures nor economic policies pursued in 1982-86 produced a significant turnaround in the Polish economy. The economy did not reach the pre-crisis levels of global output; in 1988, national income produced stood at 99.0% of that in 1978, and national income produced per capita at 91.6%.[1] Applying the Marxist criteria for delineating phases of the business cycle, the Polish economy—since it had not reached the peak of the previous cycle—was still in the phase of depression. The defeat of the government's plans for the economic reform, which led to the announcement of the "second stage of economic reform," and recent strikes showed that the crisis was not confined to the economy but extended to the whole complex of relations between the socialist state and society. Put differently, Poland's political economy of state socialism was in crisis.

The 1988 April-May and August-September strikes in Poland revealed the limited political capacities of the state to impose necessary adjustment costs and circumvent political constraints on economic policy making. While the opposition's credibility was undermined by its inability to launch a general strike, the situation did little to boost the government's strength. Its strategy of containing the wave of strikes through denying political demands and accepting the economic ones undermined the implementation of the second stage of economic reform. The wage increases granted would inevitably increase disequilibria and, therefore, contradict the objectives of the ill-conceived "price-income" operation.[2]

The underlying causes of limited political capacities in reviving the economy stemmed from the institutional legacies of state socialism which displayed substantive resistance to change. The persistence of these institutional arrangements was manifested by two fundamental inconsistencies in economic and political strategy pursued by the Polish government after 1982. The first inconsistency involved a tolerance of political opposition and diversity combined with a simultaneous rejection of reforms that would make pluralism politically meaningful. The changes in the political and legal framework failed to broaden the political base of the Jaruzelski regime. They produced social apathy and indifference which could guarantee dominance but not leadership. If the authorities wanted to preserve the institutions of state socialism, nothing short of genuine enthusiastic social support and mobilization would turn the economy around. Given the state of relations between the rulers and ruled, this was rather unlikely. The alternative was to overhaul command planning, the economic pillar of state socialism.

The second inconsistency in the policies pursued in the 1980s was related to the introduction of economic reform measures congruent with a market economy in a nonmarket environment. The program of economic reforms adopted by the Ninth Extraordinary Party Congress was not free of internal conceptual incoherences. They were, however, exacerbated in the course of program implementation. Government documents published in early 1987 to initiate a public debate on the second stage of economic reform described the overall objective in terms of introducing a viable combination of planning and an effective— to borrow a term from the government's "Theses on Designing Organizational Structures"—"self-regulatory market mechanism."[3] This was also the objective of the first stage of reform and indicated economic and political realities were "reform-proof." The pattern of progression and regression observed in Poland since the first attempt to reform the economy in the post-1956 upheaval period had again prevailed.

The purpose of this chapter is neither to describe a sequence of political and economic measures implemented by the Polish authorities, nor to analyze point by point their impact on economic performance in the 1980s.[4] Instead, I will focus on three critical questions. First, what were the major characteristics of the political economy of state socialism and how did they shape the state's directive capacity? Second, what major impediments to reform surfaced in Poland in the 1980s? Third, to what degree did the economic reform measures implemented in the 1980s mark a departure from "traditional" state socialism and how did they contribute to the improvement or deterioration in the directive capacity of the state?

Note that in posing the issues in this perspective there are three important consequences. The first consequence is that my query focuses on the rules, or framework, that guided economic activity in any society that adopted the Stalinist economic system. The rigidity of the social and economic structures of this system, strongly reminiscent of the traditional, status-oriented society, bore responsibility for the continuation of the Polish crisis. The patterns of behavior and organizing principles of state socialism, on the one hand, were a major impediment to economic efficiency and, on the other hand, granted the policy makers rather narrow opportunities for action. Reform, then, was conceived as a change in organizing principles and patterns of behavior.

The second consequence is that assessment of the departure involved not only purely economic issues but encompassed a complex of political, social, and economic processes defining state socialism. Finally, the third consequence is that in order to explain the problems encountered in implementing the economic reform measures, one should take into account the institutional setting of state socialism. Many episodes of abortive economic reforms in Poland and other East European countries suggest that impediments were rooted in the design of the state-socialist political and economic order.

II.   IMPLICATIONS OF THE FUSION OF
STATE AND ECONOMY

State socialism is rooted in the political and economic order that
Stalin built in the Soviet Union in the 1930s. The Stalinist system
was shaped by authoritarian political procedures extended to the
economy: an administrative mechanism of resource allocation
replaced the market. The commitment to the rule of law was replaced
by ad hoc rules defined by the authorities. The legal order became
a direct tool of governance by subjecting it to the discretional
interpretation of higher authority. The introduction of *nomenklatura* and the hegemony of the party over major institutional systems
amounted to the rejection of democracy. Faced with the weakening
of ideology and the erosion of central controls over society and the
economy, Stalinist state structures and capabilities changed. Many
(e.g., Nove 1986; Commisso and Tyson 1986) claim that in spite of
numerous attempts at changing the system, its essence, consisting
of a unique symbiotic relationship between party-state and economy,
still prevailed. To determine whether this description fit Poland in
the mid-1980s is one of the objectives of this essay.

   Inclusion of the economy into the direct realm of state activities
has a number of consequences. First, the dominance of state over
the economy and the politicization of resource distribution has
removed the stimulus for efficiency and innovation provided by
markets. Among the most important objectives of the state,
capitalist and socialist alike, one can hardly find economic
efficiency. It is overshadowed by concerns with political stability,
internal order, and the security of the state. Some authors observe
that efficiency has always been a secondary consideration in the
choice of state policies. This creates no problem in the market
economy where competition enforces microeconomic efficiency. In
state socialism, however, the subordination of the economy to the
state creates a conflict between imperatives of economic efficiency
and political interests, usually solved in favor of political interests.
In addition, since the essence of direct state involvement in the
economy is to protect *state-owned* enterprises from failure
(shielding them from domestic and foreign competition) the
motivation to innovate and increase efficiency is further weakened.
As Hewett (1986, p. 14) reminds: "Economic insecurity plus
economic autonomy are parents of innovation."

Second, the fusion of state and economy generates commitments which reduce the political flexibility of the state. The party apparatus and economic bureaucracy derive privileges and benefits from direct "interference in wealth creation"—to borrow an apt term from Winiecki (1987, p. 55). Any change that limits access to the economy is strongly resisted and constitutes a threat to the stability of the political order of state socialism. This helps explain why reforms in Eastern Europe and the Soviet Union have either failed or fallen short of their goals.

Third, the fusion of state and economy imposes on the state the burden of responsibility for economic developments far exceeding the responsibilities of governments which operate in a market environment. The paradox is that it weakens the state by making it responsible for all the shortcomings of the economy. A cross-country study (Coleman and Nelson 1984) comparing Poland with several Latin American countries indicates the degree of workers' alienation in the "worker state" is much higher than in developing state-capitalist societies. The state's omnipresence and its aspiration to control everything not only reduces its ability to change, but also breeds alienation and apathy.

Fourth, subordination of the economy to the state necessarily eliminates the market as a mechanism for resource allocation. State socialism is left with the only other mechanism available, a bureaucratic mechanism according to Kornai (1986b), or simply a nonmarket allocative mechanism (Wanless 1985).[6] Whatever the adjective, the menu of economic policy instruments available to state decision makers is essentially reduced to direct microeconomic administrative intervention, hence the principle of direct manual controls. The absence of markets and the price mechanism make the use of instruments of indirect intervention— monetary policy (regulating the money supply and interest rates) and fiscal policy (controlling flows of income)—virtually impossible.[7] The major instruments available are material balances and central allocation, "planning from the achieved level," and various forms of coercion or paternalism. To be sure, there are prices, interest rates, and taxes, but they do not directly shape management decisions in the socialized enterprise sector. The survival of enterprise management does not depend on profit maximization, but on its ability to coexist with the state and party administration.

Hierarchical multilevel structures, an inevitable component of administrative mechanisms, are not only inherently inflexible, but also require much more information than the market mechanism to effectively control the economy. As an economy moves up the development ladder, information needed to sustain directive capacity dramatically increases. With the modernization of the economy, the party's desire totally to control society and the economy becomes more difficult to fulfill. Many (Birman 1978; Wilhelm 1979; Winiecki 1987) argue the information processing requirement alone makes central planning impossible. Socialist states face what Nove (1986, p.143) succinctly described as "the impossible [in terms of information processing—BK] scale of centralized microeconomic planning." Because of this information barrier, economic actors gain some degree of autonomy, which then sets the stage for bargaining.

Bargaining magnifies distortions in state socialism to a much greater degree than in a democratic, market-based society. In the absence of markets, there is no reference point to measure the deviations from economically efficient allocations and those resulting from bargaining. The results of bargaining are neither directly subjected to market appraisal nor publicly known. They are free from direct accountability to the public and to the constraints of economic efficiency.[8]

While flexibility of the socialist state is curtailed by the exclusive reliance on hierarchical multilevel structures to control the economy, state socialism is endowed with a mechanism that reduces threats to its survival, albeit at substantial costs in terms of economic efficiency. The mechanism is the parallel administrative arrangements of the party and state hierarchies. The party apparatus may provide a check on the natural tendency of bureaucracy toward expansion and corruption exhibited in all societies. Some claim that the party apparatus functions as a substitute for both public control and political accountability of the elites ruling in democratic societies. In relation to the state administration, it acts as a controller, ad hoc coordinator, and stimulator.

The functional unity of political and economic mechanisms produces a precarious social equilibrium. Stability requires an effective suppression of group interests and the existence of economic disequilibria within a socially tolerable range.[9] On the other hand, the political stability of state socialism depends on providing job security. It is the same mechanisms of shortage generation that lead to inadequate supplies of capital goods and production inputs that also provide full employment. Full employment and shortages are inevitable outcomes of internal mechanisms underlying the fusion of state and economy, rather than of deliberate public policies. Any attempt to dissect factors contributing to shortage generation inescapably conflicts with factors contributing to state socialism's legitimacy, that is, with full employment, job security, and rationing.

These very factors are also responsible for allocative and productive inefficiencies. For instance, Kornai (1986a) contrasts the necessary conditions for economic efficiency with "the ethical principles of a socialist economy," and concludes that they are mutually exclusive, thus supporting a classic argument of Friedrich Hayek.[10] Polish economist Lipowski (1987), by demonstrating the incompatibility between state planning and market processes, arrives at a similar conclusion. As recent debate on the second stage of economic reform in Poland suggests, official thinking was changing as well. The authors from the Committee for the Review of Organizational Structures of the Government-Party Commission, having enumerated the necessary organizational changes that should effect the diversity in organizational structures (priority of economic over bureaucratic considerations, direct links between producers and international markets, etc.), concluded these "are not a feature of political system, but they stem from the character of contemporary productive forces in the changing world economy" ("Tezy w sprawie ksztaltowania..." 1987, p. 1). It remained to be seen whether the implicit recognition of a dialectical contradiction between productive forces and production relations in the Polish economy would produce institutional change eliminating the contradiction.

III. HURDLES TO ECONOMIC REFORMS: LIMITED ADAPTIVE CAPACITIES OF STATE SOCIALISM

Two components dominate the relationship between economic reform and directive capacity. The first is an institutional

component encompassing the changes in the institutional
framework and rules of the game between the state and economic
actors, whereas the second relates to public economic objectives
and means to attain them. Meaningful institutional change
implies not only a modification in the institutional framework of
state socialism, but also in the menu of public policy instruments
available to policy makers. Leaving aside various attempts to
improve administrative procedures of planning and management,
the general thrust of economic reforms has been to complement
and/or replace administrative commands with financial levers
(Fallenbuchl 1988; Nuti 1987). The objective of economic reform
is to improve productive and allocative efficiency and thereby to
increase directive capacity. During the transition to a reformed
system, public economic policies include both institutional
changes and specific goals, and a sequence of actions to attain
them. The correspondence between institutional and legal changes
and the instruments and procedures used by the state to attain the
objectives of economic policies is critical for successful economic
reform.[11]

The economic reform officially depicted as the "Second Stage
of Economic Reform," was the fourth attempt at a comprehensive
change in the principles of a command planning system. The first
undertaking aimed at eliminating the most obvious drawbacks of
command planning followed the political crisis of October 1956;
the second, the workers' revolt in December 1971; and the third
followed the labor unrest in 1980 and the imposition of martial
law in December 1981. None of them brought about a meaningful
change.

The failure of economic reforms suggests that within the
institutional arrangements of state socialism there is limited room
for change. The changes that improve directive capacity and
productive and allocative efficiency are a direct threat to the very
foundations of state socialism. It is suggestive that the first two
attempts at comprehensive reform took place during periods of
relative political liberalization when fundamental institutions of
state socialism were challenged.[12]

The third reform, although its original blueprint was designed
during a period of unprecedented freedoms, does not fall into this
pattern. The most ambitious endeavor to implement it took place
in 1982-83 during the period of "normalization," that is, of

recentralization of political controls. While the period between late 1981 and mid-1984 witnessed a number of innovative reform measures, in subsequent years there was stagnation. The pattern of progression and stagnation came full circle in May of 1988 with the approval by the Sejm of a package of special powers for the government to push through its economic reform program.

Despite the relatively modest political component of the reform measures, all fell short of being fully implemented. Each left a legacy of new regulations and unsolved problems for later years. Further, they cannot be easily dismissed as just an example of politics of succession or, in the case of the first stage of the economic reform in the 1980s, as a *novum* in the politics of normalization. Each contributed to the change in emphasis on the components of state socialism that should be changed and to what extent. The common denominator of each economic reform was the emphasis on changing the rules underlying the principle of inclusion. Let us examine the economic reform measures introduced during the first stage in the 1980s in the context of the principle of inclusion and implications for the state's directive capacity.

Distinguishing the reform pursued in the 1980s was a perception among the authorities that a radical change in the rules of interaction between the state and the economy was the last resort for overcoming the crisis. While Gierek was able to contain the crisis in 1971 by tapping external resources, this option was not available to the government in the 1980s. The depth of the economic crisis and the legitimacy crisis of communist rule was fully revealed by the Solidarity self-limiting revolution. This set a new tone for the debate on the economic reform program.

In contrast to the earlier programs of economic reform, the blueprint of the Party-Government Commission for Economic Reform, formally accepted by the Ninth Extraordinary Party Congress in 1981, recognized the necessity for major changes not only in planning and management instruments, but also in the framework of party-state involvement in the national economy.[13] It called for changes in the institutional tenets of the economic system by introducing strict and transparent rules of state economic intervention. This was by far the most comprehensive and radical blueprint designed to modify the tenets of state socialism.

At the core of the reform blueprint was the transfer of some powers from the government to society and economic actors, and the development of new instruments of controlling national economy. The blueprint included a change in the role of the state economic administration, an increased role of the Sejm, and significant financial and decision-making autonomy of self-managed enterprises. The scope of central command planning was to be reduced mainly to budget-financed social infrastructure and large-scale projects in key economic sectors. Greater social participation in choosing the objectives and the means to attain them was envisioned. The social participation was to be achieved mainly by changes in enterprise regime. The enterprises were to be independent, self-managed, and self-financed. The banking system was to be reformed by establishing competing commercial banks controlled by the Central Bank. Wages and bonuses were to be directly linked to production and productivity growth, whereas the state would guarantee minimum wages. In brief, direct state microeconomic intervention was to be gradually supplemented with indirect macroeconomic controls operating through markets. Thus, had the reform followed the directives outlined in the document, "Kierunki reformy gospodarczej," the principle of fusion of the state and economy would have been eroded, if not entirely severed.

The program was not only substantially circumscribed in the course of implementation, but its scope was curtailed. Laws providing a legal framework for a reformed system lost their edge because of frequent ad hoc suspensions and exceptions, or because of, as Pajestka (1985) claims, softness in their implementation. Laws were easily bent, fudged, and forgotten, an indication that the principle of bending the rules was not eradicated. In addition, public economic policies, prompted by political rather than economic considerations, tended to undermine the provisions of various legislative measures.

The implementation of the economic reform program as outlined in "Kierunki reformy gospodarczej" was to be spread over a period of two to three years. The implementation began on January 1, 1982. The legal framework was set by two fundamental laws on state enterprises and workers' self-management enacted by the Sejm in 1981. The law on state enterprises substantially reduced the scope of direct intervention by the state.[14] The so-called founding organizations (ministries) were made responsible for setting up a new enterprise regime depicted by the famous three

"S's": self-management, self-financing, and self-dependence. Instead of a plan assigning targets to an enterprise, economic activities were to be conducted on the basis of plans adopted by enterprise employees. The law provided for exceptions retaining production quotas related to national defense or international agreements. In these cases, the founding organization was obliged to provide the necessary input to fulfill these quotas. Public utility firms exempted from the law were to remain subject to direct administrative controls.

The law on self-management, delineating one of the three S's, gave the workers' council, directly elected by enterprise employees, powers to make decisions on all important issues concerning management of the enterprise. Except for enterprises of "basic national importance," councils were empowered to hire and fire directors. Then, with the imposition of martial law, which lasted from December 13, 1981, to July 22, 1983, all powers of workers' councils were transferred to either the military commissars or directors. Although the issue of self-management remained high on the official agenda and the councils regained powers provided for in the law of 1981, the loophole offered by the "basic national importance" consideration was used by the state to retain the *nomenklatura* over the appointments in major state-owned enterprises.[15]

These two acts, the legislative pillars of the reform, fell short of being fully implemented. Their intentions were distorted not only by loopholes and exemptions but above all by a flood of legal acts and their interpretations restricting the three S's. In addition to more than 300 laws setting the legislative framework of the reformed economic system, there were about 12,000 interpretations by 1985.[16] This astounding number of interpretations was an inevitable outcome of loopholes and imprecision in the legal acts, and of delegating powers of their interpretation to the state apparatus. As Kleer (1988) observed, the state apparatus sought to interpret the laws with a single objective of minimizing losses in its privileges, incomes, and power. The variety of contradictory laws, combined with administrative decrees inconsistent with the two basic laws, did not alleviate the softness of the Polish legal order nor advance the economic reform. The legislative hybrid was a manifestation of an array of developments eroding the program of economic reform.

Assuming the government was committed to implementing the economic reform as envisioned in "Kierunki reformy gospodarczej," was the legislative hybrid evidence of weak directive capacity? The government neither developed the program detailing the sequence of measures nor displayed determination to implement the reform. Commenting on the special powers act, the Polish "official" economist Kleer bluntly noted: "Though over the last years political elites and government have been persistently stressing their willingness to implement far-reaching economic and social reforms, nonetheless—at least between 1984 and mid-1987—they were not sufficiently determined to implement them" (Kleer 1988, p. 4).

A growing gap between rhetoric and policy suggests that in the government's assessment, political and economic costs of fully implementing the reform exceeded the benefits. Although martial law witnessed fervent activity by the Sejm to create a new legal framework compatible with the program of economic reform, its implementation was not granted a top priority. In fact, economic reform was one of many policy actions designed to effect the "normalization" without simultaneously increasing the potential for political instability.[17]

Although the Polish authorities have been praised for rejecting both the Husak variant of normalization based on massive reprisals and the Ceaucescu approach to "solving" the debt crisis by imposing extreme hardships on the population, the government's relatively flexible approach of seeking to coopt rather than coerce various social groups in many instances undermined the economic reform. The Polish government pursued policies aimed at minimizing the loss of power (or the economic burden) of those who might directly threaten political stability, but which fell far short of instituting a promised mixture of planning with self-regulatory markets.

Several sectors of the economy and areas of public policy making were outrightly exempted from the reform. These industries, declared to be either public utilities or of national importance (in order to conform with the law on state enterprises), included the cement, coal, power, sugar, and meat producing sectors. The reform could have survived the reduction of its scope. More significant was that the reform measures, despite the vehement opposition of the Government's Consultative Economic Council and Socio-Economic Council of the Sejm, did not target the institutional framework of investment decisions.[18] As a consequence, highly capital-intensive investment projects have retained their "priority" status in central plans, and investment policies have followed the same pattern as in the 1970s.[19] The emphasis has been on energy-intensive rather than on energy-saving investment.

In spite of widespread criticism and frequent promises made by government officials, the 1986-90 investment plan or its 1988 component have not yet been revised.[20] According to the Consultative Economic Council Report, the coal industry's share of total investment outlays increased from 7.6% in 1971-75 and 11.1% in 1976-80 to 17% in 1981-85. The coal industry remains the largest single recipient of subsidies from the state budget. The corresponding shares for the energy producing sector were 8.7%, 10.4%, and 15.5% (KRG 1988). Similar proportions are indicated in the 1986-90 National Social and Economic Plan. The authors of the report wryly observe that these proportions are higher than in the Stalinist 6-Year Plan of "socialist construction" in 1951-55, which focused on the development of the energy and resource industrial base. Thus, coal and energy-producing sectors absorbed roughly one third of total investment expenditures in the socialized sector in the 1980s. It left the state with few resources to restructure the debt-ridden economy.

Neither did it enhance chances for a meaningful economic reform. In fact, this increased the bargaining position of the heavy-industry lobby. Subjecting investment decision making to economic criteria would most likely reduce the flow of resources to these industries (because of the low levels of profitability) and, therefore, they are generally believed to favor recentralization. There is some evidence that the heavy-industry lobby sought to undermine reform. For instance Crane (1988, p. 11) indicates the Ministry of Metallurgy and Engineering sponsored several initiatives to recentralize controls in their industries. Close links between heavy industry and defence also strengthened their leverage within the state.

Ironically, since large plants, which have been bastions of Solidarity, are mostly in heavy or defence-related industries, the bargaining position of "metal eaters" has been enhanced by the government's strategy of buying labor peace. Wage rates and government subsidies continued to be the highest in these sectors, even though labor productivity was not. These sectors have received preferential treatment, although their costs of production exceed international prices—in some cases by three to four times (e.g., steel). This congruence of interests of the heavy industrial "proletariat" and metal eaters, combined with a failure of the reform to curtail excessive energy consumption, enhanced the bargaining position of heavy industry. It also contributed to inflation and the rapidly deteriorating competitiveness of Polish products in international markets.

Between 1983 and 1986, in spite of steady growth in the average real wage, real wages of about half the workforce declined. The most substantial increases in wages were not in those sectors which experienced the largest increases in productivity, but in those which had the largest average wages to begin with. Among the sectors that received preferential "wage" treatment, one may find industries of the extractive and heavy-industry sector. For instance, between 1982 and 1986 the largest gains in wages were obtained by employees in coal mining, iron metallurgy, and engineering industries. A correlation analysis of Poland's top 500 corporations in 1986 indicated the existence of a weak link between wages and labor productivities.[21] The problem was acknowledged by the Executive Committee of the Official Trade Union which noted that the growing disparity in wages in various industries "unfortunately, often bears no relation to economic performance" (Jeziorański 1987).

Instead, it bears a rather strong relationship to the size of industrial plants. In fact, the large plants, strongholds of the Solidarity movement like the Gdansk shipyard or Lenin steelworks in Nowa Huta near Cracow, seem to predominate in the sectors obtaining the lion's share of increases in wages.[22] This suggests real incomes fell for employees of small industrial plants rather than the large ones, which could organize highly visible and economically costly strikes. This vulnerability to the demands of the industrial "proletariat" (confirmed by the government's readiness to grant wage increases to striking workers who did not demand political concessions), reveals the inability or unwillingness of the state to free itself from capture by various anti-reform social groups and seriously impeded the state's ability to overhaul the traditional command system.

In contrast to the political sphere, the state was not, except for the demands to reinstitute workers' councils, subjected to societal pressures to effect the program of economic reform. To the contrary, each reform measure contemplated by the government generated suspicions that its true intention was to increase (to borrow a term from Marx) the "rate of exploitation." A recent statement, ironically from W. Martyniuk (the Vice Chairman of the official Trade Union Organization), captures the prevailing disposition toward the government's reform measures. In reference to the government's plans to raise prices and impose income taxes, he said that "union members believe the government's price and income policies will lead only to higher prices, more inflation, and a further decline in real incomes" (Polish Radio; Warsaw; January 13, 1988). Since the recent price-income operation failed to change price relations between manufactures, energy, and agricultural products, he indeed was right.

Another impediment was related to the incompatibility between the social and political assumptions underlying the program of economic reform adopted by the Ninth Party Congress and imperatives of the normalization process. While the program envisaged Solidarity and active social participation unfettered by the interference of the state, the essence of normalization was integration through vertical, instead of horizontal, linkages and social atomization.[23] In the wake of martial law all powers of self-management bodies were transferred to the military commissars or directors. The program was not corrected to allow for the socio-political realities of the post-Solidarity period. This apparent incongruity, between the political content of the program and centralization of political controls effected under normalization, was not corrected.

Given that these structural impediments to the economic reform program were not overcome, the conditions for a shift away from the principle of inclusion, that is, from direct to indirect controls, were not obtained. The impact of draconian price increases in early 1982 (intended to restore market equilibria and to set ground for a price reform) was diluted first by the government's decision to pay compensations in late 1982, and later by the failure to introduce institutions compatible with promised enterprise autonomy.

Social resistance, combined with the reluctance of a party-state bureaucracy faced with an impossible task of "reforming itself," provided little incentive for the introduction of economic reform. Hence, the list of meaningful changes in the political realm forced upon the government by societal pressures, although still falling short of introducing genuine political accountability of the government, is much longer than a comparable list of economic changes.[24] This also explains the paradox pointed out by Polish economist Sołdaczuk that the improvement in the economic situation precipitated a drift away from the reform program.[25] Yet, in many important aspects the interface between the state and economy has changed.

IV. THE SCOPE OF CHANGE: DISINTEGRATION OF STATE SOCIALISM

A number of indicators suggest a considerable reduction in the scope of central planning. Formally, since 1982, central plans have been replaced by forecasts. There are no longer obligatory targets for state-owned enterprises. Enterprises still construct plans and provide information to the state administration, but enterprises may alter them at their own discretion.

A considerable portion of investment decision was transferred to enterprises. The ability to start new projects was linked to financial results (for access to credits). Between 1983 and 1986, the share of investment made by enterprises in total investment outlays increased from 51 to 56.2%. The access to credits, the main source remained the Central Bank, depended, at least in principle, on creditworthiness.

Such innovative measures as auctions of hard currency and currency-retention quotas (allowing an exporter to retain a portion of its hard currency export revenues) reduced the isolation of domestic producers from international markets. The number of enterprises authorized to hold hard-currency retention quota accounts increased from 1,629 in 1983 to 2,389 in 1986; their share in imports grew from 9.4 to 11.3%, and in exports from 10.7 to 13.8% in the same period. This suggests that the state's involvement in direct control of foreign trade fell. Similarly, the law allowing enterprises that meet certain requirements to apply for foreign trade permits weakened the traditional foreign-trade monopoly by the state.

Another area which, nota bene, was affected by each of the successive waves of economic reforms was central rationing. The scope of central rationing, measured by proportions of inputs centrally allocated, fell. For instance, the scope of raw materials and intermediate products subject to direct rationing fell significantly, from 60% in 1984 to 45% in 1986. This measure alone may be misleading, however. The introduction of "purchase orders" and the compulsory designation of suppliers effectively reduced progress toward genuine decentralization.

Further, a number of indicators unequivocally points to a retreat of the reform. The state's involvement in the redistribution of purchasing power among economic actors increased. Subsidies, which initially fell as a result of price increases in 1982, started to grow again. And, so did the number of loss-making enterprises. Similarly, the increase in the concentration and centralization of production flew in the face of the spirit of the economic reform program which envisaged a significant curtailment of the degree of monopolization of the economy.

The most telling indicators of the regression of the economic reform are those related to the state budget's role in managing the economy. The magnitude of income redistribution among enterprises is a good indication of financial dependence of enterprises on central planners. In view of the emphasis of the economic reform blueprint on increasing the autonomy of enterprises, it should be disappointing to the authorities that the proportion of national income distributed through the state budget was actually higher in 1985 than before the reform in 1978 (Albinowski 1987). Since 1983, the budget has been commanding an increasing share of net income of industrial enterprises. By 1986, the ratio of budgetary revenues derived from net income of enterprises increased to about 40%—the average level recorded in 1958-72 (Wojciechowska and Zytniewski 1987). These revenues were increasingly used to subsidize mainly coal mining and food processing. These two sectors account for about 86.5% of budgetary subsidies.

That direct administrative mechanism, a unique trait of state socialism, has not been weakened is also illustrated by expansion in employment in the area of central economic administration in

Poland. The streamlining of central administration in 1981 did not reverse a trend of employment growth in the state administration. During the first stage of economic reform, employment in central economic administration grew faster than the employment in the socialized sector as a whole. Its increase was also higher than the increase in national income produced.

Since there are no grounds to posit that the increase in employment in central economic administration was caused by a sudden fall in bureaucratic productivity, the increase must be due to the administrative burden of the reform measures. This contradicts the intentions of the authors of "Kierunki reformy gospodarczej..." who wanted to reduce the state's direct involvement in the economy. The implementation of the reform program, according to which direct central controls were to be replaced by indirect tools of control, should have reduced the administrative burden of central economic administration. Yet, in spite of introducing various, explicitly indirect tools of controls such as tax rates, credit policy, and the exchange rate, the administrative burden has increased. The conditions calling for discretionary intermediation of resources by the state were not eradicated. The reform measures introduced, instead of simplifying, significantly complicated the task of management of the economy.

V. CONCLUSION

To what extent did the reform measures implemented in the Polish planning and management erode, or invalidate, the organizing principles of state socialism? First, this short story of the frozen reform has confirmed the existence of a close relationship between power structure, forms of social control, and domination, as well as the factors accounting for negative legitimation, bargaining, and shortages. The reform measures fell short of establishing a clearly defined boundary between the economy and the state. As a result, the distribution of resources remained highly politicized. Following Usher (1981), one may argue that the incomplete reform did not eliminate the tension between the conditions accounting for negative legitimacy and the conditions for improving economic growth performance.[26] One pervasive manifestation of this was the growth of subsidies. A further manifestation was ambivalence in the government's approach to the private sector which, because of economic considerations was allowed to grow, but subjected to administrative nuisances. This search for solutions to improve economic efficiency without undermining the power of the state (derived, inter alia, from discretionary management of shortages) eventually sidetracked the original economic reform program. The measures implemented have the potential for undermining the symbiosis between government and business and thus the unitary logic of state socialism.

The growing awareness among Polish officials of the necessity to create conditions for domestic convertibility of the Polish zloty[27] indicates that the principle of inclusion will be directly challenged. A strong zloty or remonetization of the economy would amount to the removal of institutional arrangements responsible for Kornai's mechanisms of shortage generation. Monetization entails subjecting the interaction between the state and the economy to well-defined universal rules.

Second, there have been no studies published—to my knowledge—on how the role of the party apparatus in managing the economy has been affected by Solidarity, martial law, and economic reform. The picture is again fuzzy. On the one hand, the government sought to expand the use of law as an instrument of governance. Indeed, there is some fragmentary evidence pointing to a stricter observance of the law. For instance, laws were introduced that allow enterprises and citizens to challenge the decisions of the administration. The shift toward greater legal symmetry in the relations between citizens and administration helped the government to curb the power of local administration.

On the other hand, because of informal leverage of the "founding organs" (due to their discretionary intermediation in resource allocation), greater legal symmetry did little to enhance the autonomy of enterprises. Within the state itself the economic administration was strengthened while the party apparatus was weakened.[28] Some even claim that the "regional Poland of the 1970s has been replaced by a 'Poland of Branch Ministries'."[29] In addition, an examination of various legislative measures enacted in the 1980s strongly suggests that the tradition of fuzziness and loopholes, that is, leaving the interpretation to the state administration, persists. These observations suggest that although the form may have been altered, the legal system has not yet eradicated conditions conducive to bending the rules.

Third, partial remonetization of the economy and limited autonomy granted to enterprises demonstrated that a transplantation of control tools of market provenance leads to an inefficient hybrid of controls necessitating direct manual controls. Markets cannot be simulated "instead of being allowed to develop" (Marer 1987, p. 184). This concluding observation on the Hungarian reform of the 1980s applies also to the case of the Polish reform which vastly complicated the task of management—not only for the state, but also for other economic actors.

Finally, the government's readiness to bend to wage demands, even though they put the whole reform in jeopardy, illustrated its inability to suppress group interests which is crucial to the effectiveness of the socialist state (Poznanski 1986). It also demonstrated something much more important: the reform fell short of introducing effective political mechanisms of conflict mediation that would recompensate for the loss of the ability to subdue group interests.

NOTES

1. It is interesting to note that national income produced in private sector in 1987 exceeded the 1978 level by 9.6% whereas of the state-owned 96.% was 3.2% below the 1978 level. The share of the private sector in national income, which amounted to 17.2% (agriculture—8.2) in 1987, is still too small to make a significant difference. (Data from *Rocznik statystyczny*, Warsaw: Central Statistical Office, 1988, and Podstowowe dane statystyczne o Polsce 1946-1988, Warsaw: Central Statistical Office, 1989.)

2. This term is used in Poland to describe the government's policy of raising prices, mainly the price of food products, and then wages to compensate for the price increases. It remains to be seen whether the government coalition-solidarity opposition accord, signed on April 7, 1989, will solve this problem.

3. See the government official documents: "Tezy w sprawie II etapu reformy gospodarczej" (Theses on the Second State of Economic Reform), *Rzeczpospolita*, Warszawa, April 17, 1987; "Tezy w sprawie ksztaltowani struktur organizacyjnych" (Theses on Designing Organizational Framework of the Economy), *Rzeczpospolita*, May 12, 1987. For the assessment of economic reform by the Provisional Council and Provisional Coordinating Commission of NSZ "Solidarność," see *Stanowisko NSZZ "Solidarność" w sprawie sytuacji i kierunkow przebudowy gospodarki polskiej* (NSZZ "Solidarity" Standpoint on the Situation and Restructuring of the Polish Economy), mimeo, Gdansk-

Warszawa, April 1987. The assessment by OPZZ ("official" Trade Union's Confederation) has been presented in *Alternatywna koncepcja realizacji reformy gospodarczej: czesc II rozwiniecie* (Alternative Approaches to the Economic Reform), mimeo, Warszawa, September 1987.

4.   For a detailed analysis of the reform measures, see Gomulka and Rosowski (1984); Fallenbuchl (1985); Nuti (1987); and Mieszczankowski (1987). Crane (1988) gives an assessment of the impact of the reform on economic performance.

5.   The analysis in this section draws heavily on Kaminski (1989).

6.   Wanless (1985, p. 4) distinguishes two kinds of nonmarket allocation mechanism: the (National) Plan and the (State) budget mechanism. This distinction is highly misleading. The plan is a product of state administration. In addition, although enterprises are accounting cost units, costs and revenues do not determine—because of subsidies and price equalization accounts—their retained profits

7.   As Portes (1983, p. 150) points out there are macroeconomic aggregates, like household money balances, which "cannot be planned centrally at the microlevel." However, it does not follow that they are "planned indirectly at the macrolevel." Because of the persistence of administered prices and soft budget constraints, monetary policy plays a more circumscribed role than in market economies.

8.   In addition, since information is not readily available to central planners, it undercuts the effectiveness of central planning. The process may be described as follows: in the phase of plan construction producers seek to maximize input/ output ratios and hide information about their actual production possibilities frontiers. In the process, they want to assure cooperation of the local party apparatus and the local trade union administration. Those two, theoretically, having at their disposal alternative communication channels may undermine an enterprise strategy. Central planners, on the other hand, seek to elicit maximum effort and effect coordination. Some have claimed (Birman 1978; Wilhelm 1979) planning within this institutional framework is impossible.

9.   Since state socialism is deprived of effective political mechanisms, its performance is critically dependent on its ability to suppress them. Poznanski (1986) observes that one of the causes of the Polish economic crisis was the inability of the Gierek regime to effectively suppress group interests.

10.   It is worth noting that Kornai has drawn his conclusion from contrasting the economic efficiency conditions with the conditions of the *reformed* Hungarian economic system.

11.   For instance, if othe reform grants financial autonomy to enterprises, the state's direct involvement in rationing of inputs undermines the reform.

12.   It gave rise to the assertion of a link between pressures toward economic decentralization and relaxation of political controls (Nuti 1979).

13.   See "Kierunki reformy gospodarczej-projekt: Projekt ustaw o przedsiębiorstwach państwowych-o samorządzie przedsiębiorstwa panst- wowego," published by the CC PUWP's official daily *Trybuna Ludu*, Warszawa, July 1981.

14.   For a discussion of its major provisions, see Fallenbuchl (1988, pp. 120- 121).

15.   The list of enterprises exempted from the right to appoint directors increased from 200 in late 1981 to 1,371 in 1985. For illluminating insights on workers' self-management before and after the imposition of martial law, see Holland (1988).

16.   Jeziorański (1985) quoted in Fallenbuchl (1988 p. 118).

17.   As Bielasiak (1988, pp. 103, 104) succintly observes: "This emphasis on economic action, however, should not be confused with the entire program of the state of war ... Economic reform was but one component of a complex process of political, social, and economic policies designed to stabilize the country by means of control over society by the state."

18.   See the interview with Professor Czeslaw Bobrowski, former Chairman of Consultative Economic Council, "Nie liczę na przełom ..." (I do not expect a turning-point ...), Życie gospodarcze, No. 51/52, 1987.

19.   See a letter signed by Mieczyslaw Lesz, Życie gospodarcze, No. 51/52, 1987, p. 11. The blueprint for Katowice steel works calls for transporting steel to other steel works, although the second melting requires 60% of original energy input. Lesz, like many other economists, argues that the current investment plan should be overhauled.

20.   For instance, highly controversial projects like the steel plant "Katowice" which is to be expanded in accordance with the blueprint prepared in the 1970s as well as coal mine "Stefanów" have been included in 1988 CPR (Central Annual Plan). As far as the "Stefanów" project is concerned, this view—although very carefully worded—is shared by experts from the World Bank. According to the World Bank report (*Poland: Reform, Adjustment and Growth, Volume 1: Main Report*, Washington: The World Bank, 1987) the Stefanów mine should be abandoned "... if its capital costs are truly as high as $350/ton of annual capacity" (p. 51). Szpilewicz (1987) is less cautious: having examined costs and benefits of coal extraction from the Lublin coal deposits (Stefanów coal mine is part of it), he draws the following conclusion: "It does not pay off to invest in Lublin coal deposits, the sooner we put an end to this ruinous procedure—the better" (p. 6).

21.   According to one study (Baczko 1987), the correlation coefficient in 1986 was +.312. There was, however, a very significant variation in correlation among various sectors. The correlation coefficient for metallurgy equalled .261, while for rubber, cement, and electronic industries it was over 0.5.

22.   The enterprises drawn from the list of 500 largest corporations published in Zarządzanie monthly (June 1987) and ranked according to wages include five steelworks, two shipyards, a copper mining company, and two companies in metallurgy.

23.   For an illuminating analysis of links between normalization and the blueprint of economic reform, see Bielasiak (1988).

24.   Persistent societal pressures forced the authorities to adopt measures that produced a significant improvement in the human rights situation and extended individual rights. For instance, new institutions, a Constitutional Tribunal, an Administrative Tribunal, and a Sejm Ombudsman were set up to give citizens some protection against the abuses of power by the administration. Openness of the official mass media, tolerance of underground publications as well as a recent decision (January 1988) to stop jamming programs broadcast by Radio

Free Europe point to the reconciliation of the authorities to the loss of the "information monopoly."

25. Quoted in Fallenbuchl (1988, p. 119).

26. Usher (1981) argued that in democracies the growth of the state's involvement in the distribution of resources tends to exacerbate conflicts and thereby to undermine consensus and erode legitimation. As argued earlier, under state socialism it accounts, inter alia, for social compliance and stability accomplished through political instruments of atomization and vertical linkages.

27. As it was described in the report of the Polish National Bank (Program ..., 1987). Also see, for example, Kaleta (1987) and Lipowski (1987).

28. This observation is indirectly supported by Mieszczankowski's article (1987b) critical of excessive authority of founding bodies over enterprises. Given the disintegration of the Communist Party during the Solidarity period and after the imposition of martial law, the decline in the influence of the party apparatus was inevitable.

29. Professor Sobczak's observation in Wieczorkowska (1987).

REFERENCES

Albinowski, S. "Cudów [niestety] nie ma" (There Are No [unfortunately] Miracles). *Życie gospodarcze* 16 (1987).

Baczko, T. "Nieprawidłowości w systemie motywacji" (Improper motivation system) *Zarządzanie* 6 (1987).

Bielasiak, J. "Economic Reform and Political Normalization." In *Creditworthiness in Poland: Western and Polish Perspectives*, edited by P. Marer and W. Siwinski. Bloomington, IN: Indiana University Press, 1988.

Birman, I. "From the Achieved Level." *Soviet Studies* 2 (1978).

Comisso, E., and L. Tyson. "Preface." *International Organization* 2 (1986).

Crane, K. *Polish Economic Policy and Western Economic Leverage.* Santa Monica, CA: The Rand Publication Series, July, 1988.

Coleman, K.E., and D.N. Nelson. *State Capitalism, State Socialism and the Politicization of Workers.* The Karl Beck Papers in Russian and East European Studies, University of Pittsburgh, Paper No. 304 (1984).

Fallenbuchl, Z.M. "The Present State of Economic Reform in Poland." In *Creditworthiness in Poland: Western and Polish Perspectives*, edited by P. Marer and W. Siwinski. Bloomington, IN: Indiana University Press, 1988.

Gomulka, S., and J. Rostowski. "The Reformed Polish Economic System." *Soviet Studies* 3 (1984).

"Gorbachev's Economic Reform: A Soviet Economy Roundtable." *Soviet Economy* 3 (1987).

Hewett, E.A. "Reform or Rhetoric: Gorbachev and the Soviet Economy." *The Brookings Review* (Fall 1986).

Hirszowicz, M. *The Bureaucratic Leviathan.* New York: St Martin's Press, 1980.

Holland, D. "Workers' Self-Management Before and After 1981." In *Creditworthiness in Poland: Western and Polish Perspectives*, edited by P. Marer and W. Siwinski. Bloomington, IN: Indiana University Press, 1988.

Jeziorański, T. "Poparcie i obawy" (Support and Fears). *Życie gospodarcze* 49 (1987).

―――――. "Galimatias" (Jumble). *Życie gospodarcze* 50 (1986).

Józefiak, C., quoted in Jeziorański, T. "Przyśpieszenie, jak i kiedy?" (Acceleration, How and When?). *Życie Gospodarcze* 14 (1987b).

Kaleta, J. "Jak uzdrowić złotowkę?" (How to Cure the Zloty?). *Odrodzenie*, Krakow (August 8, 1987).

Kaminski, B. "Directive Capacity of Socialist State." *Comparative Political Studies* 1 (1989).

―――――. "Pathologies of Central Planning." *Problems of Communism* (March-April 1987).

―――――. "Dying Command Economy: Solidarity and the Polish Crisis." *Journal of Contemporary Studies* (Fall-Winter 1986).

Kaminski, B., and K. Soltan. "Evolutionary Potential of Late Communism." Mimeo, University of Maryland, College Park, 1988.

Karpińska-Mizielińska, W. "Reforma w oczach kadry" (Reform in the Eyes of Management). *Życie gospodarcze* 36 (1986).

Kleer, J. "Czas nadzwyczajny" (Urgency Time). *Polityka* 21 (1988).

Kornai, J. *Contradictions and Dilemmas: Studies on the Socialist Economy and Society*. Cambridge, MA: The MIT Press, 1986a.

―――――. "The Hungarian Reform Process." *Journal of Economic Literature* (December 1986b).

―――――. *Economics of Shortage*. Amsterdam: North Holland, 1980.

Kostro, E. "Okolice upadłości" (The Issue of Bankruptcy). *Zarzadzanie* (September 1987).

Kotowicz, J. "Popyt niesterowalny" (Uncontrollable Demand). *Życie gospodarcze* 22 (1987).

Kowalik, T. "Jesli ma się udać..." (If it's to come true). *Zarządzanie* 12 (1987).

KRG-1988, "Konsultacyjna Rada Gospodarcza: Rewizja inwestycji" (Consultative Economic Council: Revision of Investment). *Życie gospodarcze* 2 (1988).

Kulesza, M. "Samorząd terytorialny i własność komunalna" (Territorial Self-management and Municipal Ownership). *Życie gospodarcze* 23 (1987).

Lipowski, A. "Plan a rynek" (Plan versus Market). *Polityka* 17 (1987).

Mieszczankowski, M. "Krótka historia reformy" (Short Account of the Reform). *Życie gospodarcze* 20 (1987).

Misiak, M. "Wyniki finansowe przedsiębiórstw w 1986 r" (Financial Performance of Enterpises in 1986). *Życie gospodarcze* 10 (1987).

Nove, A. *Socialism, Economics and Development*. London: Allen & Unwin, 1986.

Nuti, D.M. "Poland: Current Development and Prospects of Economic Reform." In *The Economies of Eastern Europe and Their Foreign Economic Relations*, edited by P. Joseph. Brussels: NATO, 1987.

Pajestka, J. "O reformie po 3 latach" (About the Reform after Three Years). *Życie gospodarcze* 37 (1985).

Polański, Z. "Spirala" (The Spiral). *Życie gospodarcze* 39 (1986).

Portes, R. "Central Planning and Monetarism: Fellow Travellers?" Pp. 140-165 in *Marxism, Central Planning and the Soviet Economy. Economic Essays in Honor of Alexander Erlich,* edited by. P. Desai. Cambridge, MA: Cambridge University Press, 1983.

Poznanski, K. "Economic Adjustment and Political Forces: Poland since 1970." *International Organization* 2 (1986).

"Program umacniania złotówki" (Program To Strengthen Zloty: Summary of the National Bank of Poland Report). *Rynki Zagraniczne* (August 6, 1987).

Strange, Susan. "Protectionism and World Politics." *International Organizations* 39, 2 Spring (1985).

Szpilewicz, A. "Czy warto inwestować w Lubelski węgiel?" (Does it pay off to invest in Lublin coal?). *Życie gospodarcze* 48 (1987).

"Tezy w sprawie II etapu reformy gospodarczej: propozycje dyskusji" (Theses on the Second Stage of Economic Reform: Proposals for Discussion). *Rzeczpospolita* (April 12, 1987).

"Tezy w sprawie kształtowania struktur organizacyjnych gospodarki" (Theses on Designing Organizational Structures of the Economy). *Rzeczpospolita* (May 12, 1987).

Usher, D. *The Economic Prerequisite to Democracy.* New York: Columbia University Press, 1981.

Wanless, P.T. *Taxation in Centrally Planned Economies.* New York: St. Martin's Press, 1985.

Wieczorkowska, A. "Kondycja władzy terenowej: rozmowa z prof. Karolem Sobczakiem z Uniwersytetu Warszwskiego" (The State of Local Authority: Interview with Karol Sobczak, professor of the University of Warsaw). *Życie gospodarcze* 21 (1987).

Wilhelm, J. "Does the Soviet Union Have a Planned Economy?" *Soviet Studies* 2 (1979).

Winiecki, J. *Economic Prospects-East and West. A View from the East.* London: The Centre for Research into Communist Economies, 1987.

Wojciechowska, U. "Wazna lekcja: VI ankieta Instytutu Gospodarki Narodowej" (Important Lesson: The 6th Survey of the Institute of National Economy). *Życie gospodarcze* 18 (1987).

Wojciechowska, U., and M. Żytniewski. "Deficyt i dotacje w przemysle" (Deficit and Subsidies in Industry). *Życie gospodarcze* 12 (1987).

Zychowicz, E. "Tajemnice zamówien rządowych" (Mystery of Government Contracts). *Slowo Powszechne* (June 13, 1987).

AN ASSESSMENT OF
THE ECONOMIC REFORM
IN POLAND'S
STATE-OWNED INDUSTRY

Keith Crane

I. INTRODUCTION

The previous chapter by Kaminski focused on questions concerning major impediments to reform in the 1980s, and the degree to which the economic reform measures implemented in the 1980s marked a departure from "traditional" state socialism.[1] This chapter assesses the effectiveness of the reform in Polish state-owned industrial firms. This sector was chosen because of the central role played by the state sector in the Polish economy and the importance attached to industry by the government. State-owned firms dominated production. Their continued ownership by the state was one of the tenets of socialism. Consequently, if the reform was to succeed, it had to make these firms more responsive to changes in relative prices and more concerned with efficiency.

Kaminski provided a detailed description of the reform and a macrolevel analysis of its success. This chapter focuses on how the reform functioned at the enterprise level, it discusses the way in which the center attempted to direct enterprises, how enterprises reacted to these instruments, and concludes with a look at the economic outcomes of this process and the implications of these outcomes for the success of the reform. Of particular interest are the contradictions that were introduced into the reformed system because of the competing economic policy goals (full employment, low relative prices for consumer basics, and high relative wages for favored groups of workers) that were pursued by the Polish government. Because ideas, outlines, and plans for reforms in Poland have been a dime a dozen, this chapter describes what the center appears to have attempted to do and then discusses how state-owned enterprises reacted, rather than dwelling on particular theoretical outlines. In this fashion a clearer picture of the reform emerges. Moreover, by focusing on "revealed preference," what the center actually chose to do, rather than policy statements, the problem of determining actual intentions from contradictory policy statements is avoided.

II.   THE ROLE OF THE CENTER ACTORS

The center was not a single-minded institution with set goals. It consisted of a number of institutions—the Politburo, the Council of Ministers, and functional and branch ministries and organizations—each with its own functions and interests. The Politburo decided overall economic policy, but under Jaruzelski the Council of Ministers determined much of the content of policy.

Although the Sejm had a greater legislative role after 1980, most Polish law was generated by the Council of Ministers through decrees. These decrees determined the structure of the reform. While the Sejm passed about 300 laws on the reform between 1982 and 1985, the government issued roughly 12,000 decrees of which 8,000 were issued by the Finance Ministry (Kaminski 1985, p. 30). To put this in perspective, there were less than 6,000 state or cooperative-owned enterprises in all of Polish industry during this period, implying two decrees per industrial enterprise.[2] These decrees represented the revealed preference of the central authorities.

The most important functional ministries were the Ministry of Finance and the Ministry of International Economic Cooperation

(Ministry of Foreign Trade). The Ministry of Finance set regulations on prices, implemented tax policy, and determined which enterprises were eligible for tax rebates and subsidies. As a result, it became the most important ministry in Poland.

The Ministry of International Economic Cooperation continued to have the same position within the new system as its predecessor, the Ministry of Foreign Trade, had within the old. It had, however, become more active in terms of exchange rate policy, providing information and supervising the increased number of firms with foreign trade rights. Interview data indicate that the Ministry of Foreign Trade took a more active role in encouraging exports. Fourteen respondents among a group of 56 enterprise managers gave this ministry positive marks; eight criticized it for failing to react to the needs of the enterprises and to market exports more strongly, the rest did not comment.[3]

The National Bank also changed its role. Formerly, it merely handled transactions and issued money as needed to finance enterprise investment and the budget deficit. The bank was given targets for credit and for the issue of currency. It also evaluated the potential for an enterprise to repay a loan from the proceeds of an investment. In the past credits had been granted passively on the orders of the Council of Ministers or Planning Commission.

The Planning Commission still used the balance method to draw up plans so the mechanics of plan formulation did not really change. Branch ministries provided the commission with lists of expected output levels and input demands for "key" commodities. The commission attempted to balance requests with expected supplies. Plans, however, were no longer compulsory for enterprises and were drawn up in variants to provide the Council of Ministers and Sejm with a choice. Its importance declined after the passage of the reform.

State-owned enterprise managers in Poland continued to be appointed and judged by the "founding organ," which was generally the branch ministry or, in the case of smaller firms, the local government. The branch ministries, which included a superministry—the Ministry of Industry, founded in 1987—and the ministries of agriculture, communications, and transportation, nominated and approved managers, and dismiss managers at will and set their bonuses and salaries. They frequently demanded information from the enterprise on the enterprise's plan, production, and use of materials (Wojciechowska 1986, p. 193). Consequently, managers were primarily beholden to the branch ministries. Somewhat surprisingly, however, 24 of 31 enterprise managers who commented on their relations with the branch ministry, evaluated them positively (Wojciechowska 1986, p. 207). These managers argued that their relationship with the branch ministries was substantially different from the pre-reform period. Ministries often interceded with the Ministry of Finance concerning tax and subsidy questions and attempted to provide the enterprises with inputs. They were perceived more as partners than as opponents, especially since enterprise managers argued that the power of the ministries to order particular actions was now much more limited than before.

Under the ministries were the associations. These organizations replaced the old *zjednoczenie,* an intermediate trust. Most of the associations were voluntary, although those in heavy industry also tended to be compulsory. Voluntary associations were primarily concerned with allocating inputs and planning investment in the industry. Membership costs were paid from profits, so enterprises had to have a strong incentive to join because of the important uses profits could be put to elsewhere. In later years cooperatives, technical institutes, and even private artisans joined them in order to secure input supplies. Compulsory associations played a far different role. For example, the association for electricity generation was highly centralized, and coordinated investment policy. It also had an important role in allocating inputs and determining production (Wojciechowska 1986, p. 241).

Like the branch ministries, most enterprise managers positively evaluated the role of the associations. According to the managers, the associations represented the interests of the enterprises to the center and also provided scarce inputs and additional investment funds.

III.   POLICIES AND POLICY INSTRUMENTS

Aside from the goals of increasing economic efficiency, attaining market equilibrium, and improving foreign trade performance, the center also attempted to lower the rate of inflation to single-digit levels while preventing factory closures and unemployment and preserving real wage levels for sensitive political groups—workers in heavy industry and mining. The center found it impossible to pursue these goals simultaneously. The Council of Ministers was highly sensitive to the possibility that economic dissatisfaction generated by the failure to attain these goals would lead to demonstrations that could threaten the government. Consequently, economic policy and reform measures often appeared to be dictated by immediate concerns about the popularity of particular decisions. This led to the introduction of ad hoc, often contradictory, decrees, making economic policy and the instruments used to pursue it inconsistent with the principles of the reform. An analysis of these economic policies follows, explaining how they affected the implementation of the reform.

A. Monetary Policy

Despite the existence of plans for the supply of credit and the issue of currency, monetary policy was still accommodatory.[4] If an investment ran over budget, the bank usually accommodated the increased demand for credit, thus leading to an increase in the money supply despite the existence of a target for the supply of credits. The government budget deficit continued to be financed by printing money. Consequently, when enterprises experienced unplanned losses and were subsidized from the budget or by new loans, the money supply rose, feeding into the continued growth of nominal aggregate demand.

The reluctance of the government to adopt an active monetary policy was probably motivated by the desire to forestall plant closures. Important firms were protected from financial difficulties. The government also did not adopt a harder policy because of its reluctance to halt investment projects once started and its inability to fight off special interests.

B. Prices

The counterpart to monetary policy was price policy. It was a primary concern of the Council of Ministers. The council stipulated three types of prices: fixed, regulated, and contract. Fixed, government-set, prices were used for a wide range of consumer goods and basic industrial inputs such as foodstuffs, public transport, utilities, ores, petroleum, and coal. Regulated prices could only be changed after consulting the Ministry of Finance. Contract prices were set between firms or by the market.

In recent years neither regulated nor contract prices functioned well. Because of the center's unwillingness to control the money supply, it relied on price controls to limit the "reported" rate of inflation. These controls were extended from regulated and fixed prices to contract prices by stipulating that prices must be constructed on the basis of "justified costs," that is, prices had to be set on the basis of costs plus a mark-up. In other words, these prices were cost-plus, but only part of "justified" cost increases could be passed along in prices. Prices were not tied to market demand and, thus, frequently failed to clear the market. Those that did often contained a highly variegated turnover tax. Consequently, prices adjusted poorly to changes in demand and failed to provide enterprises with accurate reflections of relative costs or demand.

C.   Allocation of Industrial Inputs

Because monetary policy was accommodatory and prices were not permitted to rise to clear markets, enterprises faced excess demand for most of their products. Since markets were not allowed to function, some other method of allocating inputs had to be used. The center fell back on a version of the old system employed in traditional Soviet-type economies. As of 1986, roughly half of fuels and major materials, and an even higher percentage of imports, were still centrally allocated. Other formal and informal measures were instrumental in allocating much of the remainder.[5] Producers of inputs such as steel products, coal, and electricity had to sell all or almost all of their output to central wholesalers. The wholesalers did not operate as profit-maximizing enterprises. They decided to whom to sell depending upon instructions from the Planning Commission, branch ministry requests, and orders from the Council of Ministers. Branch ministry requests in turn were decided on the basis of requests from associations and large enterprises. Bargaining power and past patterns of resource allocation were therefore the primary means of deciding who got what in this system.

The center attempted to better ensure that its preferences, rather than the preferences of the branch ministries, were enforced through the introduction of a system of "government orders" for products that the government decided were priority items. Enterprises bid for these orders and if their bid was accepted, they were guaranteed the necessary inputs to manufacture the products.

In practice, the system replicated many of the features of the old centrally planned system. In most cases the orders were not for government consumption. The government contracted for the entire output of the industry and then sold the output through the state wholesale network. Consequently, the enterprise faced a monopsony, rather than multiple buyers. Additionally, the government did not select its priorities carefully. Most enterprises received at least one government order for a large share of output. Supplies of inputs frequently did not meet the quantities promised by the government, so contracts could not be honored and the whole system of shortage was perpetuated.

D.   Wage Policy

Because monetary policy was accommodatory and the government used price controls to keep the recorded rate of inflation lower than it otherwise would have been, excess demand was endemic to the system. This extended to the demand for labor as well. To keep the rate of increase in nominal demand from accelerating, the government adopted an income policy to control wages. This policy was exercised by levying a punitive tax on nominal wage increases above a specified level (12% in 1987, for example). These taxes, called *Państwowy Fundusz Aktywizacji Zawodowej* (PFAZ), were paid from profits; they ran 200% or more on wage increases over the threshold level. In order to encourage firms to shed labor, however, the government taxed increases on the total wage bill, not individual wages. Consequently, firms that shed workers could increase wages by more than the threshold level by distributing the wage fund among the smaller pool of remaining workers.

Such a system penalized firms that wished to hire new labor and thereby slowed restructuring. Taxes were so high that the marginal product of an additional worker was rarely great enough to make

it worthwhile to pay the tax. Price controls also prevented the firm
from increasing prices to raise profits, and thereby increased the
wage bill. In the interest of encouraging some restructuring the
government allowed partial exemptions to the PFAZ tax based on
increases in value added, on output or exports, and in some
instances on enterprise-specific exemptions (Wojciechowska 1986,
p. 72). Thus, if an enterprise increased exports, it could offer higher
wages to its employees without incurring the tax. Exemptions,
however, were frequently granted for individual firms on the basis
of petitions. Thus, PFAZ taxes varied widely from firm to firm in
an arbitrary fashion.

In general, the enterprise managers interviewed by Urszula
Wojciechowska were highly critical of PFAZ. Although 46.5%
argued that such a tax was necessary, even these individuals felt
it was too progressive, led to bargaining with the central
authorities concerning tax relief, and in general did not achieve
the purpose for which it was designed.

E.   Fiscal Policy

Because the Polish government financed the budget deficit by
printing money, fiscal policy consisted of tax and expenditure
policies; internal debt management was not an issue. The Ministry
of Finance set tax rates, subsidies, and many prices. Thus, it had
a multitude of fiscal policy instruments from which to choose.
There were three main taxes: PFAZ, profit taxes, and turnover tax.
Enterprises also had to turn over a share of amortization which
was akin to a tax on capital.

Taxes commanded a very large share of enterprise resources. In
1985 in a sample of 2,211 Polish firms, PFAZ taxes averaged 15.9%
of the wage bill, profit taxes took 47.0% of profits on average (the
median was 52.7%) and ranged from 5.1% to 70.0% of total profits.
Turnover taxes averaged 4.8% of production sold.[6] In this same
sample enterprises paid from 7.2% to 78.0% of amortization to the
national budget in 1985 (Wojciechowska 1987, p. 23). In other
words, the government set highly variegated, seemingly arbitrary
tax and amortization retention rates.

Subsidy rates also varied greatly. Of the 2,211 enterprises, 1,063
received subsidies or tax relief. Subsidies averaged 345% of, and

ranged from .1% to 1117% of, the reported profits of these enterprises (Wojciechowska 1987, p. 16).

Subsidies were given to cover the costs of producing items with fixed prices. These products were usually either raw materials (coal, coke), agricultural inputs (fertilizer), or food products (milk products and meat). Some enterprises also received export subsidies.[7] In some cases high-cost producers were also given subsidies to make up the difference between their costs and the official price based on costs of lower-cost producers.

The central government did not work out a coherent subsidy policy. In many cases government organs individually tailored subsidies for enterprises. In general, the enterprises that had the largest losses in an industry received the largest subsidies. Consequently, subsidies acted as an instrument for leveling out differences among enterprises. Those enterprises performing the worst were rewarded; those that performed the best were in effect penalized.

F.   Investment Policy

Because the government took such a large share of profits and amortization from the enterprises, only half of the total investments in the state and cooperative sector were provided by the enterprises.[8] The other half was determined by the central and local governments, social funds, and cooperative housing associations. The construction and machine-building industries also faced excess demand, however, so even when a decision was made to start an investment project, the materials and means to construct it were frequently not available. Thus, the government faced a two-fold decision: what to invest in and which of the selected projects should actually be implemented.

These decisions were still determined by bureaucratic battles. Although the National Bank had been given a more important role in assessing investment projects, the actual choice of government funded projects was still determined by the Council of Ministers where rate of return was only one criterion. At lower levels, the ability of managers to obtain materials and construction workers for a project depended heavily on their bureaucratic clout and on their relations with the contractor. Market forces played a very weak role in determining the allocation of capital.

G.   Foreign Trade Policy

The center used exchange rates, subsidies, tax relief and hard currency accounts to motivate enterprises to export. Exports under CMEA treaties, however, were often made legally compulsory. The most important of these instruments were hard currency accounts. Of the 56 enterprises interviewed by Wojciechowska, 85% said that these accounts were the primary reason they exported (Wojciechowska 1986, p. 92). They were used to purchase inputs (60% of expenditures), spare parts, and machinery. The importance of these accounts reflected both the continued acute shortages facing Polish enterprises and the continued overvaluation of the zloty.

In January 1987, the government froze sums accumulated in these accounts and set up a new system. Under the old system enterprises earned entitlements to purchase hard currency through exporting. The amount of the entitlement earned by a dollar of exports varied across enterprises. In the new system enterprises actually owned the hard currency. The new measure, however, effectively froze several hundred million dollars of entitlements earned by Polish enterprises after 1982, which they planned to spend in 1987, creating supply problems that disrupted production. Although enterprises would supposedly be able to exercise these entitlements in coming years, managers were skeptical of their ability to exercise their rights with a subsequent diminution in incentives to export.

Under the new system enterprises could sell their hard currency on an inter-enterprise market run by the Ministry of Finance. In the auctions enterprises were able to sell holdings at three to four times the official rate of exchange, a price similar to that prevailing on the black market.

Imports were primarily allocated using quotas, although those purchased with enterprise retention quotas became increasingly important. The Planning Commission and Ministry of Foreign Trade generated a foreign trade plan in which imports were allocated on the basis of past usage and the preferences of the Council of Ministers. Branch ministries and associations then frequently allocated hard currency allotments among enterprises, although some enterprises were assured of some imports by the Planning Commission or Ministry of Foreign Trade. This system made it very difficult to reallocate imports efficiently because neither the Ministry of Foreign Trade nor the Planning Commission had the information needed to make the most efficient allocation of hard currency imports.

IV.   THE ENTERPRISES

To this point the analysis has focused on the composition and goals of the center and the ways in which it attempted to steer enterprises. This section attempted to summarize how enterprises reacted to these measures.

A.   Control of Workers' Councils

In the original outline of the reform published in 1981, workers were to have a deciding voice in the management of the enterprise through workers' councils. These councils in conjunction with the branch ministry were to hire and fire the director of the firm and take an active role in making major decisions.

Reality was quite different with significant consequences for the operation of enterprises. Interviews with managers indicated that workers' councils were listened to and did play a role in the life of the enterprise (Wojciechowska 1986, p. 259). They, however, functioned more as an advisory board than as an executive or legislative body. They tended to concentrate on wage and work-related problems, but in some instances also discussed investment issues as well.

Representatives of active workers' councils who attended seminars at the Institute of Sociology in Warsaw stated that they had some influence on personnel policy. In one case they were able to force the resignation of an incompetent manager in charge of investment, but they also noted that participation in the council took a large amount of time and that perseverance was vital. In most of the enterprises interviewed by Wojciechowska, more than 50% of the members of the workers' councils were workers, but in only one quarter did this percentage exceed 60%, so management was also well represented. The councils often tended to be dominated by party members. In 20 of the 56 enterprises more than 40% of the workers' councils were party members (Wojciechowska 1986, p. 259). This contrasted with 8% of workers as a whole.[9]

B.   Founding Organs

The power to hire and fire managers continued to lie with the "founding organs," which were either the branch ministries, local governments or, in some cases, other enterprises. In some instances the choice appeared to be influenced by the workers' councils. Managers' salaries and bonuses were also determined by these organs. Salaries were set at the national level and fell into different grades, like those in the civil service in the United States. The ministry decided into which grade a manager fell. Because the government changed these levels slowly, sometimes highly skilled workers could earn over 20% more than directors (Wojciechowska 1986, p. 66). Salaries were not tied to the profitability or performance of the firm, in contrast to workers' wages which were highly correlated with profit per worker. Bonuses were also determined by the "founding organ." Enterprises in the light and chemical industries received a "complex evaluation" twice a year based on sales, exports, labor productivity, the average level of wages, capital productivity, capacity utilization, the effectiveness of repair work, the material intensity of production, the energy intensity of production, costs, changes in financial indicators such as changes in the development fund, profits and losses, absenteeism, and the accident rate. Points were assigned for each category. Other enterprises were evaluated on an ad hoc basis. Seventeen of 22 enterprise managers who were evaluated using the "complex" method thought well of the exercise, but others criticized the method for being opaque (Wojciechowska 1986, p. 196).

The inconsistency of this system with the goal of increasing enterprise efficiency is illustrated by the tale of the Pokój Steelworks. The enterprise was threatened with bankruptcy in 1986, losing its credit rating. After receiving credits from enterprises outside the sector, presumably clients, it was able to stave off bankruptcy and put together a recovery plan based on closing the blast furnace and concentrating on producing shaped and rolled products. The ministry demanded that the works continue to produce 220,000 tons of steel each year, because the Polish economy required it, even though it was the highest cost producer in Poland. The management and the local community wanted to close the 150-year-old steel-making section.[10] The ministry argued that it would be more expensive to import the shortfall in production, than to continue operating the steel works. In other words, exchange rate and price policies were irrational in this sector, because the highest cost producer that made large losses was assumed to produce steel at lower cost than importing it.[11] The ministry, however, was able to insist that the plant continue to operate because it was the founding organ and because of a national resolution aimed at maintaining steel production.

C. Management Objectives

Although enterprise managers were not asked what their goals were, the above discussion of the role of the ministry and the workers' councils coupled with newspaper accounts of enterprises indicate that the primary goal of the enterprise manager was to stay in the good graces of the branch ministry and, to a lesser extent, of the workers' council. As shown by the entries in the "complex evaluation," the branch ministries had several goals. The weights of these entries varied over time as policies and personnel changed. Because of the government's emphasis on preserving labor peace, however, the ministry's primary goal often boiled down to keeping the work force content. For the enterprise manager this meant increasing workers' wages.

Between 1982 and 1987, the second two most important goals of managers appeared to have been increasing production and increasing after-tax, after-subsidy profits. These goals were a product of the incentives provided by the center and the constraints under which enterprise managers operated.

1. Increasing Production

In 1982, the primary economic policy goal of the central government was to stop the fall in output. Branch ministers were under great pressure to increase production. They transmitted this pressure verbally to enterprise managers. Because of continued shortages, enterprise managers continued to be under great pressure from the branch ministries and customers to increase output.

After 1983, this pressure was applied through discussions of enterprise plans and through tax reliefs. In 1983, enterprises were permitted to raise wages above the centrally stipulated threshold for each percentage point increase in gross sales at comparable prices (Lipinski and Wojciechowska 1987). This system was transformed into tax relief based on increases in value added measured in comparable prices (Wojciechowska 1986, p. 72). Enterprise managers were induced to increase output through personal pressure and financial means.

2. Increasing After-Tax, After-Subsidy Profits

One of the major objectives of Polish managers was to increase after-tax, after-subsidy profits. This objective was not one imposed so much by the ministry, as it was a necessary condition for maintaining the solvency of the enterprise and increasing production.

Polish enterprises did not face a "hard budget constraint" as defined by Kornai (1980). The government was willing to bail out all large loss-making firms with subsidies or by forgiving loans. Enterprises that continued to post losses, however, found life became difficult. A few enterprises went bankrupt, the first a small metalworking firm in Zabrze. Moreover, the number of firms in financial difficulties rose. Firms that fell into financial difficulties were overseen by an appointee of the National Bank and had to work out a program to restore the enterprise to financial health. In effect, the old manager found his former power curtailed or that he was out of a job. For these reasons, avoiding losses was an important objective for enterprise managers.

Profits were also important because they facilitated maintaining the size of the labor force. After 1982, when the Polish government offered early retirement to many people in their fifties, Poland suffered endemic excess demand for labor (Lipinski and Wojciechowska 1987, p. 28). Workers, especially the highly skilled, moved quickly to those enterprises that paid the highest wages (Wojciechowska 1986, pp. 64, 70). Consequently, if the enterprise was to continue to operate, managers had to increase the wage bill to retain workers.

Profits and tax relief provided the two most important avenues for increasing the wage fund. As noted above, relief on the payment of PFAZ, the wage increase tax, was granted for increasing exports, for value added or for reducing energy or for raw material usage.

Of the 56 enterprise managers interviewed by Wojciechowska, 26.8% reduced payments to PFAZ by increasing value added,[12] 7.1% increased overtime (these payments were not subject to tax), 1.8% increased exports, and 1.8% reduced the use of energy or raw materials. The other enterprises either did not receive relief on the PFAZ tax or were granted individual relief from the Ministry of Finance (Wojciechowska 1986, p. 72). Almost half the enterprises requested individual relief in 1985 and over half of these requests were granted. Relief had no correlation with financial results, but appeared to be determined by the force with which the enterprise manager argued for them (Wojciechowska 1986, p. 72).

More aggregate data also show the importance of tax relief in determining the financial results of Polish firms.[13] In 1986 income tax reliefs were given for 21.3% of the gross taxes of the 500 largest Polish enterprises. Most of the reliefs, 54.1%, were granted because of increased exports. Energy savings and quality awards accounted for only 2.7% and 3.9% of the reliefs. Arbitrary grants of individual reliefs comprised an important fraction of the remaining reliefs. Only 28 of the 500 largest Polish enterprises were not granted some form of tax relief.

Although managers actively pursued wage tax reliefs, profits were a more important determinant of wage increases. There was a strong positive correlation between profit margins and wage levels (Table 1). The industrial branch was an important determinant of wage levels as well. Profits were also pursued because they were an important source of investment funds. As shown in Table 1, profits were positively correlated with the rate of increase in funds available for investment. Of the enterprises interviewed by Wojciechowska (1986), 41.0% financed their investments from the development fund, which was financed out of profits. The second most important source of funding was subsidies from the national or local governments (30.0% of the enterprises); bank credit was used by only 14.2%. The remainder apparently did not respond to this part of the survey.

In the classic centrally planned system, enterprise managers pushed for investments in new capacity because the larger the enterprise, the higher the manager's salary. Investments also tended to facilitate the fulfillment of plan targets because they could remove short-run bottlenecks. The incentives for investment in the

Table 1.   The Relationship Between Profit Margins
and Wages in 1985

Profits as a % of Total Sales				
Loss-Making	0-5	5-15	15-30	>30
Monthly Wage				
Mean	17900	18100	19100	19600	20300
Median	18100	17700	18700	19200	19900
Rate of Increase in the Development Fund				
Mean	-13.1	31.2	35.6	61.1	81.8
Median	-15.9	1.6	20.1	27.3	36.7
# of Enterprises	15	333	971	631	261

Source: Urszula Wojciechowska, Grazyna Pasznik, and Andrzej Szeworski. *Sytuacja ekonomiczna przedsiębiorstw przemysłowych w 1985 roku, Raporty.* Warsaw: Instytut Gospodarki Narodowej, 1987.

Polish reformed system were not altogether the same. The enterprise managers interviewed by Wojciechowska (1986) said they invested to increase production; improve the quality of products; develop exports; improve the technological level of production; conserve on labor, energy, and materials; and protect the environment. Ministerial and customer pressure to expand production provided another incentive to invest. Investing in order to remove bottlenecks was another incentive. Both these motives made it possible to increase profits or expand production. The former enabled the enterprise manager to keep his own job and his work force happy; the latter pleased the ministry.

3.   Other Goals

Profits could be pursued by increasing sales of profitable items, curbing production of loss-making items, raising prices under the assumption that sales fail to decline, or by reducing costs. Aside from the pursuit of profits, the reduction of inputs of energy and materials in production was an additional indicator used by the branch ministry to evaluate enterprise managers. Enterprises also received wage tax reliefs for reducing costs. Although enterprise managers said that from .5 to 8.0% of increases in profits stemmed from reducing costs, the majority argued that cost reduction was a poor way to increase profits (Wojciechowska 1986, p. 21). They often found that the central authorities forced them to lower prices after cost reductions, thus eliminating the incentive to reduce costs. Reducing material inputs in production was also given as a reason for declines in quality.

Increasing exports was another goal of enterprise managers.[14] The primary reason for exporting given by 85% of the 56 enterprises interviewed by Wojciechowska was hard-currency accounts, although tax relief was also mentioned (Wojciechowska 1986, p. 97). These accounts gave the manager a great deal of freedom because he could use the monies to purchase inputs, machinery, or spare parts which were in short supply. The resulting removal of the bottleneck permitted production to run more smoothly and produce higher profits.

Of the managers interviewed by Wojciechowska, 65% said exports to CMEA countries were more profitable than sales on the domestic market or hard-currency exports, providing an incentive to direct exports to the east (Wojciechowska 1986, p. 79). Despite a widening differential between the dollar-ruble exchange rates, this difference in the profitability of hard-currency and ruble exports did not diminish.

D. Management Constraints

Although after-tax, after-subsidy profits were important for Polish firms, Polish managers had several avenues along which they might be pursued. To some extent managers followed the path of reducing costs and innovation. Because of the many obstacles managers faced in adapting production, however, lobbying the center for tax relief and investment grants and subsidies was possibly of greater importance in determining the financial health of the enterprise. Although one reason enterprise managers devoted so much of their energies to lobbying was that the rate of return is high, the other reason was the multiplicity of constraints which limited their managerial freedom.

1. Prices

Price controls appeared to have had a debilitating effect on profitability and on more rapid enterprise response to changes in demand and input costs. In general, the larger the share of fixed priced goods in total sales, the lower the profitability of the enterprise (Wojciechowska 1987, p. 35). Neither subsidies, tax relief, nor annual increases in fixed prices compensated enterprises for the greater profitability possible from selling goods that had contract prices.

Of the 56 enterprises, 51 faced excess demand for their products. On average managers said that in 1985 they could have sold 50% more than they were able to produce (Wojciechowska 1986, p. 15). Enterprises in the most advantageous position were purveyors of inputs. Investment-goods producers had faced saturated markets in previous years. Some consumer-goods producers faced more equilibriated markets in 1985 as well.

Enterprises also were constrained by the center in terms of clients. Of the enterprise managers interviewed, 82% said that they did not have a choice of client. They were either forced to sell all their output to a central wholesaler or were constrained by traditional ties or multiyear sales agreements with other enterprises.

2. *Labor*

In 1985 half the enterprise managers interviewed by Wojcie-chowska claimed that they lacked sufficient workers, especially skilled workers (Wojciechowska 1986, p. 9). Lack of workers was considered the primary constraint on the level of output by 70% of enterprise managers (Wojciechowska 1986, p. 76). Because of the lack of workers, capacity utilization averaged 72.5% and was especially low in the machine-building sector (62.4%) where the average number of shifts was 1.44 as opposed to over 2 in the other industries (Wojciechowska 1986, p. 35).

The reasons for excess demand for labor were easily traced to Polish monetary policy and wage controls. As noted above, almost all enterprises faced excess demand for their products. Because of wage controls, the marginal product of labor exceeded wage levels so enterprises sought workers. Even in cases where enterprises lost money due to price controls, the pressure to increase output coupled with ministerial willingness to cover losses increased the demand for labor. In most cases, however, price regulations were lax enough that enterprises could raise prices to ensure a profit,

Table 2.   Decapitalization in a Sample of
Polish Industrial Enterprises
(% of Total Capital Stock)

	Year		
Industry	1983	1984	1985
Metallurgy	60.2	62.3	64.8
Machine Building	44.4	47.6	49.5
Chemical	45.5	47.0	49.3
Textiles	64.4	64.5	65.7
Food Processing	43.0	44.1	42.7

Source: Urszula Wojciechowska and Jan Lipinski. *Funkcjonowanie Przedsiębiorstw w 1985 Roku, Raporty.* Warsaw: Instytut Gospodarki Narodowej, 1986.

even though the resulting prices did not clear the market. Consequently, labor shortages persisted.

3.   Capital Stock

During the 1980s, Polish enterprises complained of decapital-ization, that is, their capital stock wearing out and not being replaced. According to enterprise managers, this had reached substantial proportions (Table 2). Enterprise managers com-plained that they lacked both financial and physical resources for investment. Although not as important a constraint on production as labor and input shortages, 20% of the managers interviewed argued that the quality and size of the capital stock was a binding constraint on the volume and quality of production (Wojcie-chowska 1986, p. 10). Moreover, because of the lack of development funds or inability to import machinery, enterprises were constrained to repair older machinery, even though the cost was greater than the replacement of the older machinery by new (Wojciechowska 1986, p. 32).

4.   Inputs

Of the managers interviewed by Wojciechowska, 50% stated that problems with supplies constituted an important, binding constraint on production. Most of the enterprises received almost all their inputs through obligatory deliveries ordered by the center.

These deliveries were often obtained under central government programs or through government orders (Wojciechowska 1986, p. 43). For example, in metallurgy an average of 14.5% of supplies were contracted for on a free basis; the rest came from obligatory deliveries by suppliers.

Despite preferential treatment or government orders, more than half the enterprises which participated in government programs (half the sample) argued that they had great problems with supply in terms of quantity, delivery times, and quality. Most enterprise managers said their contacts with government institutions in charge of supply were poor (Wojciechowska 1986, p. 43). Poor supply was credited with production disruptions, deterioration in the quality of output, and forced substitution. Supply irregularities make it very difficult to change output assortment and led to very large inventories because enterprise managers feared they would be unable to procure inputs on time in the future.

5. Imports

Imports continued to be a major constraint on production in Poland. In 1985, several enterprise managers stated that lack of funds to purchase parts and Western machinery curtailed production and efficiency (Wojciechowska 1986, p. 100).

Like other inputs, imports were in short supply. In 1985, the bulk of expenditures on hard currency imports (over 80%) was determined by the Ministry of Foreign Trade in conjunction with the Planning Office, the branch ministries or the associations. This share subsequently fell. Funds were budgeted and then distributed according to "need," not willingness to pay. Moreover, when the Foreign Trade Bank faced shortages of hard currency, imports were delayed, leading to production delays as needed components did not arrive on time (Wojciechowska 1986, p. 101).

Hard-currency accounts provided a way around shortages. Not surprisingly, enterprise managers with these funds appeared to use them in a highly efficient manner. They purchased goods that removed bottlenecks in production, that is, had very high marginal rates of return. These enterprises sometimes sold suppliers hard currency in exchange for guaranteed supplies.

V.   ASSESSING THE REFORM

A.   Managerial Assessment

The Polish managers interviewed by Wojciechowska were also asked for their opinion concerning the reform, specifically on the independence of enterprises, the degree to which the enterprises were self-financing, and the role of self-management. The survey concluded with a general evaluation of the reform. Although 18 of the 56 managers said that they had more independence under the reform, and only 6 argued that independence had not increased, even those that positively evaluated their independence argued that it was severely constrained. Thirteen directors argued that the government issued too many regulations and changed them too often; 11 argued that the government prohibited them from expanding; 9 said that their independence was curtailed because they were not permitted to set their own prices, while 7 saw their independence curtailed by financial instruments (Wojciechowska 1986, p. 252). Several enterprise managers also offered the opinion that the center had gained decision making power at the expense of the enterprises and that this situation would continue to get worse (Wojciechowska 1986, p. 254).

Of the respondents (22 enterprises), 39% said that they were self-financing; 58% stated that possibilities in this area had become very restricted. In general, enterprises argued that they were unable to be self-financing because of lack of funds (14 enterprises), the tax system (10), the price system (10), increases in raw materials and input prices (6), credit policy (6), the PFAZ tax (3), and payment problems stemming from clients' failure to pay promptly (4) (Wojciechowska 1986, p. 256). Although one could argue that tax policies made it extremely difficult for enterprises to cover their own investment costs, managers seemed somewhat confused over what constituted self-financing. According to the study, they generally sought explanations for their financial problems in outside forces. The fact that many firms actually had financial problems, not a serious difficulty in traditional centrally planned systems, indicated that in a general sense enterprises had to be self-financing, that is, profitable.

An interview within the Polish National Bank also added force to the argument that enterprises were self-financing. The interviewee argued that many enterprises did not apply for bank credits for investment, but preferred to finance investments out of current profits. In many cases this led to very long construction times; construction proceeded as funds became available. He explained that enterprises disliked bank financing because managers put a very high premium on assuring future profits so they could continue to raise wages. Bank finance tied down part of this uncertain future stream of profits that might be needed to increase workers' wages. By investing as funds became available, the enterprise manager maintained his freedom to control future profit flows.

This interview also demonstrated the high level of uncertainty faced by enterprise managers. If an investment was likely to be highly profitable, one would think managers would have borrowed to finance it, but in the face of shifting regulations on price formation and input availability, the payback to most investments was so uncertain that managers were unwilling to incur the debts necessary to finance them.

Twenty-two of the enterprise managers criticized the lack of possibilities to finance their own development; only one cast a positive light on the possibility of self-finance. The criticisms focused on the confiscatory nature of taxation and the tight controls on prices. High profit taxes and the payment of a large portion of amortization to the national budget sharply limited their own resources.

1. Workers' Councils

Forty enterprise managers evaluated enterprise councils positively, thirteen had mixed views, and only one evaluated them negatively (Wojciechowska 1986, p. 260). Most disagreements concerned wages. Councils voted on the enterprise accounting balance, the division of profits, the annual plan, and the system of wages. Workers' councils had a very limited role in the selection of managers. Most of their influence was confined to promoting the consideration of several candidates (Wojciechowska 1986, p. 261). The ultimate decision appeared to be made by the enterprise director or the branch ministry.

Workers' councils' representatives and managers both argued that the influence of the workers' council depended on how active its members were. The more active the council, the greater their influence.[15] Enterprise managers appeared to credit them with a substantial amount of authority. When asked who made the key decisions for the enterprise, 33 managers said the management, 18 said the management in cooperation with the workers' council, 4 said the workers' council and only one said the proprietary organ (the branch ministry). Forty-three managers said they consulted the party organization and 33 consulted the labor unions as well (Wojciechowska 1986, p. 262). Managers were divided concerning the role of the councils. Some argued that they should fulfill their statutory role, which would make them a decision-making body. The other group argued that they should have been just a consultative group.

The second and third elections for workers' councils indicated a declining level of interest by the workers themselves. Ministerial reports found voter participation was down in 1986 in comparison to previous years and some elections had to be held two or even three times because of low voter turnouts. The primary reason appeared to be that the councils took up too much time and did not bring either benefits or satisfaction to the participants (Dryll 1987, pp. 1-4).

2. General Managerial Evaluation

Fourteen managers evaluated the reform positively; the rest of the 56 were critical. The critics argued that the reform had not been implemented as planned; many fundamental features still did not exist. The sharpest criticism was directed toward the center for its unwillingness to trust decisions made by enterprise managers. One manager in particular criticized the center for constantly changing regulations, for being too soft—not making enterprises suffer the consequences of the decisions taken by their directors. He argued that there was a lack of freedom to make decisions and of responsibility for them once made (Wojciechowska 1986, p. 265). Another manager argued that the center was pleased with the reform, but enterprise managers were not. The enterprise manager still approached the center as a penitent, pleading for materials, imports, investments, and tax relief.

When asked which social group most opposed the expansion of the reform, 28 managers placed the blame on the central administrative bureaucracy; 7 argued that production workers were the greatest barrier. Eleven managers argued that the major problem was that the instruments employed to steer the economy were ineffective. In general, managers stated that due to outside constraints the thrust of the reform, the improvement of economic efficiency, was impossible (Wojciechowska 1986, p. 265). If efficiency was to be improved, constraints on hiring labor, investing, and procuring inputs had to be removed.

B.   Economic Performance

The opinions of enterprise managers, although illuminating, are not the most unbiased means of evaluating the reform in state-owned industry. The reform may have functioned well, despite the comments made by enterprise managers, if it served to redirect investment and labor to more productive sectors and if it induced increases in factor productivity. The Polish statistical yearbook (*Rocznik statystyczny*) contains information on investment and employment by industrial sector and capital and labor used in industry as a whole. These data coupled with data on profitability provided in Wojciechowska (1987) are used below to assess the effectiveness of the reform in improving Polish economic efficiency.

The following two periods were chosen for comparing factor productivity growth: 1975-78, the years before the economic crisis, but also years when the government began to try and tighten its belt; and 1983-85, the first three years after the reform. Factor productivity growth was defined as the change in the ratio of net industrial output to the three inputs (the stock of fixed capital, hours worked in industry, and electricity consumption by industry). Table 3 compares factor productivity growth for these two periods. Despite the apparent superior performance in terms of capital productivity growth and improvement in the efficiency with which electric power is used in the reform period, the figures mask the tremendous declines experienced in factor productivity in Poland. The ratio of Net Material Product (NMP) produced by socialized industry to capital was 65% lower in 1985 than in 1975, implying an enormous decline in capital productivity. The ratio of NMP produced in socialized industry to electrical consumption produced in socialized industry was 20% lower in 1985 than in 1977,

Table 3. Factor Productivity Growth in
Polish Socialized Industry

Year	Net Material Product		
	Net Output/ Capital	Net Output/ Labor	Net Output/ Electricity
1975	0.401	0.343	0.038
1976	0.401	0.371	0.038
1977	0.388	0.397	0.039
1978	0.364	0.412	0.039
1979	0.330	0.407	0.038
1980	0.303	0.395	0.036
1981	0.249	0.367	0.033
1982	0.232	0.383	0.032
1983	0.238	0.384	0.032
1984	0.242	0.406	0.032
1985	0.242	0.422	0.033
	Average Annual Rate of Increase		
1975-78:	-2.42	4.62	0.60
1983-85:	0.64	3.22	0.63

Source: Data from *Rocznik statystyczny.*

again indicating a decline in efficiency, although this ratio may merely reflect a change in the composition of energy consumption. On the other hand, the ratio of NMP produced in socialized industry to hours worked was 3% higher in 1985 than in 1979, showing an absolute rise in the productivity of labor. In sum, socialized industry did not become notably more efficient after the introduction of the economic reform.

A second indicator of the success of the reform is whether resources were reallocated to more efficient sectors with the advent of the reform. Wojciechowska (1987) provides information on profits as a percent of gross sales and on profits per worker. Although these categories are not equivalent to rates of return and are heavily influenced by capital/labor ratios, they provide a rough indication of relative profitability.[16] By comparing sectors ranked by profitability with their shares in total employment and investment in socialized industry, some indication of the success of the reform in reallocating resources toward more profitable sectors can be realized.

Table 4. Investment and Employment Shares and the Profitability of Socialist Industry

Industry	Gross Profit Margins-% 1985	Profits Per Worker (thousands of zlotys) 1985	Percent of Investment		Percent of Labor Force	
			1975-78	1983-85	1975-78	1983-85
Light	33.5	248.8	5.1	5.2	17.7	15.2
Other	30.5	296.0	1.5	1.6	2.4	3.3
Electricity Generation	27.3	3460.1	8.7	15.5	1.7	2.3
Machine-Building	27.1	348.3	25.1	22.3	33.4	34.0
Chemical	19.4	502.1	12.1	10.0	7.1	6.6
Minerals and Wood Products	17.4	203.7	10.9	7.4	12.1	10.6
Metallurgy	9.8	550.9	16.8	5.8	5.4	5.0
Coal	2.5	141.9	8.4	16.2	7.9	10.0
Food	-2.6	332.5	9.2	11.9	11.3	11.8

Source: *Rocznik statystyczny 1986*, and Wojciechowska, Pasznik, and Szeworski, 1986, 46-47.

Table 4 contains the average share by industrial sector of investment and employment in socialized industry for the 1975-78 and 1983-85 periods, gross profit margins, and profits per worker. The industries are arranged in descending order.

The table shows that capital and labor flows have been the reverse of what one would expect based on profitability considerations. The coal and food industries had the worst profitability performance, yet these two industries and electricity generation registered the largest gains in the shares of investment. Both industries also registered strong increases in their shares of employment at the expense of apparently more profitable industries. These figures may merely reflect the irrational Polish price system in which goods facing high excess demand, such as meat and coal, had relatively low fixed prices and therefore were not profitable. They also reflect industry specific technologies, for example, the relatively fixed capital/labor ratios in electricity generation. Perhaps, the low profitability of the sectors to which capital and labor were being reallocated also reflect the high costs of old production technologies; new investment may have been profitable. The figures reflect, however, the very limited role of profits in determining the allocation of investments and labor. Prices in Poland still did a poor job of reflecting relative efficiency and scarcity, a consequence of the central government's pricing policies.

VI.   CONCLUSIONS

Neither the data nor the interviews provide a favorable impression of the efficacy of the reform. Markets, an important mechanism for the proper functioning of the reform, had limited roles in resource allocation. The signals received by enterprise managers appear to have been of very poor quality. The combination of controlled prices and the accommodatory monetary policy led to excess demand in almost all markets. Tighter controls on input prices than on output prices preserved a highly distorted price system. As a consequence, planners appear to have used relative rates of return to a very limited extent when choosing investment projects and providing wage subsidies. The reform appears to have done little to restructure the Polish economy toward an output mix that would more efficiently use available resources.

Wojciechowska notes that a major problem in the reform was the frequency with which regulations were changed and the poor flow of information between the center and enterprise managers. Even the managers of the large enterprises interviewed by Wojciechowska frequently did not understand or were not aware of new directives. There was also very little coordination between the central plan and enterprise plans. Because the state allocated such a large share of inputs directly, this lack of knowledge led to large efficiency losses and poor planning (Wojciechowska 1986, pp. 275-292).

The major problems faced by enterprise managers were supply uncertainties. Production was frequently constrained by shortages of labor and intermediate goods, especially imports. These shortages reflected the excess demand endemic to the system and the absence of a price system that reflected relative scarcities and permitted the highest bidder to purchase scarce goods and services.

Excess demand in the system stemmed from the central authorities' unwillingness to impose hard budget constraints on enterprises. The ad hoc grants of subsidies and tax reliefs, which increased the budget deficit (and excess demand), served to reward poorly performing enterprises and provided substantial incentives for enterprises to lobby for these relief measures rather than focus on changing internal operations.

The interviews brought across the quick responses of enterprise managers to changes in incentives and the close attention they paid to trade offs. For example, the authorities provided tax reliefs for conservation of energy and materials and also for products which were deemed deserving of "quality symbols." Enterprise managers claimed that the costs of producing higher quality products were greater than the benefits of the tax reliefs or the increases in prices permitted for products that were given the quality sign (Wojciechowska 1986, p. 21). In other words, managers had calculated the relative costs and benefits of the program and decided against participation.

One can also see the quick response of enterprise managers in the alacrity with which they responded to operational programs. Enterprises participating in these programs received higher priority in the allocation of inputs than those that did not. Consequently, despite the narrow thrust of some of these programs, most enterprises participated in one or more of the operational programs (Wojciechowska and Lipinski 1986, p. 21).

Considering these two examples, the hypothesis that the mentality of consumers, producers and, especially, managers must be changed before reform can function is false. The argument, somewhat akin to the argument that socialism will work well when people have developed a "socialist" mentality, was used to mask the real problems with the reform: the many constraints on production and investment imposed on enterprise managers by the center. Whether state-owned enterprises would have still functioned poorly in a market system is open to question. The argument that they failed under the reform, however, reflects the inability of the center to introduce market conditions in the economy, rather than attitudinal problems of managers and consumers.

This leads to the question: why did the center fail to introduce these conditions? This paper argues that macroeconomic policy concerns other than efficiency led to the introduction of a plethora of policy instruments (PFAZ, individual subsidies, and tax reliefs) that sharply reduced the effectiveness of measures to improve efficiency. If monetary and fiscal policy had been less accommodating, perhaps there would have been less pressure to introduce these efficiency-reducing measures. In my view, however, the Polish central authorities were unwilling to bear the political costs of some loss of power and of antagonizing some interest groups by implementing sterner measures. This unwillingness was the primary reason for the failure of the reform markedly to improve economic efficiency.

NOTES

1.   Kaminski, 1989, p. 4.

2.   *Rocznik statystyczny*, 1987, p. 216.

3.   Wojciechowska, 1986, p. 225. The sample is composed of 16 enterprises in the electrical and machine-building sectors, 13 in light industry, 8 in the chemical industry, 7 in metallurgy, 5 in food processing, 3 in minerals, 2 in wood and paper, 1 in the fuel industry and 1 in the "other" category.

4.   Interview data, by author with officials of the Polish National Bank, Spring 1987.

5.   *World Bank*, Vol. I, 1987, pp. 20-21.

6.   Wojciechowska, et al., 1987, p. 16. These authors conducted an annual statistical analysis of over 2,000 (out of a total of 5,496) Polish industrial enterprises based on data from the Polish Statistical Office. The firms in the sample produced most of Polish industrial output.

7.   Wojciechowska, 1986, p. 160.

8.   In 1983, enterprises provided 48.6% of total investments in the state and cooperative sectors, 1984, 51.6%, and in 1985, 52.4% (*Mały Rocznik Statystyczny*, 1987, p. 125).

9.   Interview data, Wojciechowska, 1986.

10.   Stanislaw Zielinski, "Shutdown the Steelmaking Plant or Liquidate the Entire Steelworks?" *Trybuna Ludu* (April 10, 1987): 3, as translated in Joint Publications Research Service, "JPRS Report: East Europe." *JPRS-EER* 87-100 (June 25, 1987): p. 102.

11.   Tadeusz Jaworski, "Interview with Undersecretary of State in the Ministry of Metallurgy and Machine Industry." *Trybuna Ludu* (April 10, 1987): 3, as translated in Joint Publications Research Service, "JPRS Report: East Europe," *JPRS-EER* 87-100 (June 25, 1987): p. 102.

12.   Enterprise managers primarily increased value added by changing the assortment of production from less profitable to more profitable goods. However, because of excess demand, profitability was often a function of the rigor of price controls, not changes in supply and demand. Enterprise managers shifted production from products where the permitted profit margin was less to those where it was more (Wojciechowska 1986, p. 73).

13.   The following information was taken from Marek Dąbrowski, "Changes for the Better?" *Zarzadzanie* 6 (June 1987): 44, as translated in Joint Publications Research Service, "JPRS Report: East Europe," *JPRS-EER* 87-138 (September 10, 1987): p. 117.

14.   Although enterprise managers were rewarded for import-substituting production, no particular rewards appeared to be given for reducing the use of hard-currency imports, per se. Possibly this was due to the limited ability of the enterprise to determine the quantity of imports received.

15.   Interview data, Wojciechowska (1986, p. 262).

16.   For example, the electric generating industry registered the highest profits per worker because it was very capital intensive.

REFERENCES

Campbell, R. *The Soviet-Type Economies: Performance and Evolution.* Boston: Houghton-Mifflin, 1974.

Dąbrowski, M. "Changes for the Better?" *Zarzadzanie* 6 (June 1987): 44, as translated in Joint Publications Research Service, "JPRS Report: East Europe." *JPRS-EER* 87-138 (September 10, 1987).

Dryll, I. "Self-Management Does not Want to be the Loser." *Życie gospodarcze* 22 (May 31, 1987).

Gey, P., J. Kosta, and W. Quaisser. *Crisis and Reform in Socialist Economies.* Boulder, CO: Westview, 1987.

Kaminski, B. "The Dying Command Economy: Solidarity and the Polish Crisis." *Journal of Contemporary Studies* 8, No. 1 (Winter/Spring 1985).

Kierunki reformy gospodarczej. Warsaw: Książka i Wiedza, 1981.

Kornai, J. *The Economics of Shortage.* New York: North-Holland, 1980.

Lipinski, J., and U. Wojciechowska. *Process wdrazania reformy gospodarczej.* Warsaw: Panstwowe Wydawnictwo Ekonomiczne, 1987.

Mały Rocznik Statystyczny. Warsaw: Glowny Urzad Statystyczny, 1987.

Poland: Reform, Adjustment and Growth. Volumes I-II. Washington, DC: World Bank, 1987.

Rocznik statystyczny. Warsaw: Glowny Urzad Statystyczny, 1986.

Wojciechowska, U., and J. Lipinski. *Funkcjonowanie Przedsiębiorstw w 1985 Roku, Raporty.* Warsaw: Instytut Gospodarki Narodowej, 1986.

Wojciechowska, U., G. Pasznik, and A. Szeworski. *Sytuacja ekonomiczna przedsiębiorstw przemysłowych w 1985 roku, Raporty.* Warsaw: Instytut Gospodarki Narodowej, 1987.

Zielinski, S. "Shutdown the Steelmaking Plant or Liquidate the Entire Steelworks?" *Trybuna Ludu* (April 10, 1987): 3, as translated in Joint Publications Research Service. "JPRS Report: East Europe." *JPRS-EER* 87-100 (June 25, 1987).

REFORMING THE MONETARY AND BANKING SYSTEM IN POLAND

Karol Lutkowski

I. INTRODUCTION

This chapter identifies and discusses the central issues involved in the attempt at economic reform in Poland, with particular reference to changes being introduced in the monetary system. It is assumed that the essential task of the monetary system is first, to provide a stable, preferably convertible, currency; second, to stimulate the mobilization of resources for productive purposes; and third, to encourage the efficient use of resources. Sadly, the performance of the Polish monetary system, when judged by these criteria, has been highly unsatisfactory during the past decades, especially the late seventies and eighties. Evidence of this was in the large and persistent internal and external disequilibria, double-digit inflation, and the continued absence of convertibility of the national currency, the zloty.

The relative neglect of money in theoretical models of the centrally planned economy has stimulated debate on whether or not the weakness of the currency is predominantly a reflection of maladjustments and deficiencies in the real sector. Money has never been completely "passive" in the real centrally planned economy, however. Evidence indicates that depreciating the currency may have profoundly adverse effects on economic growth and society, not only in the market economy, but in the centrally planned economy as well. Polish experience provides a glaring illustration—the existence of a large and thriving "shadow economy" is one of the more visible phenomena.

Theoretical implications lie outside the scope of this chapter. But it is necessary to point out that the debate on monetary reform largely centers on the following fundamental questions:

1.   Is the rapid depreciation of money caused mainly by ill-conceived economic policies or by the structure and mode of functioning of the system of economic management?

2.   Assuming that the system of management plays a role, are inflation-generating factors in the real sector of the economy or the monetary sector?

The second of the two questions leads directly to the core of the problem. Was the rapid growth of the volume of money in circulation, far in excess of the level compatible with market equilibrium, caused mainly by the excessive demand for credit by the real sector of the economy? Or, was it brought about by the permissive attitude of the banking sector, which creates too much credit in response to demand for it and has imperfect monetary controls, which have been unable to check the growth in the volume of credit? In contrast to the traditional view, ascribing a passive role to the banking sector and stressing the importance of the demand for credit, the supply of which was virtually infinitely elastic, the official concept of the reform introduced in 1987 recognized the significance of both demand and supply factors.

The deficiencies of the highly centralized banking system inherited from the early fifties, and of the weakness of the control instruments applied hitherto, provided justification for the radical reform of monetary systems. The reform of the structure and principles of the operation of the banking system took place within the framework of the so-called second stage of reform. Moves toward relaxing the constraints imposed upon payments across the national frontier were planned for a later period. Before proceeding to the discussion of the specific contents of the reform program it may be useful to consider the most characteristic features of the Polish banking system, as it operated prior to 1987.

Although the central bank of the country, the National Bank of Poland (NBP) was not the only banking institution, the well-known *tendency* of the centrally planned economies of Eastern Europe to hinge their monetary system on a universal "mono-bank," unifying all spheres of banking activities into a single institution, appeared in Poland as well. The NBP had precisely those characteristics. It was the central issuing institution, enjoying the monopoly right to create money, and at the same time was the exclusive source of credit to the state enterprise sector.

There were two important exceptions. The food sector was financed by another banking institution, the Bank of the Food Economy, which was also the supervisory and refinancing organ for a multitude of small operative banks granting credits to private farms and artisan workshops. The Bank of the Food Economy was somewhat unique since it sometimes acted as a "bank of banks," a role usually reserved for the central bank. The other exception concerned the foreign trade sector and the private transfer of money to and from abroad. These activities were within the domain of two specialized banking institutions, Bank Handlowy S.A. and Bank Polska Kasa Opieki S.A.[1] These few large banking institutions, however, have been subject to the supervision of the NBP, which totally refinanced their credit activity. Credits granted by them were limited to the size of the credit quota alloted to them by the NBP. Therefore, the only mode of money creation in the socialist economy consisted in the NBP's granting of credit.[2] Cash creation came later, in circumstances determined by banking rules, when a deposit holder made a withdrawal. State enterprises were legally required to keep their funds with a single office of the NBP and settle all their claims and obligations in credit money through the use of their bank accounts. Enterprises were limited in granting or receiving commercial credit from other enterprises.

Credit needs of enterprises were, in principle, directed exclusively to the bank. This was intended to ensure better supervision of the activities of the enterprises and better control over the money supply. The changes considered, discussed below, indicated that the bank had not been notably successful in these activities.

This is one of the intriguing paradoxes of the former Polish banking mechanism: its extreme degree of centralization could easily lead one to expect that control over the money supply and the behavior of the enterprises must have been nearly perfect. Neither elaborate credit planning nor equipping the central bank with appropriate legal powers prevented uncontrolled developments that undermined the realism of credit planning and turned the bank into a relatively weak partner forced to meet often unwarranted credit demands of enterprises. The effort to reform the banking structure by separating the issuing function from the crediting function and increasing the possibility of enterprise choice among competing banks resulted from post-war experience with the highly centralized banking sector. The analogy of the centrally managed banking system as a "central nervous system" transmitting information between enterprises and the center proved to be unrealistic. Disappointments resulting from the chronic divergence between the elegant simplicity of the theoretical model and its actual performance provided the impetus behind the present reform attempt.

II.   THE BANKING SYSTEM

It is crucial to examine the sphere of relations between the bank and the state enterprise sector because the most difficult problems of monetary control lie here.

State enterprises had been fed two types of credit: long-term and medium-term *investment credits,* and short-term *turnover credits* used to finance their stocks of raw materials and finished goods, current production, and financial claims. Factors determining the demand of enterprises for those two types of credit simultaneously had brought about growth in the stock of money in circulation.

The volume and branch distribution of investment financing was a decision of the central planning authority. The most important instrument of regulation was the administrative order, not financial checks and stimuli. The enterprises were not materially interested in low project costs, their speedy implementation, or their overall economic efficiency. There appeared a tendency to underestimate the efficiency of financing and to make it look most attractive from a social point of view in order to get it accepted at the central level. The chronic phenomenon of the unduly stretched "investment front," surpassing estimated costs of projects and having a large backlog of unfinished projects, testified to the imperfect control over both real and monetary processes in this crucially important sphere of economic activity.

Under these circumstances the banking sector was passive. The bank was charged with evaluating projects under consideration to ensure efficiency standards were met, and ensuring that implementation was in accordance with the plan. Nonetheless, the bank had no real powers of its own and the enterprises had no real reasons to fear its sanctions. Real decision-making power lay elsewhere. The bank remained a passive provider of money to projects adopted on grounds other than their financial profitability.

Through the mid-sixties investment projects had been financed by the state budget. In the late 1980s, bank credit was substituted as the most important source of financing. Crucial decision-making powers, however, remained with the central authorities so that the role of the bank continued to be secondary and passive. Investment financing had been and remained one of the most important but imperfectly controlled channels through which an excessive quantity of money flowed into active circulation.

Excessive credit absorption was a feature of short-term credits, which comprised the second channel of financing. Here the autonomous decision-making powers of enterprises were much broader, but another flaw of the former economic system of management was revealed. State-owned enterprises were free from the peril of bankruptcy. They could always count on subsidies and rescheduling of credits and various tax exemptions. The bank was equipped with a set of economic sanctions to be applied in glaring cases of negligent performance. These sanctions, however, never went so far as to endanger the very existence of an enterprise until recently. Unprofitable enterprises were common, but little changed since output prices were rigid and often out of line with costs. In addition, the continued central system of distributing certain scarce resources complicated matters. The source of enterprise deficits— inefficient work or the influence of external factors—was impossible to determine.

A second important point is that the most important thing for enterprises was not earning profits and avoiding losses, but achieving plan targets. In view of the frequent irregularity of supplies, it was useful to keep relatively large stocks of essential supplies, including liquid financial means, in bank accounts. The relative insensitivity of enterprises to monetary stimuli and the virtual certainty of being rescued from financial difficulties made them indifferent to the price of credit. An interest charge could easily be added to the overall costs of operation, and, importantly, it had no direct influence on employee salaries and fringe benefits. Salaries and benefits did not depend upon the size of profits. The inevitable tendency to hoard stocks of supplies and liquid financial means developed into excessive credit absorption not easily stemmed with instruments at the bank's disposal.

Confronted with pressures on its printing press, the central bank found itself in a paradoxical situation. One of its main tasks was to supervise the overall economic efficiency of enterprises, as reflected on their bank accounts. Yet central control over enterprises has been relaxed due to the abolition of the strict administrative regulation of the components of circulating capital. As a result, enterprises progressively gained greater freedom of action in their everyday activities. The weight of bank credit as a source of financing the growth of circulating assets increased.

Beginning in the early fifties, participation of bank credit in the financing of circulating assets was mandatory. It remained so until the introduction of new legislation on the state enterprise and the new banking law, a part of the package of laws implementing the current reform. The mandatory participation of bank credits in financing current needs of the enterprises, instead of strengthening the bank's role by giving it better insight into internal processes of the enterprise, diminished its influence upon the quantity of money in circulation. Combined with the virtual impossibility of enterprise bankruptcy and the indifference to efficient use of financial resources, the mandatory participation of bank credit in financing the outlays of enterprises made the supply of money practically infinitely elastic. Automatic bank credit contributed to the undermining of the stability of the zloty. This was the rationale for the radical change, at least in principle, in the relation between the central bank and the state-owned enterprise, which was embodied in the new legislation. The reform—if implemented in a consistent and energetic way—could create a much improved framework for more stable money in the future.

In part, it was the broad institutional framework within which the banking system in Poland operated that stimulated excessive demand for credit, bringing about excessive growth of the money stock and inflation. Undeniably, powerful forces were at work in the Polish system of economic management, creating an excessive demand for credit. Deficiencies in the structure of the money creating institution are also important, however. Much remains to be improved on the supply side of the monetary system too— the mandatory participation of bank credit in enterprise financing was part of the problem. As far as the institutional structure of the banking system is concerned, the real problem is whether or not the central control over the quantity of money in circulation is strengthened or weakened by a strongly centralized banking system, with a universal mono-bank as an extreme, limiting case.

The Polish experience indicates that such a highly centralized banking structure is more vulnerable to pressures from the "real" sector of the economy. These pressures weaken rather than strengthen the control over the money supply in comparison to a more decentralized banking structure, within which the issue of money is kept institutionally separate from crediting tasks. The Polish reform concept was correct in its diagnosis that the banking structure should be reformed and that the role of the central bank should be strengthened in relation to the real sector. This can be accomplished precisely by delegating the financing functions to the lower tier of the banking system. The banking structure should also be strengthened in relation to the Ministry of Finance, and the first concrete steps in that direction have already been taken. At the same time, the instruments of monetary control should be appropriately adapted and developed. Whatever the merits or demerits of monetary theory in the capitalist free-market economy, the socialist-planned economy has much to gain from carefully pondering its message as an antidote to the neglect of the role of money in planned economies. The general thrust of the Polish reform attempt goes in the right direction insofar as it tries to improve the monetary mechanism by encompassing both demand and supply-side facets, paying due regard to strengthening the mechanisms of monetary control at the disposal of the central bank.

Let us now turn to a discussion of changes envisaged in the Polish banking system. Following is a discussion of the modifications in the broader framework of the system of economic management and their bearing upon the factors determining the demand for credit.

III. THE DEMAND FOR CREDIT: ENTERPRISE AUTONOMY, INTEREST RATES AND CURRENCY CONVERTIBILITY

The pillar of the reform may be seen in new financial system of the state-owned productive enterprises, which formed the fundamental segment of the national economy. Enterprises were formally freed from administrative orders issued by the central authorities and should, in principle, be guided by means of market signals. In principle, they should be able to cover their costs out of their receipts. They also face the possibility of bankruptcy in case of inability to meet their financial obligations and should generally operate on a profitable basis over a prolonged period. Legislation in the late 1980s on improving the financial situation of the state-owned enterprises and their insolvency prescribed an appropriate procedure to be applied if enterprises are not profitable, and this procedure did in fact lead to bankruptcies of inefficient enterprises. If applied with sufficient vigor and consistency, this could be an important break with the long-standing tradition of financial laxity and general neglect of efficiency criteria typical of enterprises over the past forty years.[3] This is the *economic autonomy principle* embodied in the legislation on the state-owned enterprises.

An enterprise is now able to decide freely on the distribution of its net financial profit between the bonus fund and the development fund. Additions to its fixed and circulating capital stock are financed and long-term development credits are repaid from the development fund. Excessive contributions to the bonus fund, at the cost of the development fund, are guarded against by a sharply progressive wage-fund tax. The wage-fund tax was reformed in the meantime and, most probably, will be more effective.

The enterprise is no longer obliged to finance part of its capital with bank credit. If it chooses, it may rely entirely on its own funds. It is no longer obliged to transact business with a single bank office. In principle it may choose among various banks, when they come to be established. Nor is the bank obliged to grant credit to an enterprise. Having been put on an equal footing legally, each must decide whether to conduct a transaction. Theoretically, if an enterprise gets credits it must ultimately repay them out of its own funds. This is the "self-financing principle." Quasi-automatic financing by bank credits has been formally abolished. Credit granting should take place on the basis of creditworthiness although the meaning of that notion in practice has turned out to be an extremely controversial problem given market disequilibrium and a distorted price and cost structure.

While speaking of financial constraints, the inevitable question of the role, actual and potential, of the *rate of interest* arises. To what extent have enterprises been sensitive to the price of credit? What conditions should first be fulfilled if the rate of interest is to play an important role as an instrument of regulating the supply of money by the banking system? Does the reform project envisage such a role for the rate of interest now or in the future? The reform is an open-ended undertaking, with numerous problems left to be decided on the basis of accumulated practical experience.

As is well known, the rate of interest has neither been the determining factor of the overall volume of investment, nor has it been the instrument of resource allocation in the centrally planned economy. Strategic decisions concerning investments have always been at the discretion of the central-planning authority, with only a minor role for the enterprise. It is true that in times past efforts were undertaken to make the rate of interest an important parameter of action, at least as far as decentralized investment decisions were concerned. This was particularly true of short-term, turnover credits, which were less strictly controlled from the center than investment funds. In spite of all efforts, however, the rate of interest has remained an ineffective instrument of monetary control. Enterprises have never had difficulties in simply adding interest charges to the overall costs of operation, especially in a chronically unbalanced market. Again, it should be noted that wages and salaries never stood in direct relation to the amount of financial profit. Payments were conditional upon achieving plan targets and insolvency was practically impossible.

All these factors rendered the rate of interest impotent. With enterprises playing for safety by accumulating sufficiently large stocks of supplies, including monetary reserves, and the general tendency to start an excessive number of investment projects, typically at underestimated costs and unrealistically planned gestation periods, an overabsorption of credits was bound to develop. Can the rate of interest become more effective now?

Certain obstacles preventing effective operation of the rate of interest have formally been removed. In principle, enterprises have become economically autonomous and bear financial responsibility for the outcome of their overall activity. Intervention of the central-planning board has been eliminated and creditworthiness has become an important criterion of credit granting. Nonetheless, numerous important features of the old system persisted and exerted their influence: the market was in profound disequilibrium (repressed inflation), requirements of financial solvency were diluted by widespread use of subsidies and tax privileges, essential raw materials and foreign exchange were rationed, a vast proportion of the overall investment quota was still being financed automatically by the banking system through so-called centralized investments, and the connection between wages and profits was still loose or nonexistent.

It is believed that financial profit is unreliable as an indicator of efficiency of the socialist enterprise in a situation of persistent and large market disequilibrium and distorted price controls, divorced from the cost structure. Thus, it was officially taken for granted that preconditions for making the rate of interest the chief instrument of monetary control were absent and likely to remain so in the foreseeable future. It, however, is fully in accord with the spirit of reform to place it in such a central role.

The project of reform left open the question of the role of the rate of interest. Efforts became concentrated on finding the most appropriate practical interpretation of creditworthiness and economic efficiency as applied to the operation of state-owned enterprises. While market equilibrium and a more adequate price structure are important, efforts must also be made insure an active role for the rate of interest. Dismantling the rationing of essential supplies, correcting the distorted price structure, and creating a more direct and credible link between wages and profits are essential. It would be useful to have this important efficiency criterion working even imperfectly rather than not at all.

Currency convertibility was also often presented as being both desirable but unattainable in the foreseeable future. At least part of the restrictions on foreign exchange transactions among enterprises and the bank could have been abolished without any harm. The system of foreign exchange retention quotas could have been liberalized without undue shocks to economic structures.

In the absence of movement in that direction, the supply of credit was rationed according to the assumptions of the credit plan and the supplementary cash plan. This had hitherto proven to be an imperfect check on money growth and would have remained so if not supported by an effective economic mechanism.

Similar considerations apply to another important macroeconomic variable, the rate of exchange. The rate of exchange had been prevented from exerting its influence upon the internal price structure to a sufficient extent. The inflationary potential of a transition from an insulated to a more open internal price system should not be underestimated, especially since the external value of the zloty had been reduced to a more realistic level in the late 1980s. The dangers of such a move may be exaggerated, however, because the inflationary impact could be reduced if the transition were a part of a broader package of measures aimed at stimulating productivity.

The problems of the actual and potential role of the rate of interest, the desirability of striving toward ultimate convertibility of the currency, and the need for a more flexible rate of exchange policy had not been lost in the reform project. They were, however, largely left as highly debatable issues to be solved at a later stage. Initial steps in this direction have been made in the sense of creating a more favorable institutional framework for bringing them into play at a moment judged more propitious. The question of timing and of the depth of changes that have already been made is subject to controversy.

The tasks achieved so far have been considerable. Efforts have been concentrated on introducing the new economic and financial system of the state-owned enterprises and on redefining the relations between the enterprises and the bank with emphasis on the basic preconditions for better control over the supply of money and limits on the demand for credit side. Excessive credit absorption can now more easily be controlled than in the past.

IV.   THE SUPPLY OF CREDIT

Far-reaching changes are also envisaged on the side of the supply
of credit as well. The banking legislation of 1983 opened up the
possibility of a profound reorganization of the banking system.
The measures taken within that framework indicated the direction
of changes to come. According to official pronouncements at the
time, the crediting or financing function of the banking system
would be separated from its money-creation function. The central
bank would retain the monopoly right of issuing money and
would hold monetary reserves of the banks and refinance their
activities. It would also act as the bank of the state, but would
normally not have direct contacts with the enterprise sector.
Deposit holding and granting credits to enterprises would be done
by a number of commercial banks which would compete among
themselves for potential clients. That would be a natural corollary
to the freedom granted enterprises to choose banks with which to
hold their accounts and transact credit deals. The centralized
banking system would thus be split into a two-tier structure: the
central bank and the subordinate but organizationally and
economically autonomous commercial banks.

The number of commercial banks remained to be determined
on purely practical grounds. In the late 1980s there were about five
or six larger banking institutions, in addition to a multitude of
small cooperative banks scattered throughout the country. The
first concrete steps had already been taken in the field of foreign
trade and export production financing. In addition to the Foreign
Trade Bank, Bank Handlowy SA, a bank called the Bank for
Export Promotion was created. Because the spheres of activity of
the two banks partially overlapped, the competitive principle was
actually introduced into the Polish banking structure. Another
development was that the network of saving institutions was
separated from the organizational structure of the central bank and
transformed into an independent banking institution. Within the
limits of the credit quotas alloted them by the central bank, the
commercial banks would be free to grant or to refuse credits to
individual enterprises on the basis of the merits of each case.

Further developments in the direction of a market-type structure
of the banking system and modes of its regulation were not
excluded by the banking legislation. They depend on the progress

within the other sectors of the national economy. Examples of such progress include the emergence of a more diversified ownership structure and the creation of industrial bonds and government securities. At the root of the concept of institutional reform lies the conviction that narrowing the scope of activity of the central bank, while insulating it from direct pressures of the enterprise sector, will strengthen its control over the supply of money.

The position of the central bank as the highest monetary authority has also been strengthened in relation to the Ministry of Finance and the administrative apparatus of the state in general. Until 1983, the National Bank of Poland, Narodowy Bank Polski, was directly subordinate to the Ministry of Finance. This dependence has been abolished. The chairman of the NBP is appointed by the Sejm on the suggestion of the government and is no longer subordinate to the Minister of Finance. The chairman participates in meetings of the government and is subordinate, ultimately, to the Sejm. It is to the Sejm that he presents the draft of the credit plan, including the envisaged growth in the quantity of money. The same applies to the General Guidelines on Credit Policy for the coming year. The chairman of the NBP is also obliged to report to the Sejm on the actual implementation of the credit plan and is in a position to give his advice on the budget draft. The central bank is now formally charged with the task of watching over stability of the currency and is expected to come forward with an appropriate stabilization program. The position, as well as the responsibilities of the central bank, have been strengthened and broadened.

V.   CONCLUSIONS

Taken together, the changes in the mechanism of the demand for credit and the changes in the mechanism of money supply add up to a considerably improved monetary framework for future growth with stability. If this goal still seems remote, it is partially due to the remaining imperfections of the mechanism of monetary control. Fundamental structural weaknesses hampering the smooth functioning of the monetary system still exist. Some important monetary channels are still extremely loosely controlled. The so-called soft financing has been manifested in the wide and often arbitrary use of subsidies and exemptions, as well as in the nearly automatic financing of budgetary deficits. To the extent that centralized investment was also nearly automatically financed by the banking system, credits have actually become a substitute for the budgetary subsidy. The transition to the new system is a prolonged and difficult process with many obstacles on the road to its full implementation.

NOTES

1.   A third bank, the Bank for Export Promotion, was created with a sphere of activity partially overlapping that of the old Commercial Bank Ltd. This was, however, a first step toward the reform of the structure of banking. The fact is significant in so far as it brings an element of competition into the sphere of activity in which the spirit of competition had been alien.

2.   Apart from buying foreign exchange, which may also be regarded as a sort of credit granted to the country issuing the currency in question.

3.   The operation of this principle was hampered by the centrally administered distribution of raw materials and other productivity inputs, as well as by the system of state contracts for the output of some branches and enterprises. The most important remnant of the old system of management (and the most injurious to the stability of the national currency) was the widespread and rather arbitrary use of subsidies and tax exemptions. Besides distorting the economic efficiency calculus and paralyzing motivation they imposed a heavy burden on the state budget. The enterprise most likely to find itself in dire financial straits was a relatively unimportant small economic unit with insufficient support on the part of an industrial lobby, unable to extort subsidies and tax privileges from the central authorities.

PART II

INTERACTION WITH
THE WORLD ECONOMY:
OPPORTUNITIES AND LIMITATIONS

PROBLEMS AND PROSPECTS FOR EAST-WEST ECONOMIC RELATIONS

Jozef Sołdaczuk

I. GENERAL POLITICAL AND ECONOMIC CONDITIONS OF EAST-WEST TRADE

The second half of the eighties, in contrast with the first half, was characterized by a gradual return of détente and an improvement of conditions for development of economic relations and trade between the East and the West.

The improvement of political relations between the Soviet Union and the United States was of primary importance. Improved relations led a breakthrough in the disarmament negotiations between both superpowers. Of vital importance were the far-reaching peace proposals put forward by Warsaw Pact countries, aimed at reducing armaments and military forces, and promoting an atmosphere of trust and mutual reliance in Central Europe.

These proposals were validated by the program of deep social, political, and economic reforms undertaken in the USSR and in other Eastern European countries, especially in Hungary and Poland. A positive evolution also took place in the NATO countries. This is demonstrated by both specific initiatives and peace proposals, as well as the resolution of emerging tensions and conflicts through negotiations and political dialogue.

Experience after World War II indicates that an improvement in East-West relations usually leads to an improvement in economic relations and faster trade growth. In contrast, a deterioration in political relations and increased tension among countries of both systems have led to a loss of interest in economic cooperation, and further limitations and obstacles to East-West trade.

The latter situation occurred during the early eighties, after the Soviet military intervention in Afghanistan and after martial law was introduced in Poland in December 1981. The NATO countries reacted by imposing economic restrictions in finance and credit, trade, and the transfer of technology, aimed at the Soviet Union, Poland, and to a large extent the remaining countries of Eastern Europe. The current deep political changes in the USSR and in Eastern Europe and the improvement in political relations and the lifting of Western restrictions and trade barriers, together with an ongoing normalization of credit and financial relations, enhanced the already improved conditions for the development of economic relations between the East and West.

There is a growing understanding that the solution of the very complex economic problems of the modern world requires establishing worldwide economic cooperation. This was evident in the discussions during the Seventh United Nations Conference on Trade and Development, held in August 1987. The resolution, or at least mitigation, of two complicated problems will be possible only with complex economic cooperation on a world scale. These problems are the rapidly increasing external indebtedness of the least- and medium-developed countries, and the prevention of greater disproportions in per capita income between the developed and developing countries.

One factor which could lead to improvement is the potential development of trade and economic cooperation within the East-West-South triangle. Greater cooperation between these groups could set the stage for resolving the complicated economic problems of *all* countries.

The need for complex international cooperation also arises from mounting threats to man's natural environment. Problems connected with protection and conservation are complicated.

Because their solutions generally require large material, technical, and financial outlays, overcoming them, or even reducing them, by having particular countries undertake autonomous projects is not always possible. Very often these problems require the cooperation of several countries on a regional or even international scale. The growing understanding of all emerging problems, needs, and dangers results in a lasting improvement in political and economic relations between East and West.

Such possibilities of cooperation are surfacing, especially in Europe. Countries of Western Europe have always been significantly more interested in developing trade and economic relations with the USSR and Eastern Europe, than the United States has been. This is because Eastern Europe constitutes for the former countries an important, though only supplementary, source of energy, raw, and semi-processed materials. Eastern Europe also serves as an alternative export market for Western Europe's industrial, farm, and food products. The percentage of total trade turnover of Eastern Europe to Western Europe was about 6%, which is not high. Potential possibilities exist for increasing this percentage. The recently developing fierce competition in international trade between Western Europe, the United States, and Japan, and competition from the newly industrialized countries increase Western Europe's interest in economic cooperation and markets in Eastern Europe.

During the period of increasing political tension in East-West relations at the beginning of the eighties, Western Europe was considerably more restrained in imposing barriers to East-West trade than the United States. Western European nations clearly did not want to return to cold war practices. Even though they accept maintaining strategic control over sensitive modern technologies exported to Eastern Europe and the USSR, they oppose the exaggerated and excessively widened interpretation of the strategic exports category, preferring to limit it to items of strictly military significance.

West European countries in general hold the view that positive economic and commercial cooperation may improve the political atmosphere and better promote fulfillment of political interests. Thus, during the early 1980s Western Europe undertook new initiatives directed at improving and animating economic and commercial East-West relations.

The USSR and countries of Eastern Europe have an even larger degree of interest in developing economic relations and trade with the West, particularly with Western Europe. This is reflected in the high share (22-27%) of Western Europe in the total trade turnover of the USSR and the rest of Eastern Europe. East European countries have emphasized that there are larger possibilities for developing complex commercial cooperation, and for developing a more universal, all-European international division of labor. Doing so, they stipulate only that mutual economic relations should be based on principles of noninterference with internal affairs, equal treatment, and mutual benefit.

The formal agreement between the European Economic Community (EEC) and the Council for Mutual Economic Assistance (CMEA) should create a favorable base for faster development of mutual trade and cooperation in industry, farming, food production, services, and finance.

East European countries implementing economic reforms aimed at restructuring their economies toward decentralized, market-type economic systems, are deeply interested in modern, efficient methods of management and marketing, as well as in effective Western economic policy instruments. East European countries also have a growing interest in joining worldwide economic organizations. For example, Hungary in 1981 and Poland in mid-1986 have rejoined the International Monetary Fund and the World Bank. Another example is the Soviet Union's interest in participating in the General Agreement on Tariffs and Trade (GATT) activities. All this should create better and more durable foundations for the development of East-West trade and economic cooperation.

II.   THE LEVEL AND PATTERN OF EAST-WEST TRADE

In 1986 East-West trade turnover was as follows: exports of East European countries (including the USSR) amounted to $47.2 billion, while imports totaled $51.3 billion. These flows constituted 2.35% of world exports and 2.45% of world imports.[1] In comparison with the level in 1975, exports (valued in dollars at current prices) have increased 218%, while imports have increased by 59%. However, in relation to world exports and imports the level of East-West trade was lower in 1986; in 1975 the respective shares were 2.53% and 3.72%. In comparison with 1980, exports of East European countries (including the USSR) were 10% lower in 1986, while imports decreased by 3.5%. In 1980 the shares of East-West exports and imports in world trade amounted to 2.68% for both flows, respectively.

The contraction of East-West trade during the first half of the eighties was a consequence of an entanglement of numerous economic and political factors that influenced the trade of certain East European countries. A direct cause was the reduction, or stagnation, of export revenues. The reduction of export reserves limited Eastern Europe's ability to import, thereby depressing total East-West trade turnover. Factors causing the insufficient growth, stagnation, or contraction of exports from Eastern Europe were generally of an internal nature. These stagnating countries have not yet managed to move onto the stage of intensive development, envisaged for implementation as early as the 1970s. This stage of development is based on accelerated labor-productivity growth and increased economic efficiency. The process of restructuring, modernizing, and adapting the economies to changing conditions of the world economy was too slow. That is why those countries have not managed to prevent falling further and further behind the West in technology. The growth of both the export capacities and competitiveness on foreign markets was insufficient.

The decline of the political climate, unfavorable Western business cycles, growing protectionism, and unfavorable ratios of export prices to import prices prevailing in most East European countries during the early eighties also contributed to an unsatisfactory growth in East European exports to the West. The ability to import from Western countries was also limited by an increasing difficulty in obtaining foreign credit as the indebtedness of Eastern Europe to the West continued to grow. In 1981 indebtedness reached a total of $95.4 billion gross and $81.0 billion net, while in 1987 it grew to about $110 billion gross and $83.6 billion net.[2] Difficulties in obtaining new loans in the West were also caused by political factors, particularly in Poland. The cost of obtaining foreign credit grew parallel with indebtedness until 1984, in connection with a rise in interest rates on international financial markets. The burden of foreign debt servicing grew, decreasing the current ability of Eastern Europe to import from the West. The interest of Eastern Europe, particularly the USSR, in imports from the West was also diminished by intensified strategic control, which included limitations on exports of the newest technologies to the USSR and to the rest of Eastern Europe.

These factors affected the trade of East European countries with the West in various ways. The collapse of trade turnover with the West did not occur at all in East Germany. On the contrary, East Germany has generally had a relatively stable rate of economic growth, about 4% annually. East German exports to the West have grown continuously, almost doubling from 1980 to 1987. Easy access to foreign credits, especially from West Germany, enhanced the level of East German exports. As a result, among East European countries, East Germany has grown to become the second-highest exporter and importer with the West, with the USSR leading the way.

In 1984 the Soviet Union reached a peak of $30.1 billion in its level of exports to the West. At the time, this constituted 54.6% of total East European exports to the West. The relatively high level of the Soviet Union's exports to Western countries in 1984 was due mostly to high fuel prices, especially oil, on world markets. The collapse of oil prices in 1986, together with a downward trend in raw material prices since 1984, brought about a nearly 33% reduction in the value of the Soviet Union's exports to the West. This reduction also decreased the overall exports of Eastern Europe. Such a strong reduction was a consequence of the commodity structure of the USSR's exports to the West, in which fuels and raw materials constituted, in 1986, 85% of total exports. In comparison, the share of fuels alone in all export revenues amounted to 66%. Of the total Soviet exports to Western countries, industrial products constituted only 13%, semi-finished industrial products accounted for 10%, machinery and finished industrial products accounted for 10%, while machinery and finished consumer goods accounted for only 3%. A mere 2% of exports generated by the Soviet Union were agricultural and food products.

Such a skewed structure implies export revenues in foreign exchange are highly dependent on changes in business activity and in prices on world markets. This in turn highly influences the USSR's ability to import and, during periods of unfavorable prices on world markets, limits the size of trade turnover between the

USSR and the West. To change the situation, the USSR has been making radical changes by diversifying exports to the West through growth of industrial exports.

Although the Soviet Union experienced a sharp fall in export revenues, its imports decreased only 7% from 1984-86. Because of its enormous economic potential, together with large resources of fuels and raw materials that are attractive to the West, a huge sales market, and considerable reserves of gold and foreign exchange, the USSR has enjoyed a high credit rating on the international financial market. Therefore, it will be able to maintain for some time a high level of imports, regardless of unfavorable price changes and temporary contractions of export revenues. In other East European countries, with the exception of East Germany, lower exports to the West from 1980-82 caused a more pronounced fall in imports.

The deepest fall in exports and imports occurred in Poland. The value of exports decreased from 1980-82 by $2 billion, or 33%, while from 1980-83 imports fell by as much as $3.5 billion, 53% of the total. A sharp contraction of Poland's trade with the West was the result of a deep economic and social crisis, which peaked from 1980-82. Compared with pre-crisis levels, the crisis caused a 17% reduction in industrial production and a 25% reduction in national income. Additionally, a year of bad harvests, coupled with an insufficient supply of equipment for agriculture, caused a reduction of 11% in farm production. The fall in both industrial and agricultural production decreased the supply of products for the domestic market, leaving even fewer products available for exports. Acute internal supply shortages and strong inflationary pressure, connected with a wave of strikes, wage increase demands, and simultaneous decreases in labor efficiency, created a situation where internal needs absorbed the supply designated for exports. A gradual regaining of export volumes to the West began in 1983, but until the end of 1986 it was not possible to regain the 1980 export revenue levels. The levels in 1983 were approximately $1.5 billion lower than in 1980. In addition to the internal difficulties, the West imposed restrictions [for example, limiting access to markets and the U.S. suspension of Most Favored Nation (MFN) status] following the declaration of martial law in Poland, contributing further to the decline in import and export volume.

A marked acceleration of Poland's export growth to the West began only after the abolishing of martial law in July 1984. During the period from 1984 to 1986, exports to the West grew on average by 6.6% a year. In the first seven months of 1987, when total exports grew by 6.2%, exports to non-CMEA countries increased by 11.2% in constant prices and in value terms by 14%. Hard currency exports, placed mainly in Western markets, increased by 20% in value terms, and was a significant step forward in restoring Poland's export position with the West. A fundamental factor contributing to improvement of the growth of that trade was the gradual restoration of industrial and agricultural production in Poland during 1984-86 to levels above those before the crisis. Equally important was a gradual, though slow, implementation of the economic reform in Poland since 1982. The step-by-step restoration of cooperative links between Poland and the West, broken off from 1981-82, is also a positive factor in the increase of Polish exports to the West. The ongoing normalization of political and economic relations, the admission of Poland to the International Monetary Fund (IMF) and the World Bank, together with the restoration of Poland's most-favored nation status by the United States in 1986, should promote full restitution of economic relations with Western countries and enhance their further development.

Besides Poland, Romania also experienced a very serious contraction of exports from 1980-82—a total drop of $1 billion, or 21% of the total. Even more severe was the drop in imports—$2.8 billion, or 66%. Such a decrease was the result of acute import restrictions introduced in Romania to protect the balance of payments and to generate a sufficient surplus for servicing and repaying foreign debt. With tremendous effort, Romanian exports were restored in 1986 to their previous levels. Imports subsequently increased, but to a much smaller extent. In 1986 the value of imports was only 50% of the 1980 level. This allowed Romanian foreign indebtedness to decrease from $10.2 billion to $6.4 billion.

From 1980-86 Bulgarian exports also fell by about $900 million, hurt by falling prices of agricultural products on world markets. At the same time, Bulgarian imports from the West increased by about $900 million. This raised the level of indebtedness in 1986 to $4.3 billion gross and $3.2 billion net. Czechoslovakia and Hungary experienced stagnation of their trade with the West from 1980-86, both in exports as well as imports.

The overall value of East European exports, excluding the USSR, grew from 1980-86, after a decline of $24.2 billion. This growth occurred only because of a systematic increase in East German exports. The depreciation of the American dollar from 1982 to 1986 also favorably affected Eastern exports. With fewer Soviet exports, the remaining share of East European exports to the West grew to 53.6%, overturning the pattern of 1984. The trend in imports also reversed, although in this case it was the share of Eastern Europe which declined to 48.4% while the share of the USSR grew to 52%.

The commodity structure of East European (excluding the USSR) exports to the West differed significantly from that of the Soviet Union. Industrial products accounted for 56% of exports, while fuels, raw materials, and agricultural products accounted for 44% of total exports. Within industrial products, 21% of exports were semi-finished goods, 11% were machinery and transport equipment, and 24% were consumer durable goods. Within raw materials and agricultural products, fuels (for the most part, coal) constituted 19% of total exports, raw materials accounted for 12%, while agricultural and food products accounted for 11%. East European countries have a more diversified commodity structure of exports and are considerably less dependent on exports of fuels and raw materials. However, because semi-processed products exported from Eastern countries are generally characterized by high material- and energy-intensiveness, they should be included in the raw materials category. East European countries, therefore, also stress the necessity to change further the structure of exports by increasing the share of industrial goods, especially technology-intensive products. Taken together, the share of industrial goods for direct consumption of machinery, capital equipment, and transportation equipment amounted to only 35%.

In contrast to their differentiated export structures, the commodity structures of imports from the West by Soviet and East European countries were very much alike. In both cases industrial goods constituted 76% of total imports while agricultural products and raw materials, including fuels, accounted for 24%. The composition of both product groups was a bit different. Raw materials and agricultural products dominated Soviet imports, accounting for 17% of the total, while the respective shares of raw materials and fuels were 6% and 1%. In imports of the remaining

East European countries raw materials for industry, and agricultural and food products each accounted for 10% of the total, while fuels constituted 4%. In the industrial goods group, semi-finished products accounted for 38% of total Soviet imports and 31% of the remainder of Eastern Europe. East European imports of machinery and capital equipment, however, were higher than Soviet imports—34% and 31% respectively. Similarly, the share of final consumer goods was higher in East European imports, 12%, than in Soviet imports, where it amounted to only 7%.

What was striking in the East European imports from the West was the relatively high share of industrial products, including those of high quality, which were not manufactured in East European countries. A dominating item was the group consisting of machinery and capital equipment, together with machinery components. They perform a very important role in the process of modernizing production and raising the technological level of manufacturing in the East European countries.

III.   PROSPECTS FOR DEVELOPMENT OF EAST-WEST TRADE

In discussions of prospects for East-West trade it is usually stressed that there are great potential possibilities for the development of trade that are not being sufficiently utilized. This is manifested in the low share of East-West trade with relation to world trade—currently at 2.4% of world exports and imports. The low level of commercial flows between East and West is especially visible when compared with the economic potential of Western countries and Eastern socialist countries, including the USSR. Because the economic capacities of the West are generally known, only the economic potential of Eastern Europe, as of 1988, will be discussed below.

With the Soviet Union included, Eastern Europe is an area inhabited by 380 million professionally active people. Of those, 80% are employed in nonagricultural professions. Their general level of education differs only slightly from the level found in highly developed Western countries. Eastern Europe, excluding the Soviet Union, is inhabited by 105 million residents, with 50 million professionally active citizens. Anywhere from 75-87% of the citizens, depending on the country, are employed in nonagricultural professions.

Together with the USSR, Eastern Europe generates about 27% of the total world production of energy raw materials, 22% of electric power, 30% of steel, and about 23% of total world production of manufacturing industries. Eastern Europe without the USSR generates about 5.2% of the total world production of energy raw materials, 5.1% of electric power, 9.1% of steel, and about 5% of the world's manufactured goods. Of the total hard coal production, 7.3% is from Eastern Europe, of which 6.0% is contributed by Poland. These general figures point out that the fundamental economic potential of Eastern European countries creates more possibilities of developing trade with the West than are being realized today. The share of Eastern Europe, including the USSR, in world exports is about 9.5%, and in world imports about 8.8%. Excluding the Soviet Union, the shares of the rest of Eastern Europe amount correspondingly to 4.7% in exports and 4.2% in imports.

The level of participation of East European countries in world trade, measured by per capita value of exports and imports, is sometimes only half the analogous value of comparable Western countries. Of Eastern Europe, the most engaged in trade were East Germany and Bulgaria, with exports and imports each at about $1,500 per capita. That is comparable to levels of Italy's exports and imports, yet only half the levels of West Germany and Denmark. Similarly, Czechoslovakia and Hungary, with exports and imports ranging from $900-1,100 per capita, trade at a level less than a third of Austria. Romania and Poland have a per capita trade level that is one-half to one-third the level of Spain. Exports per capita in the Soviet Union are less than half the level of the United States, while imports amount to only one-fifth of U.S. totals.

This very low level of Eastern European participation in the international division of labor is a consequence of underestimating the benefits of international specialization, even within the CMEA. This was reflected in assigning a higher priority to the development of import substitutes.

The ongoing discussion in Eastern Europe of the need to move from extensive to intensive development has raised the question of promoting international specialization, within the CMEA as well as with countries of different political systems. Raising the technical level, modernizing production, and accelerating the growth of overall economic efficiency are fundamental factors in promoting international specialization.

Plans set up in the seventies to implement the new development strategy stressing the need for a more export-oriented development of East European economies and new directions of international specialization and cooperation in production, have not been successful. The main reason was that new development strategies were implemented without a fundamental reform of the economic and management systems. More recently, similar strategic goals and tasks aimed at restructuring Eastern Europe's national economies have been more closely tied to the deep reform of their economic systems and policy instruments. Restoring a kind of market-type, multi-property sector economy (assuming some reprivatization of part of the state enterprises), together with limiting the scope of centralized decisions and increasing the independence of enterprises and economic organizations by basing their activity on the principles of economic efficiency and self-financing, are major goals. These changes cover not only the internal economy but also external economic relations. The gradual departure from the state monopoly of foreign trade, by licensing state, cooperative, and private enterprises to perform foreign trade activities, has become more and more common practice in Eastern Europe. Forming joint-ventures with foreign capital is also allowed or intended.

Experience demonstrates that the lack of a sufficient degree of international specialization in CMEA countries was one of the important factors decelerating technological progress, lowering product quality and its level of modernity, hindering faster growth of labor productivity, and hindering overall economic efficiency. Benefits arising from the international division of labor and international specialization grow in proportion with its scope, that is, with the number of countries involved. Limiting specialization and division of labor to CMEA countries alone would narrow possibilities of gaining larger benefits stemming from international specialization.

Even though the economic potential accumulated by the East European countries is considerable, their technological level and degree of modernity in industrial production remains far inferior to the level of the Western industrialized countries. Imports of modern technology and technical know-how from the highly developed countries, together with the development of specialization and cooperation in production, should raise the technological level and quality of East European industrial production. The more intensive mutual division of labor among CMEA countries allowing wider specialization and development of large-scale production should increase the supply of specialized higher-quality export goods at world standards, decrease manufacturing costs, and improve the competitiveness of East European exports in Western markets. These processes will also increase the East European capacity to import from Western countries.

Utilizing the possibilities to develop East-West trade will require important changes in the commodity structure and the trade system. The lack of symmetry in the commodity structure of East European (including Soviet) exports and imports inhibits a more rapid development of this trade. First, production of fuels and raw materials in East European countries (excluding the USSR) is far from sufficient in relation to their own consumption needs. With their continuous economic growth, even at a moderate yearly rate of 3.0%, production of those materials will be increasingly absorbed by internal needs. Increases in export capacities of Eastern European countries will therefore depend on development of new export specializations in industry and on the increase of export capacities of agriculture and foodstuffs. In this last domain, however, there are similarly strong pressures of unfulfilled internal demand for foodstuffs, especially in Poland, Romania, and the USSR, thus limiting products available for export. At the same time, traditional exports of agricultural products and foodstuffs to the West, especially to the EEC, meet with serious barriers which are part of the common agricultural policy of the EEC. Thus, East-West trade will be mostly dependent on industrial exports from Eastern Europe to the West. New directions of specialization will have to be worked out, that is, a new division of labor with the Western countries will have to be established.

IV. PROBLEMS AND CONDITIONS WITH DEVELOPMENT OF THE ALL-EUROPEAN DIVISION OF LABOR

During the seventies, East European countries, excluding the USSR, managed to attain some progress in increasing the share of industrial products, including semi-processed materials, in their exports to the West, while reducing the share of fuels and raw materials. This direction will continue. The Soviet Union is only just beginning to undergo the necessary changes in the structure of its exports. For both Eastern Europe and the Soviet Union, the greatest possibilities for creating new directions of specialization in economic relations with the West appear in Europe. Since World War II, nearly 90% of the total East-West trade has been conducted in Europe. There are many reasons for this: 1) many years of traditional commercial, industrial, and technical cooperation, 2) knowledge of West European markets and technology by East European managers and technical personnel, and 3) many West European businessmen are familiar with East European markets and with methods of operating within them. These factors constitute favorable conditions for widening and intensifying the existing links, as well as for developing new forms of economic ties and industrial cooperation. Starting with the simplest forms of cooperation, such as licensing agreements, subcontracts with East European suppliers, and buy-back agreements, cooperative arrangements of higher complexity have gradually been introduced. These arrangements involve co-production, both of parts and components and in final products. Such contracts are usually based on long-term credits and involve supplies of Western technologies, modern capital equipment, as well as numerous production components. They are usually accompanied by agreements on personnel training and on cooperation in organization and marketing. Products manufactured under such agreements are often exported through marketing networks of Western companies. Unfortunately, during the acute socioeconomic crisis in Poland from 1980-82 which led to increasing tension in East-West political relations, a number of the cooperation agreements were broken off or not renewed. This pertained particularly to cooperation agreements with Poland, but it also had a negative impact on the relations and cooperation of Western companies with other East European countries. Numerous Western enterprises refrained from further engagement, especially in new cooperative links with Eastern Europe, awaiting clarification of the situation and improvement in the East European political and economic scene. Another contributing factor was that from 1980-82 *all* East European countries, especially

Poland, suffered increased internal economic difficulties, reflected in the lowering of growth rates, or even in stagnation of production and national income, and in an increase of external indebtedness to the West.

The policies of glasnost and perestroika and the gradual economic and political reforms in the Soviet Union, as well as in Hungary and Poland, have played an important role in the normalization of East-West relations. A new period of positive economic links and industrial cooperation is opening again in East-West relations. In particular, new possibilities of direct cooperation in capital investment between Western enterprises and industrial organizations in Eastern European countries are arising. Most East European countries introduced legislation allowing for joint-ventures with foreign capital. Although these reforms are only at a preliminary stage and there have been few significant successes, except in Hungary, they create greater opportunities for developing and deepening mutual production cooperation in the future, both on the interbranch as well as on the intrabranch level.

Focusing attention on the development of industrial cooperation and specialization does not mean that there are not opportunities for specialization in agricultural and foodstuffs production. On the contrary, new directions and specialization possibilities are emerging, parallel with those which characterized intra-European trade in this area 25-30 years ago. West European countries, especially those of the EEC, developed their agriculture intensively, not only increasing their level of self-sufficiency in food production, but also generating large surpluses of many basic agricultural products grown in moderate climates. The countries of Eastern Europe, on the other hand, have transformed themselves from net exporters to net importers of numerous agricultural products, especially grains and fodder, but also meat and dairy products. Nevertheless, East European exports to Western Europe still consist in part of the old, traditional agricultural and foodstuff exports. Many new products were also introduced. For example, in Poland new items were exported, among them horse and rabbit meat, and a wide range of fresh, frozen, or processed fruits and vegetables.

Thus, agricultural production development possibilities are much greater now and would benefit from all-European specialization. Division of labor would allow for better utilization of the specific conditions and experiences of different countries in farming and food processing. It would also increase efficiency and limit the commonly used systems of subsidizing production. This would also allow for better fulfillment of the more varied needs of consumers in both parts of Europe. It would be especially important for East European countries where the supply of food products is different in each country.

Development of an all-European division of labor would also require creating an all-European infrastructure in these areas: electric energy transmission networks; oil and gas pipelines; an all-European road transport system; railroad connections; and telecommunication systems. Another area which would also require full cooperation and intensifying turnover is in services. Compared with Western Europe, services lag behind in Eastern Europe. Efforts to modernize them will lead to cooperation in investments and the establishment of joint-ventures. These joint-ventures could include catering, tourist services, vehicle repair and service, and modern networks of banking services.

Development of full investment and capital cooperation between Eastern and Western Europe in industry, agriculture and food processing, services, and banking and finance may give rise to dynamic trade-creation effects, similar to those triggered in Western Europe during the period of development and economic integration. If adequate conditions were created and effects of this type were to be triggered, East-West trade in Europe could grow during the nineties at a faster rate than world trade. This would enhance the acceleration of economic growth in both parts of the continent and would strengthen Europe's position in the world economy.

With traditional directions of East-West specialization prevailing, East-West trade will most likely proceed at a rate not higher than the overall growth rate of world trade, and its share will at best remain on a level similar to the present one.

V. OBSTACLES TO DEVELOPMENT OF EAST-WEST ECONOMIC RELATIONS AND THE ROLE OF GOVERNMENT AGREEMENTS IN THEIR ALLEVIATION

Existing potential possibilities for development of East-West economic relations cannot conceal existing obstacles, uncertainties, and dangers. First, the uncertainty surrounding the stability of improved political relations between East and West prevails. Negative experiences of the past have given rise to skeptical attitudes in some Western and Eastern economic circles, whose members do not believe that relations are really entering a new, positive phase. This skepticism results in caution before joining more durable and extensive cooperative projects, especially joint-ventures.

Many elements of uncertainty also appear with regard to further evolution of the economic situation in both the West and in Eastern Europe. Uncertainty surrounds growth prospects in the West. Fears that accelerated inflation and higher interest rates on the international markets may reemerge. Instability on world foreign exchange markets and large swings in the relative values of major currencies also contribute to an atmosphere of uncertainty. Changes in both exchange and interest rates exert an influence on the level of indebtedness and on the current burden of East European debt-servicing payments to the West. There is a threat that the currently manifested growth in protectionist tendencies prevailing in Western countries may exert negative influences on East-West trade.

It is especially unclear how rapidly and effectively East European countries will implement indispensable economic reforms, raise labor productivity, increase economic efficiency, and improve their ability to compete on foreign markets. Whether they will be able to reorient their economies toward exports, increase their involvement in the international division of labor, raise the technical level and quality of production, and adapt to the needs and requirements of foreign customers in the West, is not known. Some business circles in the West show marked skepticism in these matters and adopt a wait-and-see attitude, holding back from engaging in capital investments and more durable cooperative ties until signs of true progress appear in the economies and exports of Eastern Europe.

Development of East-West economic relations depends on an improvement in the payments situation of Eastern Europe and on its ability to service foreign debt. The general level of indebtedness, in comparison with other debtors of the world and in relation to Eastern Europe's economic potential, is not excessive, with the exception of Poland. But during the last two years this indebtedness has grown, while the current accounts of the balances of payments of most East European countries have deteriorated. This deterioration has increased uncertainty as to what further evolution might bring. It is beyond any doubt that an improvement in the payments situation and the general economic situation of Eastern European countries will depend first of all on their own efforts. Nevertheless, creating more favorable conditions for accelerated trade and closer industrial cooperation between East and West cannot be a one-sided process. To achieve a real improvement in conditions for faster trade growth and better overall East-West economic relations, positive Western cooperation is necessary. Easier access to markets in Western countries is indispensible. A liberalization of technology transfer and full normalization of financial credit relations are also necessary.

Much can be achieved through adequate intergovernmental agreements and undertakings. This should lead to enhancing mutual trust and securing a higher degree of economic certainty and safety in East-West economic relations. Such agreements could define both the general principles and "rules of the game" in mutual relations, providing specific legal guarantees that would provide protection from sudden one-sided swings in the conditions of East-West trade. Of considerable significance would be a return to the practice of regular meetings—during which reviews of mutual relations would take place in the forum of mixed commissions or similar bodies.

Considerable progress achieved in relations between EEC and individual East European countries, should also create more stable conditions for developing East-West economic relations in Europe.

In summary, it is hoped that all parties involved will manage to work out a system of economic cooperation providing for easier resolution of emerging difficulties and tensions, promoting more rapid development of mutual trade, and improving the overall economic relations between East and West.

NOTES

1.   All data from the *Economic Survey of Europe, 1986-1987*. New York: United Nations, 1987, pp. 350-354.

2.   Ibid., p. 309.

POLAND'S FOREIGN INDEBTEDNESS

Zbigniew Kamecki

I. POLAND'S FOREIGN INDEBTEDNESS

The foreign convertible currency debt of Poland amounted to $39.2 billion at the end of 1988. About two-thirds of the Polish debt resulted from public credits or private credits guaranteed by public financial institutions of the Paris Club member countries. Developed Western countries held 80% of this debt, developing countries held about 10%, and the CMEA countries and two CMEA common banks held 8-9%. On September 30, 1988 the most important creditors among the developed Western countries were the Federal Republic of Germany, which held $7.6 billion, or 19.5% of the total; France held $4.2 billion or 10.8%; Austria held $3.5 billion or 9.0%; the United States held $3.2 billion, or 8.0% of the total; the United Kingdom held $2.9 billion, or 7.4%; and Italy held $1.7 billion, or 4.5%.[1] Of the Polish debt, 24% was the result of unguaranteed credits from Western commercial banks.[2] Because exchange rate fluctuations exert an important impact on the size of the debt, it is worth adding that 37.9% of the debt at the end of 1988 was in U.S. dollars (50.7% at the end of 1984), 23.4% in German marks (17.2% in 1984), 12.1% in Swiss francs (11.9% in

141

1984), 8.3% in French francs (5.7% in 1984), 6.9% in Austrian shillings (5.3% in 1984) and 3.3% in English pounds (2.6% in 1984).

Poland is also indebted to the CMEA countries in transferable rubles. It was not until the eighties that the ruble debt appeared. At the end of 1988, the debt reached $6.5 billion in transferable rubles.[3] This debt created various problems, but these problems were unquestionably easier to solve than the problems related to the convertible currency debt. First, ruble debt was much smaller; second, servicing it was relatively easier because the interest amounted to only 2-5%; third, the debt was being repaid with Polish exports that did not encounter any special sale difficulties on the CMEA market. Finally, the terms of trade with the CMEA countries, with the USSR in particular, were improving during the late 1980s.

For these reasons, this chapter will concentrate on the Polish convertible currency debt. The need to service the debt makes it currently impossible to finance all the necessary imports. This causes, in turn, an under-utilization of production capacities, decapitalization of production equipment, shortages of many products on the domestic market with a simultaneous deterioration of their quality (because in many cases the imported raw material has to be replaced with inferior domestic materials), and a decrease of national income distributed in relation to the national income produced, which then generates inflationary effects. An interview granted to the Polish Press Agency by Mr. Baka, the president of the Polish National Bank at that time, illustrates this phenomenon. According to him, if the trade surplus in convertible currencies (which amounted to $1.1 billion in 1986) could be used for the purchase of market goods instead of debt servicing, the supply on the domestic market, at the zloty exchange rate at the time, could have increased by 260 billion zloty. It would eliminate the inflationary gap, which reached 170 billion zloty in 1986, and increase real wages by about 2.4%.[4]

Poland was neither the only nor the most indebted country. It was eighth on the list of the biggest convertible currency debtors and fourteenth or fifteenth as to the size of debt per capita, and finally eighteenth as to the size of debt in relation to the national income. On the other hand, Poland occupied seventh place on the list of the size of debt in relation to the size of exports. Poland, however, was first among the socialist countries both in size of debt and in the ratio of debt to exports.

Table 1. Polish Convertible Currency Debt
(Millions of dollars at year end)

Year	Amount	Year	Amount
1971	1000	1980	24123
1972	1200	1981	25453
1973	2600	1982	24835
1974	5200	1983	26396
1975	8400	1984	26808
1976	12100	1985	29296
1977	14900	1986	33500
1978	18600	1987	39200
1979	22400	1988	39200

Source: *Zadłużenie zagraniczne Polski i drogi jego przezwyciężania. Geneza, charakter i skutki zadłużenia* (Foreign Indebtedness of Poland and the Ways of Overcoming It. Its Origin, Character and Consequences), report of the Foreign Trade Research Institute and of the Institute of the National Economy, Warsaw 1986, p. 76 and data from the Narodowy Bank Polski.

The fact that the indebtedness in 1988 had remained unchanged in comparison to 1987 resulted from the opposite factors. On the one hand, Poland did not pay a portion of interest ($2.1 billion) but, on the other hand, there was a decrease of the dollar rate of exchange (which diminished the Polish debt by $1.6 billion) and a repayment of capital ($0.5 billion).

The Polish convertible currency debt has a relatively short history—it first appeared during the early seventies. Unfortunately, the debt increased rapidly, practically without respite, and is still increasing (see Table 1). In spite of an enormous effort, Poland is not in a position to pay all the interest due. This is a situation that will persist for several years to come, increasing the debt further. It is worth adding that the debt increased despite the fact that Poland designated enormous amounts of money towards its servicing. From 1971 to 1987 the repayment of principal amounted to $23.8 billion and interest to $19.4 billion, while the long and medium-term credits received during that time amounted to $47.6 billion.[5] In other words, debt servicing done by Poland from 1971 to 1987 amounted to 90.7% of credits received. The size of the burden of debt servicing for the Polish economy can be illustrated by the fact that 54.0% of total Polish convertible currency export earnings at that period were used for servicing the debt.[6]

The increase in the Polish convertible currency debt was the result of a number of internal and external reasons. Initially, the main reason for the debt increase was the economic policy assumed by the Gierek administration, which came to power following the events of December 1970. The policy envisaged a rapid growth of the national income[7] and a broad modernization of the economy, of industry, which required a considerable increase of investment outlay.[8]

A second goal of Gierek's policy was to achieve a rapid growth of consumption at the same time. The gap between insufficient domestic accumulation and investments was to be filled with credits obtained from the West, which were to be repaid later with increased exports. This was to be achieved through the increase and modernization of the production apparatus in Poland.

Several external conditions favored such an economic policy: detente in East-West relations; credit policies of the West more favorable to the Socialist countries; easier access to Western technologies; the West's changing its policy toward imports from socialist countries; a "discovery" of the Eastern markets by the West; competition of the Western countries for gaining position in those markets; and easy credit in the West due to a surplus of capital on the international financial markets.

The economic policy of the Gierek administration meant a rapid growth of investment imports from the West, financed to a considerable extent from Western credits. In 1970, those imports amounted to only $269 million, while in 1975, their value reached $2.5 billion. From 1971 to 1980, total imports reached $17.9 billion, despite the fact that their growth was stopped during the second half of the decade.[9] The technologies purchased in the West also required raw materials and materials obtainable for convertible currencies, especially since the domestic supply of raw materials lagged behind domestic needs. As a result, investment imports caused an additional burden on the balance of payments, inducing an increase in imports of raw materials and semi-processed products for industry. These imports increased from $438 million in 1970 to $2.5 billion in 1975. During the following years, further growth of these imports was restricted in connection with mounting balance of payments difficulties. Nevertheless, despite the decline in national income that commenced in 1979, imports of raw materials and semi-processed products reached $2.7 billion in 1980. Total imports of these goods totaled $19.7 billion from 1971 to 1980, 10% more than imports of investment goods.[10] These raw material imports were also financed to a considerable extent by Western credits.

An indirect result of the economic policy chosen by the Gierek administration was the increasing import of grains and fodder. This phenomenon was the indirect result of Gierek's policy in the sense that investment means were concentrated on modernization of industry while the investment needs of agriculture were not considered to be as important. In fact, agricultural output did increase, but the increase was slow, and moreover, several consecutive years of poor crops were recorded during the late seventies. At the same time, the domestic demand for food increased dynamically, both as a result of the rapid increase in national income and because of a relatively high income elasticity of demand for food, higher in Poland than in more developed countries. When the rate of growth of food imports increased, the rate of growth of food exports declined. Imports of food amounted to only $280 million in 1970, but increased to $1 billion in 1975 and to $2.4 billion in 1980. Total food imports from 1971-80 amounted to $12.6 billion.[11] These imports were to a considerable and increasing extent financed from Western credits, and from the U.S. Commodity Credit Corporation in particular. As a result, Poland, a traditional net exporter of food to convertible currency markets, became a net importer starting in 1974. The deficit in food products trade manifested an increasing trend. It is estimated that each of the three kinds of imports outlined above, investment goods, raw materials, and semi-processed products for industry, as well as food, contributed equally to the increase in foreign debt.

The excessive scale and the excessive concentration of investment imports contributed to the increase in indebtedness as well. These imports were so large that they exceeded the absorption capabilities of the economy. The situation grew more complex because there were also large investment ventures based on domestic investment goods and domestic raw materials undertaken on a scale much larger than before. During the early seventies these ventures became a real investment boom, penetrating the whole economy, especially industry. The realization of this enormous number of ventures exceeded the capacities of building and construction, transportation, and industrial enterprises. As a result, the investment cycle of individual ventures lengthened and the results achieved were often far short of the results planned. These phenomena were caused primarily by the fact that the planning and management system of the economy became completely ineffective during the seventies.

The system was characterized by a considerable centralization of economic decisions.[12] Enterprises were subjected to industrial unions and the unions to ministries acting on the grounds of government instructions, mainly the Government Presidium and the Planning Commission. The functioning of the system was based to a large extent on instructions from the economic center and to a smaller extent on economic stimuli inducing enterprises to become more effective in planning and in carrying out the plans. The economic calculus was underestimated both on the micro and the macro levels. Such a system through its nature attached importance to quantity, not quality and economic efficiency. Efforts to stimulate an increase in labor efficiency, decrease production costs, and improve the quality of products were particularly weak. On the other hand, there were both administrative and economic stimuli to increase investments. As a result, enterprises, industrial unions, and ministries readily planned new investments, particularly those based on Western credits. This meant saving domestic means of production, increasing the number of ventures and decreasing investment discipline. It resulted not only in a great number of investment ventures being undertaken simultaneously, but also lengthened investment processes. Even more important, investments' results were worse than planned in terms of production costs, the effectiveness of production, energy, material and import intensity, and the quality of products. All of this naturally caused a demand for further foreign credits and hindered their subsequent repayment. The Gierek administration made an attempt to reform planning and management from 1972-73. This attempt was, however, rather restricted, lacked internal cohesion, and had no consequence on the general system of planning and management. The attempt was soon abandoned and the ineffective centralized planning and management system persisted until the end of the Gierek administration in the late seventies.

The increase in debt quickly caused an increase in the servicing cost. This increase was additionally strengthened by the appearance of factors increasing the debt servicing rate. First, servicing the earlier credits began to overlap and mount—a phenomenon additionally stimulated by the tendency to shorten up the maturity of credits received. As an example, in 1975 the average length of credits was six years, while in 1981 it was only three years. Moreover, during the early seventies, Poland used Western credits mainly for investment purposes. At that time, they were mostly public or guaranteed credits, granted for periods longer than commodity credits or credits from commercial banks which were exclusively used during the late seventies.

Second, the interest rate on credits granted to Poland began to increase with time. This increase resulted partly from changes in the debt structure indicated above. The interest on nonguaranteed credits and their share in the total debt also increased with time, and was higher than the interest on public and guaranteed credits. The gradual deterioration of the creditworthiness of Poland during the late seventies and early eighties, which resulted from the increase of debt and deterioration of the balance of payments, also played a role here. It resulted in a gradual increase of the spread of the Lend on Interbank Offered Rate (LIBOR) or the U.S. prime rate. Though this was an important factor, it should not be overestimated. It appeared only during the late seventies and concerned mainly new credits and credits based on market interest rates.

Third, and most importantly, the average rate of interest for Poland increased as a result of a sharp increase in rates on international financial markets during the late seventies and the early eighties. The importance of this factor was heightened in Poland by the increase in the share of nonguaranteed credits in the total debt and by the fact that a part of newly obtained guaranteed credits assumed a variable interest rate, not constant, as previously. While the average interest rate on Polish debt amounted to about 8% in 1978, it reached about 12% in 1982. This meant that Poland would have to pay nearly $1 billion more in interest in 1982. This increase would constitute about 20% of 1982 export earnings, or 17.4% of export earnings in 1978, which was assumed to be a base year. This increase in debt servicing costs would not have constituted such a problem if exports had increased rapidly enough, since the debt servicing capability of a country depends upon the ratio between the debt servicing cost and export proceeds. Unfortunately, the rate of growth of Polish exports to convertible currency markets was lower than the rate of growth of imports: the annual rate growth of exports reached 20.7% from 1971-79 and imports reached 26.1%.[13]

As a result, the trade balance deteriorated dramatically instead of improving and did not achieve a surplus to cover the debt service. In 1971 there was still a trade surplus of $109 million. In 1973, the deficit reached $1.5 billion, increasing to almost $3.0 billion annually from 1975 to 1976. It decreased slightly from 1977 to 1979 to $2.0 billion annually, but was still very high.[14] It should be stressed that the basic assumption on which the whole economic concept of the Gierek administration was based has not been met to this day, that is, that received foreign credits would be repaid with dynamically developing exports.

The relatively slow increase of exports resulted mainly from internal reasons which can be reduced to three problems. The first problem was the low efficiency of the planning and management system at that time. As was pointed out above, it caused delays in many investment ventures, including export-oriented ventures. As a result, production effects of investment were often worse than expected.

Second, the investment boom and the relatively rapid growth of population incomes combined with the delays in the increase of output, and bottlenecks in many branches caused demand to exceed supply on the domestic market during the seventies. In other words, throughout the seventies a seller's market prevailed. This naturally decreased the interest of producers in exporting, to the West in particular, where the existence of a buyer's market and the oncoming world recession caused sharp competition and high quality requirements of the purchasers.

Third, there was a clear lack of results in the government export promotion policy. The government tried to promote the development of exports, but the means applied were very weak. They were far too weak to compensate for the negative impact of the above-mentioned factors on exports. Even in situations when people responsible for a particular investment project financed from foreign credits undertook a commitment to repay the credits with exports of products obtained through the venture (called the self-repayment principle, on which a majority of imported turn-key plants were formally based) the government too easily relieved them of this obligation.

The relatively slow growth of exports to convertible currency markets, that is, the deterioration of its ratio to debt servicing costs, was also caused by external factors. First, the business situation

Table 2. The Ratio Between Debt Servicing Costs
(Interest and Principal) and Polish Exports
to Convertible Currency Markets

Year	Percentage	Year	Percentage
1971	19.4	1977	55.0
1972	17.7	1978	75.7
1973	16.9	1979	93.6
1974	23.8	1980	101.9
1975	32.5	1981	99.4
1976	41.5		

Source: Report on Foreign Indebtedness quoted above.

in the West deteriorated during the seventies and in the early eighties, reducing demand, or at least the rate of growth in demand, for many Polish exports. Second, protectionist tendencies noticeably strengthened in the Western countries during this period, exerting a negative impact on Polish exports. Third, partly because of the slump in the West, the attitude of Western partners toward Poland (and other socialist countries) changed. Initially they were interested in an increase of their exports to Poland, which were financed by Western credits, and accepted repayment of these credits with Polish exports relatively easily. Later (and it happened quite frequently), the partners tried under various pretenses to free themselves of obligations to purchase Polish products.

The rapid growth of the debt servicing cost and the simultaneous slow growth of Polish exports caused the ratio between the two to increase during the seventies. As can be seen in Table 2, Poland was still close to the ratio between debt servicing cost and export earnings generally considered safe (about 25.0%) for the balance of payments, and indirectly, for the whole economy, as late as 1974. As the ratio increased further, the government embarked on a venture called "economic maneuver," which resulted in a considerable restriction of investments, and thus of investment imports in 1976. It also attempted to reestablish the domestic market equilibrium through increasing food prices. This decision, however, was soon revoked because of a strong public protest. At the same time, there was an attempt to increase exports. These moves caused the trade deficit to decrease considerably, from $3 billion annually from 1975 to 1976 to about $2 billion annually from 1977 to 1978. This improvement, however, was absolutely too small in the face of the rapidly increasing debt servicing costs. As a result, rather than make some radical moves, the government sought new credits to improve the balance of payments situation. By the end of the seventies, practically all export proceeds were designated for debt servicing, while nearly all imports were financed by new credits. The situation worsened in 1979, when national income declined for the first time since World War II. This decline lasted until 1982. National income produced decreased by 23.6% from 1978 to 1982. Poland suffered an acute social, economic, and political crisis which led to a state of martial law in December 1981.

Such a balance of payments situation could not last. A question of basic importance arose: What to do next? Theoretically, two solutions were possible—either suspend debt servicing which could mean retaliation by foreign creditors, or negotiate with them to find a compromise. The Polish government chose the second solution, still intending to develop relations with Western countries and to make the economy export-oriented. This last point was extremely important because the lack of export orientation was one of the main reasons for the Polish economic difficulties. In choosing dialogue with the creditors, the Polish government assumed it was possible to find a compromise. Definitely both parties had certain common interests—the creditors wanted to recover their capital invested in Poland plus interest and Poland wanted to resolve the problem of indebtedness in the long run because it hindered economic development. As a result, debt rescheduling negotiations were proposed in 1980. These negotiations concluded in 1981 with two agreements, one with commercial banks (on nonguaranteed credits) and the other with the Paris Club (on public and guaranteed credits), on rescheduling the debt servicing payments due in 1981.

When the state of martial law was declared in December 1981, however, Western countries, first of all the United States, imposed restrictions on Poland, including credit and commercial restrictions. Negotiations with the Paris Club were also suspended unilaterally by the Western countries.

Poland, however, declared its readiness to continue the dialogue with creditors to settle the debt problem. To stress this positive attitude, Poland tried to fulfill obligations towards commercial banks according to the agreement of 1981, despite an extremely difficult economic situation at the time. This attempt to fulfill obligations came even though the agreement was not formally in force. The agreement with commercial banks came in force formally only after its signing in April 1982. As a result, dialogue with the commercial banks was continued despite the state of emergency. Five further agreements (including the one of July 20, 1988) were concluded. They rescheduled virtually all Polish debt in the sphere of nonguaranteed credits, with the exception of credits contracted after March 26, 1981. Among these agreements the one of July 20, 1988 was particularly important. It concerned payments of capital of about $9 billion, that is about 23% of the Polish whole indebtedness in convertible currencies from 1988-1993. They were rescheduled until 2003. Talks with the Paris Club were reconvened only in 1984 and led to four agreements on rescheduling servicing of public and guaranteed credits falling due up to 1988 inclusive.

The Polish government stressed that it was ready to undertake all efforts to assure compliance with the provisions. At the same time, it alerted its creditors to the fact that full compliance could prove difficult even with the greatest effort of the Polish economy if the creditors did not grant new credits in order to facilitate Poland's regaining its debt servicing capabilities.

Poland was not the only country to put forward such postulates. The standpoint of other debtor countries in negotiations with their creditors is the same. Moreover, the creditors usually recognize such postulates. Similar agreements concluded in recent years with Mexico, Brazil, and Argentina not only determined the obligations of these countries, but also granted a considerable amount of new credits in order to facilitate the fulfillment of the obligations.

While the commercial banks recognized, to a certain extent, the Polish conditions put forward during the negotiations and granted certain revolving credits (Poland used $961 million net from 1982 to 1988),[15] the governments represented in the Paris Club assumed a more negative attitude. Some Western countries granted credits to Poland, but the amount was rather symbolic. The amount of new medium- and long-term credits granted to Poland in 1980 reached $8.7 billion, and in 1981, $4.9 billion. In 1982, the amount of new credits dropped to $1.5 billion; in 1983, to $565 million; in 1984, to $218 million; in 1985, to $261 million; in 1986, to $294 million; in 1987, to $317 million; and in 1988, to $259 million. Few countries, if any, have suffered such a dramatic decrease in financial inflows from abroad during such a short period.

Poland was practically left to fend for itself in the fulfillment of the obligations resulting from these agreements with commercial banks and the Paris Club. The acute economic crisis in Poland made it even more difficult to fulfill the obligations. The national income produced in 1982 was 16.8% lower than in 1980, and 23.6% lower than in 1978, a year when the national income reached its highest level. National income distributed dropped by 20.0%, 27.5% in comparison with 1978. Industrial output dropped by 12.8%, investments by 31.8%, average real wages by 23.2%, exports to convertible currency markets by 31.6%, and imports by as much as 47.3%.[16]

The domestic market was completely disorganized. In this situation, preventing a further decline in the national income and improving the situation on the domestic market became of paramount importance. Thanks to a strict savings program and to a partial substitution of imports from convertible currency markets with imports from the CMEA and the USSR in particular, it was possible to accomplish this task. In 1983, an increase in the national income was recorded for the first time in four years. This increase continued till 1988.[17] The industrial output, agricultural production, and investment consumption also increased. The situation on the domestic market also improved to some extent. However, serious internal and external economic disequilibriums still persist. They were caused largely by foreign debt.

In spite of the economic difficulties, Poland tried to service its debt to the maximum extent possible. In a situation where the inflow of new credits faded, an elimination of the trade deficit and an achievement of a trade surplus were preconditions of debt servicing. A trade surplus was achieved in 1982 for the first time, $358 million. In 1983, it reached $1.1 billion; in 1984, it was $1.5 billion; in 1985, $1.1 billion; in 1986, the same $1.1 billion; in 1987, $1.2 billion; and $1.1 billion in 1988.[18] Remembering that the trade balance had been negative since 1972, (from 1975-76 about $3 billion annually, and from 1977-79 about $2 billion annually), the achievement of a trade surplus can be considered a success. It was only a partial success, however, as it was achieved mainly through drastic import cuts. It is worth adding here that the fact that national income began to grow in 1983 despite the import cuts testifies to a certain vitality of the Polish economy.

From 1982 to 1986, Poland attempted to service its debt to a maximum extent, despite enormous economic difficulties. During that period $11.4 billion were designated for that purpose, or $2.0 billion annually, out of which $2.0 billion were for principal and $9.0 billion were for interest. This amount constituted 34.0% of convertible currency export earnings during the period. Newly received credits amounted to only $3.5 billion during that period, and, therefore, the net transfer of currency abroad (payments of principal and interest less newly received credits) amounted to $8.1 billion, that is, on the average $1.35 billion annually.

The size of the economic and financial effort is illustrated by the fact that quite the opposite situation took place during the seventies. At that time, the economy witnessed an inflow of foreign capital. The average net inflow (that is, new credits less payments of principal and interest) amounted to $1.279 billion annually from 1971-80 ($1.347 billion annually from 1975-80).[19]

Despite the debt servicing effort, the fact that the U.S. dollar rate increased until spring 1985 (causing a decrease in the part of debt denominated in other currencies, and the decline of interest rates on international financial markets, which started in 1982), Polish debt increased from 1982 to 1986. The main reason was the suspension of public and guaranteed debt servicing in response to the credit blockade imposed by Western countries after martial law was declared in Poland. The main reasons for the increase in Polish debt during 1986 and 1987 were, first, the inability to satisfy all the obligations related to interest payments, and, second, the decline of the dollar which caused the debt denominated in other currencies to increase when converted into dollars. For example, in 1986 and in 1987, the Polish debt increased by more than $12.0 billion in comparison to 1984. Of that increase $9.0 billion resulted from the dollar depreciation (the difference of $3.0 billion is the difference between credits received and repayment of old credits).[20]

Because Poland cannot currently fully service its debt in the sphere of interest payments, Western countries often argue that imports should be curtailed even more, and exports to convertible currency markets should be increased in order to assure the payment of interest in full. This strategy, however, is unacceptable in the current Polish economic, social, and political situation. If exports were to increase additionally, it would drain the domestic market, leading to a decrease of not only production for the domestic market, but also for exports after some time. This would decrease Poland's ability to service debt. On the other hand, it is impossible to cut imports further. They are already below the level considered indispensable. The volume of imports from convertible currency countries was 41.5% lower in 1986 and 21.5% lower in 1988 than in 1978. If imports were further restricted, it would cause a strong decline in domestic output, including the output of exportable goods, again decreasing the debt servicing capabilities.

It is necessary, therefore, to look for other solutions—based not on the decline in national income or exports and imports, but on their growth. Increasing debt servicing capabilities at higher levels of national income, imports, and exports is very important. When these areas decline, debt servicing capabilities also decline. Thus a reasonable compromise between necessary imports, exports, and expenditures on current debt servicing should be sought.

As Polish debt increases, the valid question remains, "What should happen to the Polish debt?" Bringing the debt down to zero is not the goal. Every country can function quite well with a certain amount of foreign debt. The goal is to bring down the debt to a reasonable size in relation to national income and exports, and in particular, to a reasonable ratio between debt servicing and exports to convertible currency markets. This requires both a decrease in total debt and a considerable increase in exports. A decrease in total debt does not mean that credits already received will not have to be repaid. It does mean that while repaying those credits new credits should be secured on a reasonable scale and at more attractive terms than before to facilitate growth of the economy, to make it export oriented, and to improve the debt structure.

Decreasing the total Polish debt requires a long time, however. Consequently, the main task for the next few years is only to slow its growth. It calls for a trade surplus, as well as a balance of services and private transfers surplus, that could fully finance Polish interest payments due. In other words, the goal for the near future is to quickly eliminate the current account deficit, to assure its balance, and to gradually achieve a surplus, enabling repayment of debt. It is in the interest of all parties. The fact that Poland does not pay interest in full means only that a necessary evil has been chosen, which is still better than restricting additional imports.

This solution is not optimal, however. It causes further increases in debt to the future detriment of the economy. While receiving new credits, one gets their equivalent in the form of additional imports, but now, there are no additional imports equivalent to the unpaid interest arrears. As a result, Poland has to pay interest on interest that is becoming capitalized. Continuing this harms Polish creditworthiness, making it more difficult to obtain new credits, even commercial credit. When new credits are granted, their conditions are worse than those offered to countries with a better balance of payments situation.

Consequently, it is in the interest of Poland to balance its current account as soon as possible and then to assure its surplus.[21] It would require, however, a further improvement in the balance of services and in private transfers. This is quite possible, particularly in the case of private transfers. In addition, Polish exports would have to increase relatively quickly in comparison with the growth of Polish imports. It is, however, not an easy task because a further increase in the export of coal and of some other raw materials that have played an important role in total exports is not possible. These exports will decrease. Consequently the increase in total exports will have to result from growth in industrial and certain agricultural products exports.

Although it will be difficult to achieve this type of export growth, it is still quite possible. Investments undertaken earlier will start to produce and there are many export oriented ventures among them. There are still protectionist tendencies in many Western countries, but they exert a negative impact on exports of only a few products. Other products are free of these tendencies. There are also possibilities of increasing exports even in the case of products that are subject to protectionist actions. In many cases, Poland does not even use quotas granted by Western partners for imports of various products, for example, textiles, because of insufficient export supply. Thus the precondition to achieve the appropriate growth rate of exports necessary to assure the current account balance in Poland is to increase the supply of export products, to improve their quality, and to change the product structure of exports. To achieve this, it is necessary to accelerate the economic reform processes in Poland, particularly in foreign trade; to increase export-oriented investments; and to reestablish the domestic market equilibrium.

It is obvious that a sufficiently rapid growth of Polish exports depends mainly on Poland and that even greater efforts should be made towards this goal than have been made in recent years. Such activities will bring, however, only limited results (that is, the reestablishment of the current account balance will be delayed) if they are not reciprocated by actions of Poland's creditors. This means granting credits to Poland on conditions attractive for both parties to facilitate a more rapid export orientation of the economy, and thus, to regain debt servicing capabilities. It is essential to reach a conclusion to the negotiations with the World Bank on participation in financing specific investment projects, and with the International Monetary Fund for an economic program and credits to facilitate balance of payments improvement. The Paris Club and commercial banks should participate in this program, as they have in the case of other debtor countries.

In the longer run, the solution to the Polish debt problem will depend to a great extent on the attitude of the creditor countries towards the world debt problem. Due to its size, indebtedness became one of the basic global problems of the world economy. Polish indebtedness is only a fraction of this problem. Indebtedness is a global problem and understood as such in many circles, as illustrated by various documents such as the Vatican commission's *Iustitia et Pax*,[22] and resolution No. 41/202 of December 8, 1986 of the United Nations General Assembly. Both stress the joint responsibility of creditor and debtor countries for a solution to the world debt problem. Until now, creditor countries have refused to approach this global problem in a global way. They prefer a selective approach on a case by case basis. However, the history of international economic relations, including most recent history, reveals several instances when the initial "no" evolved with time into at least a partial "yes," and "never" into "some time." Can not the same also happen in the sphere of world indebtedness?

NOTES AND REFERENCES

1.   Source: Data from the Narodowy Bank Polski (Polish National Bank).

2.   Source: Report on the Economic situation of Poland. Statistical Supplements for 1985, 1986, 1987, and 1988. Central Office, Warsaw.

3.   Ibid.

4.   *Rzeczpospolita* (*The Republic*), March 24, 1987, p. 1.

5. See the report on Foreign Indebtedness and the data from the Narodowy Bank Polski.

6. See the report on Foreign Indebtedness, the data from the Narodowy Bank Polski, and also data of the Central Statistical Office in Warsaw.

7. In fact, the rate of growth reached a record-breaking level of 9.77% annually from 1970-1975.

8. The share of net investments in fixed capital in the national income (at prices of January 1, 1977) increased from 20.5% in 1970 to 37.1% in 1975.

9. *Rocznik statystyczny* (Statistical Yearbook), *Głowny Urząd Statystyczny,* the Central Statistical Office. Various annual editions from 1975-1983.

10. Ibid.

11. Ibid.

12. In fact, a certain decentralization took place during the seventies. However, it was done in favor of the industrial ministries. Thus, the considerable weakness of the system progressed even further as the coordinating role of the government as a whole weakened. Here, such a decentralization of the centralized system was not a positive phenomenon.

13. See note 9 above.

14. Ibid.

15. *Report on Foreign Indebtedness,* p. 67 and the data from the Narodowy Bank Polski (see notes 1, 5, 6).

16. *Rocznik statystyczny* (Statistical Yearbook) 1989, Warsaw, pp. XXXIII, XXXV, 364.

17. In 1973, national income grew by 6%, in 1984 by 5.6%, in 1985 by 3.4%, in 1986 by 4.9%, and in 1987 by 1.9%.

18. Data supplied by the Narodowy Bank Polski.

19. Ibid.

20. Ibid.

21. Ibid., p. 26. The deficit of the Polish current account calculated according to the IMF method amounted to U.S. $3.19 billion in 1981, $2.27 billion in 1982, $1.4 billion 1983, $774 million in 1984, $618 million in 1985, $665 million in 1986, $417 million in 1987 and $580 million in 1988 (data supplied by the Narodowy Bank Polski).

22. *Iustitia et Pax,* "At the Service of the Human Community: An Ethical Approach to the International Debt Question." Vatican City: Vatican Polyglot Press, 1986.

OPTIMAL EXPORT ORIENTED ECONOMIC POLICIES IN POLAND

Jan Svejnar and Richard P. Chaykowski

I. INTRODUCTION

Since January 1971, when Edward Gierek replaced Wladyslaw Gomulka as the First Secretary of the Polish United Workers' Party and embarked on the ambitious import-led growth program, the economic situation in Poland has been a focus of attention of officials in the Soviet bloc. In addition, the Polish policies have been followed by policy makers in both less-developed (Third World) and developed (Western) countries. The less-developed countries (LDC's) saw in the Polish approach an intriguing large-scale attempt by a centrally planned economy to increase growth by importing advanced technology and augmenting investment significantly beyond levels sustainable by internal resources. The idea that technology imports could enable the recipient country to secure a greater share of the world export market was shared by Poland's main LDC competitors, many of whom pursued similar technology-importing strategies.[1] The developed countries regarded Poland in the early 1970s as an attractive export market for their machinery and other technologically advanced products as well as a reasonable outlet for sizable loans. As the economic crisis set in, and Poland's debt service to export ratio started approaching unity in the late 1970s, the LDCs closely followed Poland's attempts to improve its trade balance and reschedule its sizable foreign debt. The developed countries in turn began coordinating their activities vis-à-vis Poland both in renegotiating the hard-currency debt and in imposing economic sanctions in response to the introduction of martial law in 1981.

While analysts still debate the exact causes of the Polish crisis, many agree that the severe economic difficulties experienced by Poland since 1978 were the result of inappropriate economic policies pursued both by Gomulka, during the 1950s and 1960s, and by his successors during the 1970s and 1980s.[2] In particular, while Gomulka's concern with poor export and productivity performance led to the formulation of a new export-oriented economic strategy (the "selective growth strategy") in 1968, bureaucratic rigidities and political opposition effectively prevented its elaboration and implementation.[3] Gierek's introduction of the "new development strategy" in the early 1970s aimed at improving productivity by importing advanced technology and relying on the (expected) resulting surge in exports to stop the rapid accumulation of foreign debt. The prevailing view is that the implementation of this strategy failed in large part because (a) decisions on export specialization were retained by the central authorities (especially the Ministry of Foreign Trade), (b) these decisions were made on the basis of insufficient information about export markets and the relative merits of selectively promoting specific Polish industries, and (c) the system was unable to establish priority sectors (products) and channel resources to them.[4] The inability to select and assist priority sectors plagued Gierek's "economic maneuver" of 1976-79 as well as the crisis period of 1979-1982 and the slow recovery of 1983-86.[5] Paradoxically enough, Nugent and Yotopoulos's 1982 study of 42 countries indicates that growth in the centrally planned economies depends crucially on the promotion of priority sectors.

Various studies indicate that the policy pursued by the Polish government in the last two decades has lacked sectoral focus and that its inability to make exports become the engine of growth distinguishes Poland from its main LDC competitors (for example, South Korea, Taiwan, and Brazil), who engaged in substantial technology importation but also succeeded in penetrating Western markets.[6] In this context, it is interesting to note that while many studies document the failure of Poland's policies aimed at increasing productivity through technology imports,[7] analyses of actual and optimal export policies are limited. Yet, if one takes seriously the argument that Poland could increase its welfare by adopting better export policies, this type of analysis is clearly valuable.

There are two theoretical views that should ideally be nested in such an analysis. One is based on the frequently invoked assumption that small countries like Poland are price takers in the world markets, able to export as much as they wish at world prices. This view argues that Poland's value added (or other performance indicators) can be maximized by judicious growth based on horizontal demand curves for Polish products. The other view assumes world demand (at any given price) for Polish products is limited, but that it could be augmented by superior information gathering, marketing, and export promotion measures. The Polish centralized approach to these aspects of foreign trade is seen as inferior to that of other countries (for example, the Republic of Korea or Hungary) and hence limiting the growth potential of the economy.[8]

Given the past and present nature of the Polish economic difficulties, the aim of this chapter is to identify priority sectors from the standpoint of an export policy that encompasses these two views of the world market. In particular, if resources were to be reallocated among industries or expended on increasing the demand for Polish products abroad, which sectors ought to have received and ought now to receive priority if value added or other performance indicators are to be maximized?

In attempting to answer this question, our approach is to use the most reliable data on the technological (productive) structure of the Polish economy at three distinct points in the last twenty years and identify the optimal export-based policies within these technological frameworks. Specifically, we use the 1969, 1977, and 1982 official Polish input-output (I-0) tables to identify the optimal export policies (a) immediately before the "new-development strategy," which relied so heavily on large scale investments and imports of western technology, (b) immediately after the major importations took place and the brakes of the "economic maneuver" were imposed in 1976, and (c) at the trough of the recession in 1982.[9]

Section II of the chapter describes the methodology underlying our investigation. Section III presents the main results, and Section IV draws the conclusions.

II. METHODOLOGY

The focus of our study is the calculation of five intersectoral linkages that relate an increase in any given sector's export allocation to the resulting increase in value added, employment (wage bill), household income, capital requirement, and import requirement of the economy. The conventional emphasis on economic growth suggests that the value added criterion should be used as the principal measure. Gierek's "new development strategy," however, placed great emphasis on income (wage), growth and it is therefore useful to assess which export policies would have been conducive to the fulfillment of this goal at the time. In contrast, in the 1980s the Polish planners have identified the overall shortage of labor as one of the most serious barriers to growth.[10] Of course, the labor shortage is in many respects artificial and systemically induced—most enterprises hoard excess labor. Nevertheless, in the absence of a reform that would alleviate the incentives for featherbedding, sectors with low employment linkages, other things being equal, should probably be given a higher priority now. Finally, the failure of the massive infusion of foreign capital to spur growth and the government's inability to service the mounting foreign debt have made the reduction of the capital and import requirements of the economy high priorities in the 1980s.[11] As a result, the capital and import requirement linkages have become crucial performance indicators by which to judge alternative policies.

The optimal export policies during the "selective growth strategy" of the late 1960s and the "new development strategy" of the early to mid-1970s would have emphasized sectors with high value added and household income linkages. From the late 1970s on, however, the "economic maneuver" and the crisis management ought to have stressed sectors with high value added and low employment, capital, and import linkages.

In technical terms, we assume that the production processes can be approximated by production functions which at a given point in time display constant technical coefficients and constant returns to scale. Let X_i be the annual volume of total output of industry i, x_{ij} be the amount of industry i's product absorbed annually as an intermediate input by industry j, Y_i be the amount of product i used to satisfy final demand, $a_{ij} = x_{ij}/X_j$, $i = 1,...,n$, $j = 1,...,n$. It follows that

$$\sum_{j}^{n} x_{ij} + Y_i = X_i \qquad i = 1,..., n. \qquad (1)$$

Letting X be the vector $X = (X_1,...,X_n)$, Y be the vector $Y = (Y_1,...,Y_n)$, A be the interindustry coefficients matrix of a_{ij}'s, and I be the identity matrix, the system in (1) may be rewritten as

$$X - AX = Y \qquad (2)$$

or

$$(I - A)X = Y, \qquad (3)$$

where $(I - A)$ is the Leontief matrix. Define $R = (I - A)^{-1}$ as the inverted Leontief matrix with elements of the jth column of R being the output requirements in each sector i for one unit of final demand for the jth commodity. We can then describe the relationship between the vector of total inputs (X) and the vector of total final demands (Y) by the equation

$$X = R \cdot Y. \qquad (4)$$

Moreover, it follows that

$$\Delta X = R \cdot \Delta Y, \qquad (5)$$

where ΔX represents the change in total output corresponding to the change ΔY in final demand.[12]

III. THE INTERINDUSTRY LINKAGE EFFECTS

This type of interindustry linkage analysis has been used successfully to identify optimal strategies in many LDCs, including Poland's main competitors (see Yotopoulos and Nugent 1976; and Bulmer-Thomas 1982).[13] In our investigation we calculate the interindustry value added linkage (VAL_j), the interindustry employment linkage (EL_j), the interindustry income generation linkage (YL_j), the capital requirement linkage (KL_j), and the import requirement linkage (ML_j).

The value added linkage of sector j is the total effect of a one zloty increase in the jth element in the export (or final demand) vector on the economy's value added. Letting VA_i be the ith sector's value added and X_i the corresponding total production of the ith sector, the value added linkage of sector j is given by

$$VAL_j = \sum_i (VA_i/X_i) (1 - a_{ij})^{-1} = \sum_i (VA_i/X_i)r_{ij}, \qquad (6)$$

where $r_{ij} = (1 - a_{ij})^{-1}$ is the ij'^{th} element of the inverted Leontief matrix R.

Analogously, the interindustry employment linkage is the total effect of a one zloty increase in the jth element of the export vector on the use of labor expressed in value terms (i.e., the wage bill). For the jth sector the expression Γ_j is defined as the coefficient, or the value of labor input per unit of output ($\Gamma_j = L_j/X_j$, where L_j is the jth sector's labor utilization in value terms and X_j is the corresponding total production for the jth sector). The employment linkage effect is obtained by summing over the row elements of the product of the labor coefficient and the elements of the inverted Leontief matrix:

$$EL_j = \sum_i \Gamma_i r_{ij} = \sum_i \Gamma_i (1 - a_{ij})^{-1}. \qquad (7)$$

The employment linkage EL_j thus expresses the effect of different sectors' exports (or final demand) on employment (wage bill).

The value added and employment linkages ignore the level of income, basically assuming that labor income is independent of the structure of production and effectively exogenous. To relax this assumption, we also calculate the interindustry income generation linkage YL_j, which is based on the assumption that the interindustry structure of production determines employment and that wage payments endogenously determine household income.

The income generation linkage captures the direct effects of household expenditure, as well as the indirect effects of this expenditure, on each sector's demand for intermediate products, labor, and on household income. It must be noted that the construction of the income generation linkage assumes that earnings from capital and rents are minor components of household income. In a centrally planned, socialist economy such as Poland's, this assumption is much more valid than it would be in the framework of a capitalist country.

In computing the income generation linkage, the (n x n) matrix A is augmented by one row and one column vector to form a new matrix D which is of the dimension (n + 1) x (n + 1). The row vector by which A is augmented is the vector of labor income coefficients, Γ_j, obtained from the value added quadrant of the I-O table. The extra column is the vector of the household sector's marginal (equal to the average) propensities to consume. This is obtained by dividing every entry in the household consumption column of the final demand quadrant by total household income. The transformation amounts to making the household demand endogenous while leaving the other demand components (government, investment, and export demand) exogenous. The income generation linkage YL_j is given by the last $(n + 1)^{th}$ row of the inverted matrix (I-D), that is, $(I\text{-}D)^{-1}$.

The capital and import requirement linkages are calculated analogously to the employment (wage bill) linkage. Letting K_j and M_j be the jth sector's value of fixed capital and of imports, respectively, the two linkages are given by

$$KL_j = \sum_i k_i r_{ij} \qquad (8)$$

$$ML_j = \sum_i m_i r_{ij}, \qquad (9)$$

where $k_i = K_i/X_i$ and $m_i = M_i/X_i$.

IV.   WEAKNESSES OF THE ANALYTICAL FRAMEWORK

Before turning to the empirical results, it is useful to point out two important limitations of our analysis. While these problems are well known to input-output analsts and to observers of the Polish economy, they may have a serious impact on our ability to identify optimal export policies and deserve to be clearly spelled out.

First, the assumption of constant returns to scale and fixed proportions production technology is probably an adequate first-order approximation to the true production process, but our findings have to be used with caution in sectors in which this assumption is known to be violated. For instance, Polish coal production appears to face rapidly rising marginal cost (both in terms of existing mines and in terms of opening new ones)[14] and hence an export strategy based on this sector might not generate the results predicted by our model. Second, Polish prices are highly distorted by administrative intervention, and it is likely that in many cases they do not reflect relative scarcities in the economy. In particular, many producer prices are formed on the basis of a cost-plus formula and the government pays large subsidies to keep prices of necessities and basic raw materials, including coal, below cost.[15] Welfare conclusions about the relative merits of different export policies may therefore be misleading if the producer prices which underlie our input-output tables do not reflect the relative scarcities of inputs and outputs.

The problem of distorted prices is virtually universal in Eastern Europe and the Soviet Union. It plagues all analyses that use value rather than physical data and our study is no exception. We would like to warn the reader that the problem may be a serious one and that in practical applications one ought to combine quantitative estimates with institutional insights.

A related problem is whether the price system disguises the existence of binding constraints on labor or capital capacities of particular sectors. While this is in principle possible, our maintained assumption is that labor and investment goods are not completely sector-specific and can be moved on the margin so as to support the expansion of priority sectors. Moreover, we feel that in the period of our analysis, there existed no overall shortages of labor and capital. The 1970s were the years of the investment boom and a relative abundance of labor.[16] The 1980s, in turn, have been characterized by excess capacity and, as we have pointed out earlier, even the potential labor shortage identified in the 1986-90 plan is unlikely to be very binding in view of the widespread featherbedding and low marginal productivity of labor. Our main concern is whether the production technology implied by the I-O framework is adequate and whether the use of producer prices in the I-O analysis does not take us too far from shadow price valuations.

V.   RESULTS

The calculated linkage effects based on a one zloty increase in sectoral exports are given for 1969, 1977, and 1982 in Tables 1, 2, and 3, respectively. Table 1 is based on a 15 sector I-0 table, while Tables 2 and 3 are based on 39 and 32 sector I-0 tables, respectively. The 1977 and 1982 I-0 tables are identically designed except that sectors 32-39 in the 1977 table are collapsed into one sector (material and social services) in 1982. In all calculations the employment linkage (EL_j) and income generation linkage (YL_j) have identical rankings. This means that although the linkage effects based on endogenous income determination are quantitatively different from those obtained when income is treated as exogenous, the ranking of industries is not affected by this extension. This result is important because it leads to uniform policy conclusions based on these two performance indicators.

In interpreting the results in Table 1, it is important to remember that the early to mid 1970s was a period when the promotion of sectors with high value added and income generation linkages was the government's main priority. Relatively low capital and import requirements might have been desirable, other things being equal, but the major borrowing and investment effort relegated these criteria to secondary importance at the time.

As the rankings in Table 1 indicate, apart from the category of other products and material services (1) and services (2), the interindustry value added linkage (VAL_j) is the highest in light industry (3), forestry (4), food industry (5), construction (6), agriculture (7), and wood and paper (8). The income generation linkage suggests that other products and material services (1), services (2), agriculture (3), construction (4), to a lesser extent, forestry (8), and wood and paper (9) were also important from the income generation standpoint. Finally, services, light industry, construction, wood and paper, food, and forestry had relatively low

Table 1. Value Added, Employment, Income Generation, Capital Requirement, and Import Requirement Linkages and Their Rankings in 1969

Industry	Value Added Linkage (VAL_j)	Employment Linkage (EL_j)	Income Generation Linkage (YL_j)	Capital Requirement Linkage (KL_j)	Import Requirement Linkage (ML_j)
Fuel and Energy	0.615 (12)	0.480 (13)	1.116 (13)	2.902 (4)	0.161 (10)
Metallurgy	0.669 (9)	0.583 (6)	1.355 (6)	2.723 (5)	0.489 (1)
Electromachinery	0.572 (14)	0.463 (14)	1.076 (14)	1.376 (14)	0.333 (2)
Chemicals	0.638 (11)	0.397 (15)	0.923 (15)	1.776 (10)	0.283 (4)
Minerals	0.608 (13)	0.488 (12)	1.134 (12)	2.396 (6)	0.151 (11)
Wood and Paper	0.736 (8)	0.528 (9)	1.228 (9)	1.663 (12)	0.169 (8)
Light Industry	0.820 (3)	0.505 (11)	1.175 (11)	1.307 (15)	0.145 (12)
Food Industry	0.801 (5)	0.524 (10)	1.218 (10)	2.272 (7)	0.165 (9)
Other Industries	0.561 (15)	0.607 (5)	1.410 (5)	2.100 (8)	0.234 (5)
Construction	0.765 (6)	0.654 (4)	1.520 (4)	1.687 (11)	0.127 (13)
Agriculture	0.762 (7)	0.657 (3)	1.528 (3)	3.133 (3)	0.193 (6)
Forestry	0.813 (4)	0.539 (8)	1.253 (8)	1.836 (9)	0.181 (7)
Transportation	0.647 (10)	0.571 (7)	1.327 (7)	4.399 (2)	0.091 (14)
Services	0.967 (2)	0.728 (2)	1.693 (2)	1.580 (13)	0.047 (15)
Other Products and Material Services	1.76 (1)	1.466 (1)	3.407 (1)	6.580 (1)	0.289 (3)

Note: The calculations are based on the 1969 official Polish input-output table. Values in parentheses are the rankings. Linkages are expressed in 1969 zlotys.

capital and import requirements. Given the government's goals in the early to mid-1970s, our results indicate that the optimal export policy ought to have been geared toward exportable services, light industry, forestry, food industry, construction, agriculture and wood and paper. Moreover, the results suggest that the traditional emphasis on heavy industry was misplaced from the standpoint of this policy.

Table 2 presents results from the period immediately following the great import thrust, when high value added, and low capital and import linkages were the priorities. As mentioned earlier, these results are also based on a much finer (39 sector) disaggregation of the individual sectors. As this table indicates, the ranking of the top twenty industries in the decreasing order of the value added linkage is science, technology, and state services (1), construction for production and services (2), other nonmaterial services (3), trade (4), education (5), health (6), arts and culture (7), forestry (8), recreation and tourism (9), apparel (10), coal (11), glass and ceramics (12), other food (13), plants (14), wood (15), textiles (16), material services (17), leather (18), general construction (19), and other construction (20). Products of some of these sectors are not easily tradable, but the list also contains a number of sectors that could be the subject of an export policy. Many of these sectors coincide with those identified in Table 1, but the finer sectoral disaggregation permits one to draw more precise policy conclusions. For instance, other food has a relatively high value added linkage, but meat does not. A similar distinction can be noted for instance between wood and paper or coal and fuel. These results confirm some of the earlier calculations by Polish analysts (for example, that exporting meat is inefficient), and they also justify our earlier statement that institutional knowledge is important in interpreting these results (for example, coal registers a high value added linkage but its high marginal cost makes this result misleading).[17]

The results in Table 2 also indicate that trade, forestry, plants, construction, other food, apparel, leather, textiles, wood, glass, and ceramics were among the industries that had relatively low capital and import requirement linkages, and would have been suitable candidates for an export promotion policy. Meat production has high capital and import linkages and appears inappropriate from the optimal policy standpoint. Similarly, health and education have low import requirements and high value added linkages, but

Table 2. Value Added, Employment, Income Generation, Capital Requirement, and Import Requirement Linkages and Their Rankings in 1977

Industry	Value Added Linkage (VAL$_j$)		Employment Linkage (EL$_j$)		Income Generation Linkage (YL$_j$)		Capital Requirement Linkage (KL$_j$)		Import Requirement Linkage (ML$_j$)	
Coal	0.784	(11)	0.617	(7)	1.027	(7)	1.931	(16)	0.141	(27)
Fuel	0.437	(38)	0.114	(39)	0.190	(39)	0.967	(38)	0.523	(2)
Electrical and Steam Energy	0.684	(22)	0.431	(20)	0.717	(20)	4.093	(3)	0.120	(29)
Ferrous Metals	0.426	(39)	0.300	(31)	0.499	(31)	1.662	(21)	0.546	(1)
Nonferrous Metals	0.581	(29)	0.291	(32)	0.484	(32)	1.645	(22)	0.396	(5)
Metal Products	0.579	(31)	0.350	(26)	0.582	(26)	1.293	(32)	0.336	(8)
Machines and Equipment	0.541	(34)	0.325	(28)	0.542	(28)	1.158	(34)	0.484	(4)
Fine Mechanics	0.602	(28)	0.301	(30)	0.501	(30)	0.751	(39)	0.505	(3)
Transport Equipment	0.612	(27)	0.377	(25)	0.628	(25)	1.372	(29)	0.382	(6)
Electrotechnical & Electronic Products	0.580	(30)	0.337	(27)	0.560	(27)	1.084	(35)	0.283	(10)
Chemicals	0.547	(33)	0.247	(37)	0.411	(37)	1.346	(31)	0.368	(7)
Construction Materials	0.629	(24)	0.455	(15)	0.758	(15)	2.021	(14)	0.225	(15)
Glass and Ceramics	0.780	(12)	0.446	(16)	0.743	(16)	1.487	(25)	0.210	(16)
Wood	0.760	(15)	0.418	(22)	0.695	(22)	1.428	(26)	0.167	(25)
Paper	0.538	(35)	0.288	(34)	0.479	(34)	1.531	(24)	0.268	(11)
Textiles	0.756	(16)	0.290	(33)	0.483	(33)	1.061	(36)	0.206	(18)
Apparel	0.805	(10)	0.434	(18)	0.723	(18)	1.037	(37)	0.166	(26)

Leather	0.733 (18)	0.434 (19)	0.723 (19)	1.376 (28)	0.207 (17)
Meat	0.501 (36)	0.421 (21)	0.700 (21)	2.980 (7)	0.322 (9)
Other Food	0.771 (13)	0.267 (35)	0.445 (35)	1.742 (18)	0.199 (21)
Other Industries	0.626 (25)	0.305 (29)	0.508 (29)	1.674 (20)	0.257 (12)
General Construction	0.728 (19)	0.519 (10)	0.864 (10)	1.643 (23)	0.178 (23)
Construction for Production & Services	0.892 (2)	0.640 (5)	1.065 (5)	1.991 (15)	0.226 (14)
Specialized Construction	0.569 (32)	0.402 (23)	0.668 (23)	1.250 (33)	0.139 (28)
Other Construction	0.715 (20)	0.503 (12)	0.837 (12)	1.356 (30)	0.098 (33)
Plants	0.768 (14)	0.130 (38)	0.216 (38)	1.699 (19)	0.190 (22)
Livestock	0.693 (21)	0.248 (36)	0.413 (36)	2.430 (12)	0.205 (19)
Agriculture Services	0.624 (26)	0.475 (14)	0.790 (14)	2.590 (11)	0.251 (13)
Forestry	0.830 (8)	0.438 (17)	0.729 (17)	1.928 (17)	0.098 (32)
Transport and Communication	0.671 (23)	0.485 (13)	0.807 (13)	2.943 (9)	0.203 (20)
Trade	0.875 (4)	0.560 (9)	0.931 (9)	1.401 (27)	0.078 (36)
Material Services	0.737 (17)	0.510 (11)	0.849 (11)	3.216 (6)	0.167 (24)
Housing	0.457 (37)	0.400 (24)	0.665 (24)	29.190 (1)	0.074 (38)
Education	0.863 (5)	0.749 (3)	1.246 (3)	2.660 (10)	0.078 (35)
Arts and Culture	0.843 (7)	0.871 (2)	1.450 (2)	3.477 (5)	0.096 (34)
Health	0.863 (6)	0.716 (4)	1.192 (4)	2.313 (13)	0.103 (31)
Recreation and Tourism	0.808 (9)	0.587 (8)	0.978 (8)	3.904 (4)	0.116 (30)
Other Nonmaterial Services	0.882 (3)	0.622 (6)	1.034 (6)	4.491 (2)	0.076 (37)
Science, Technology and State Services	0.969 (1)	0.875 (1)	1.456 (1)	2.946 (8)	0 (39)

Note: The calculations are based on the 1977 official Polish input-output table. Values in parentheses are the rankings. Linkages are expressed in 1977 zlotys.

171

Table 3. Value Added, Employment, Income Generation, Capital Requirement, and Import Requirement Linkages and Their Rankings in 1982

Industry	Value Added Linkage (VAL$_j$)	Employment Linkage (EL$_j$)	Income Generation Linkage (YL$_j$)	Capital Requirement Linkage (KL$_j$)	Import Requirement Linkage (ML$_j$)
Coal	0.719 (22)	0.506 (5)	1.051 (5)	1.169 (9)	0.101 (27)
Fuel	0.465 (31)	0.120 (32)	0.250 (32)	0.512 (30)	0.446 (1)
Electrical and Steam Energy	0.769 (19)	0.320 (21)	0.665 (21)	1.957 (1)	0.084 (30)
Ferrous Metals	0.670 (25)	0.413 (12)	0.857 (12)	1.491 (4)	0.379 (2)
Nonferrous Metals	0.672 (24)	0.273 (25)	0.566 (25)	1.387 (5)	0.375 (3)
Metal Products	0.609 (29)	0.256 (28)	0.532 (28)	0.786 (22)	0.213 (10)
Machines and Equipment	0.766 (20)	0.415 (10)	0.863 (10)	0.930 (16)	0.251 (6)
Fine Mechanics	0.837 (6)	0.306 (23)	0.636 (23)	0.619 (28)	0.219 (9)
Transport Equipment	0.916 (3)	0.335 (19)	0.695 (19)	1.036 (13)	0.305 (5)
Electrotechnical & Electronic Products	0.670 (26)	0.248 (29)	0.514 (29)	0.726 (25)	0.231 (7)
Chemicals	0.573 (30)	0.270 (26)	0.562 (26)	0.828 (18)	0.322 (4)
Construction Materials	0.751 (21)	0.310 (22)	0.644 (22)	1.141 (10)	0.150 (17)
Glass and Ceramics	0.824 (8)	0.498 (6)	1.035 (6)	0.824 (19)	0.143 (18)
Wood	0.785 (15)	0.474 (7)	0.985 (7)	0.764 (24)	0.112 (24)

Paper	0.636	(28)	0.242	(31)	0.503	(31)	1.057	(12)	0.210 (11)
Textiles	0.774	(18)	0.274	(24)	0.570	(24)	0.710	(27)	0.159 (14)
Apparel	0.796	(11)	0.359	(16)	0.747	(16)	0.474	(31)	0.106 (26)
Leather	0.820	(9)	0.385	(15)	0.800	(15)	0.594	(29)	0.158 (15)
Meat	0.786	(14)	0.746	(2)	1.551	(2)	1.316	(6)	0.178 (13)
Other Food	0.779	(16)	0.338	(18)	0.702	(18)	0.809	(21)	0.132 (19)
Other Industries	0.779	(17)	0.352	(17)	0.731	(17)	0.782	(23)	0.154 (16)
General Construction	0.789	(12)	0.392	(14)	0.814	(14)	0.813	(20)	0.109 (25)
Construction for Production & Services	0.992	(1)	0.404	(13)	0.839	(13)	0.866	(17)	0.114 (23)
Specialized Construction	0.642	(27)	0.246	(30)	0.512	(30)	0.717	(26)	0.086 (29)
Other Construction	0.937	(2)	0.509	(4)	1.057	(4)	1.062	(11)	0.087 (28)
Plants	0.829	(7)	0.468	(8)	0.971	(8)	0.985	(14)	0.127 (20)
Livestock	0.807	(10)	0.794	(1)	1.650	(1)	1.268	(7)	0.125 (21)
Agriculture Services	0.698	(23)	0.629	(3)	1.308	(3)	1.222	(8)	0.182 (12)
Forestry	0.852	(5)	0.325	(20)	0.674	(20)	0.946	(15)	0.069 (31)
Transport and Communication	0.378	(32)	0.412	(11)	0.857	(11)	1.784	(2)	0.227 (8)
Trade	0.912	(4)	0.265	(27)	0.550	(27)	0.467	(32)	0.041 (32)
Material and Social Services	0.789	(13)	0.427	(9)	0.888	(9)	1.590	(3)	0.123 (22)

Note: The calculations are based on the 1982 official Polish input-output table. Values in parentheses are the rankings. Linkages are expressed in 1982 zlotys.

they also display high employment linkages and therefore are not very attractive from an overall strategy standpoint.

Table 3 contains the results for 1982 and gives an indication of the relative sectoral priorities in recent years and probably also at present. Moreover, the fact that sectoral disaggregation of the 1977 and 1982 I-0 tables is very similar permits a reliable intertemporal comparison during the 1977-82 period. In terms of the value added linkage, construction for production and services (1) and other construction (2) are the leading sectors, followed by transport equipment (3), trade (4), forestry (5), fine mechanics (6), plants (7), glass and ceramics (8), leather (9), livestock (10), apparel (11), general construction (12), material and social services (13), meat (14), wood (15), and other food (16). The notable difference between the 1977 and 1982 tables is that the transport equipment, fine mechanics and meat industries gain in relative importance. These sectors, however, display relatively high capital and/or import requirement linkages and appear to be inferior targets for an export policy. The meat industry also registers a very high employment requirement linkage, thus further decreasing its appeal during the period of a (perceived) labor shortage.

Taking the labor, capital, and import requirement linkages into account, the sectors that appear to be candidates for priority in terms of an export policy are trade, forestry, construction for production and services, general construction, leather, apparel, wood, other food, glass and ceramics, and textiles.[18]

VI.   SUMMARY AND CONCLUSIONS

The aim of our investigation has been to identify key Polish sectors (industries) from the standpoint of an optimal export oriented policy based on the interindustry linkage effects.

In the late 1960s, when Gomulka unsuccessfully attempted to implement the "selective growth strategy," and in the early 1970s, when Gierek introduced the "new development strategy," the principal sectors that ought to have been given priority on the basis of our analysis were exportable services, light industry, forestry, food industry, construction, agriculture, and wood and paper. These sectors were important for value added growth and they also ranked favorably in their income generation potential. Yet, these key sectors generally did not experience above average growth in exports in the 1970s and early 1980s. In fact, the share of food in total exports dropped from 11.6% in 1970 to 8.7% in 1975 and 5.5% in 1981, that of agriculture fell from 5.3% in 1970 to a mere 1.7% in 1981 and the light industry's share was virtually stagnant at 8-9%. In contrast, machinery registered a significant increase from 31.8% in 1970 to 55.2% in 1981, thus suggesting that Poland expanded exports in sectors that had relatively low value added and income generation linkages.[19]

Fallenbuchl's 1983 examination of the allocation of Poland's imports of Western technology between 1972 and 1977 reveals the following sectoral ranking: engineering (1), chemicals (2), metallurgy (3), light industry (4), food and tobacco (5), fuel and energy (6), construction (7), wood and paper (8), minerals (9), agriculture (10), and printing (11). The orientation of this unsuccessful supply-side policy reveals priorities that only partially overlap with our rankings and suggest that technology imports were geared primarily toward sectors with low value added and income generation linkages. In particular, it demonstrates the very low priority accorded to agriculture and the relatively low emphasis on food and light industry during Gierek's new development strategy. Moreover, the high import requirement linkage exhibited by the two sectors with the highest technology import allocations (engineering and chemicals) underscores the riskiness inherent in promoting sectors with high import content and relatively low total value added linkage effects.

The more disaggregated results available for 1977 indicate that forestry, plants, trade, construction, other food, apparel, leather, textiles, wood, and glass and ceramics are key sectors. The 1977 results are broadly consistent with the 1969 findings, but they suggest that meat and paper production are not suitable sectors from an optimal export policy standpoint. The results from 1982 are similar to those for 1977, with trade, forestry, certain types of construction, leather, apparel, textiles, wood, other food, and glass and ceramics being the key sectors.

Overall, our analysis suggests that the Polish economy would have benefited significantly from an export-oriented strategy based on a relatively small number of high linkage sectors and that the priority sectors have not changed substantially over time.

ACKNOWLEDGMENTS

This research was supported in part by a grant from the National Council for Soviet and East European Research and a NSF-NATO fellowship to Jan Svejnar. We are indebted to Josef Brada, Kaz Poznanski, and Kathy Terrell for useful comments on an earlier draft. Any remaining errors are ours.

NOTES

1. See Poznanski (1984, 1985, 1986a).
2. See Nuti (1982), Brada and Montias (1984, 1985) and Fallenbuchl (1986a). In contrast, Poznanski (1986b) sees Gierek's strategy as appropriate but blames poor adjustment since 1975.
3. Ibid.
4. Ibid.
5. The fact that the growth rate of output of material goods and "productive services" fell to 3% in 1985 after registering a 6% and 5.6% growth in 1983 and 1984, respectively, and registered only 4.6% in 1986, suggests that the problems underlying the 1979-82 downturn may not be fully under control (see Vanous 1986, 1987).
6. See Poznanski (1984, 1985, 1986a).
7. See, for example, Gomulka (1978), Fallenbuchl (1983, 1986a), Brada and Montias (1984, 1985), Whitesell (1985), Kemme (1987), and Terrell (1986).
8. See Crane (1986) and Poznanski (1984, 1986) for details.
9. There are two 1977 I-O tables publicly available. The one used in this study comes from the 1981 Polish Statistical Yearbook and was selected because it contains data on imports. The 1982 I-O table was the last table officially available at the time of this investigation.
10. See, for example, Fallenbuchl (1986b).
11. See note 10 above and Vanous (1987).
12. Note that the external shift in demand may be negative, with the resulting effects being negative as well.
13. In fact, the discussion in this section follows the exposition of Yotopoulos and Nugent (1976).
14. See Fallenbuchl (1986b).
15. See note 14 above.
16. As Fallenbuchl (1986b) points out, the Polish labor force increased by 1.6 million between 1971 and 1975 and 1.2 million in the 1976-80 period.
17. We are indebted to the conference discussants for bringing this point to our attention.
18. Note that wood and glass and ceramics have relatively high employment linkages. If one feels, as we do, that the employment constraint is not binding due to labor hoarding by firms, then one can include these industries in the priority category.
19. See Kazmer (1986).

REFERENCES

Brada, J.C., and J.M. Montias. "Industrial Policy in Eastern Europe: A Three-Country Comparison." *Journal of Comparative Economics* 8 (December 1984): pp. 377-419.

_____. "Industrial Policy in Eastern Europe: A Comparison of Poland, Czechoslovakia, and Hungary." In *East European Economics: Slow Growth in the 1980's*. Selected Papers No. 1. Joint Economic Committee, U.S. Congress. Washington, DC: U.S. Government Printing Office, October 1985.

Bulmer-Thomas, V. *Input-Output Analysis in Developing Countries*. New York: Wiley & Sons, 1982.

Crane, K. "Foreign Trade Decisionmaking Under Balance of Payments Pressure: Poland Versus Hungary." In *East-European Economies: Slow Growth in the 1980s*. Selected Papers No. 3. Joint Economic Committee, U.S. Congress. Washington, DC: U.S. Government Printing Office, March 1986.

Fallenbuchl, Z.M. *East-West Technology Transfer: Study of Poland, 1971-1980*. Paris: OECD, 1983.

_____. "The Economic Crisis in Poland and Prospects for Recovery." In *East European Economies: Slow Growth in the 1980s*. Selected Papers No. 3. Joint Economic Committee, U.S. Congress. Washington, DC: U.S. Government Printing Office, March 1986a.

_____. "The Polish Economy in the Year 2000: Need and Outlook for Systemic Reforms, Recovery and Growth Strategies (The Western View)." Mimeo, 1986b.

Gomulka, S. "Growth and the Import of Technology: Poland 1971-1980." *Cambridge Journal of Economics* 2 (1978): pp. 1-16.

Kazmer, D. "The Adjustment of the Polish Economy to Scarcities in the 1970s." In *East European Economies: Slow Growth in the 1980s*. Selected Papers No. 3. Joint Economic Committee, U.S. Congress. Washington, DC: U.S. Government Printing Office, March 1986.

Kemme, D.M. "Productivity Growth in Polish Industry." *Journal of Comparative Economics* 11 (March 1987): pp. 1-20.

Nugent, J.B., and P.A. Yotopoulos. "Morphology of Growth: The Effects of Country Size, Structural Characteristics and Linkages." *Journal of Development Economics* 10 (June 1982): pp. 279-295.

Nuti, M.D. "The Polish Crisis: Economic Factors and Constraints." In *Crisis in the East European Economy: The Spread of the Polish Disease*, edited by J. Drewnowski. London: Crook Helm, 1982.

Poznanski, K. "Direct Investment by Multinational Corporations and Technological Change in Latin America and Eastern Europe." In *Multinational Corporations in Latin America and Eastern Europe*, edited by P. Marer. Boulder, CO: Westview Press, 1984.

_____. "The Environment for Technological Change in Centrally Planned Economies." World Bank Staff Working Paper, No. 718, 1985.

————. "Competition between Eastern Europe and Developing Countries in the Western Market for Manufactured Goods." In *Eastern European Economies: Slow Growth in the 1980s.* Selected Papers No. 2. Joint Economic Committee, U.S. Congress. Washington, DC: U.S. Government Printing Office, March 1986a.

————. "Economic Adjustment and Political Forces, Poland since 1970." *Industrial Organization* 40 (Spring 1986b): pp. 455-488.

Terrell, K. "Western Technology and Productivity in Polish Industry." Mimeo, Cornell University, 1986.

Vanous, J. (ed.). *Planecon Report,* Vol. 2, No. 11, 1986.

————. *Planecon Report,* Vol. 3, No. 17, 1987.

Whitesell, R.S. "The Influence of Central Planning on the Economic Slowdown in the Soviet Union and Eastern Europe: A Comparative Production Function Analysis." *Economica* 52 (May 1985): pp. 235-244.

Yotopoulos, P.A., and J.B. Nugent. *Economics of Development: Empirical Investigations.* New York: Harper & Row, 1976.

A COMPARISON OF POLISH AND HUNGARIAN FOREIGN TRADE REFORMS

Ben Slay

I. INTRODUCTION

This chapter analyzes the Polish foreign-trade reforms of 1982-86, and briefly discusses some of the changes in foreign trade introduced since mid-1986 as part of the second stage of economic reform announced by the Polish United Workers' Party's Tenth Congress during June/July 1986. The Polish reforms are then compared to the foreign-trade component of the Hungarian reforms introduced since 1968, in order to provide a standard against which reform of the Polish foreign-trade mechanism can be evaluated. The different external environmental conditions in which Polish and Hungarian reforms have been introduced are examined in the first part of this paper, following a short note on the conceptualization of foreign-trade reform. The Polish and Hungarian foreign-trade reforms are then compared to one another, first in terms of their institutional features, then in terms of foreign-trade instruments.

II. ON THE CONCEPTUALIZATION OF
REFORM OF THE SOCIALIST
FOREIGN TRADE MECHANISM

The Soviet-type foreign-trade mechanism contains *systemic* elements (i.e., the institutional structures of the Foreign Trade Ministry, Trade and Central Banks, the Chamber of Commerce, a number of various types of foreign-trade organizations [FTO's], and producing enterprises involved in import/export activities, as well as the instruments used to regulate these enterprises) and *policy* components (i.e., decisions about foreign-trade instruments' magnitudes). This conceptualization also includes the behavioral aspects of this regime, in that environmental factors, interactions between systemic elements, policy and environmental factors, and expectations about future conditions also influence decision makers. The discussion below is concerned primarily with the mechanism's systemic and policy elements (i.e., the control sphere following Kornai 1971), since they are most easily affected by reforms.

The separation of foreign-trade from the rest of an economy—any economy—is an artificial undertaking which may neglect or underemphasize the many organic links between domestic and external economic activities. The same is true for economic reform: reform of the foreign-trade mechanism must be an integral part in any serious attempt at reforming the domestic economy, while the implementation of foreign-trade reforms cannot be understood when abstracted from the fate of the economy-wide economic reform, or from general economic conditions.

III. FOREIGN TRADE REFORM IN POLAND AND
HUNGARY: ENVIRONMENTAL CONDITIONS

Factors in the economic environment can have a major impact upon the functioning of an economic mechanism, and a foreign trade mechanism in particular. This section compares the environmental conditions in which the reforms of the Polish and Hungarian foreign-trade mechanisms have been introduced.

A country's trade policy and commodity composition of trade are heavily influenced by such country-specific factors as the political system, country size, geographic location, climatic conditions, resource endowment, the relative openness of the domestic economy, and the like. Although both Poland and Hungary are relatively small European countries formerly allied with the Soviet Union, in terms of the above criteria they differ from one another in a number of important respects, which in turn have implications for the Polish and Hungarian foreign-trade mechanisms.

Poland is about three times larger than Hungary in both area (312,683 versus 93,030 square kilometers) and population (37,026,000 versus 10,680,000).[1] Poland is also much more self-sufficient in natural resources than Hungary. Poland's exploitable (hard and soft) coal reserves are the fourth largest in the world, behind the United States, the Soviet Union, and the People's Republic of China (Majewski 1983, p. 87). Sulphur, zinc, lead, copper ores, and other minerals are available domestically in quantities large enough to satisfy internal demands, although the question of how much longer this state of self-sufficiency can continue, and at what cost, is the subject of an increasingly spirited debate. By contrast, Hungary is self-sufficient only in bauxite, and must import substantial quantities of virtually all important raw materials and energy products. On the other hand, Hungary possesses the best combination of climatic conditions and soil fertility of any country belonging to the Council for Mutual Economic Assistance (CMEA) (Bernát et al. 1986), while Poland has slightly less favorable conditions for agricultural activities, particularly in terms of soil fertility. Not surprisingly, agriculture has traditionally been at the heart of Hungary's development and foreign-trade policies, while Poland's post-war development and trade strategies have relied heavily upon the extraction and export of raw materials. This is reflected both in these sectors' shares in total output and in the commodity composition of trade for both countries.

The above differences have two important consequences for the two countries' foreign-trade mechanisms:

1. The Hungarian economy is more open than the Polish economy, as measured by the share of net exports in national income (approximately 40% for Hungary and 20% for Poland). A microeconomic implication of this higher degree of openness is that foreign (especially CMEA) markets are intrinsically more

important to Hungarian enterprises than to Polish enterprises (Inotai 1986).

2.   More state enterprises and cooperatives are involved in foreign-trade activities in Poland than in Hungary. Consequently, the central planning and management of foreign-trade activities is a simpler organizational task in Hungary, due to the smaller number of enterprises to be planned and managed.[2]

The degree of internal equilibrium in which the Polish and Hungarian foreign-trade reforms were introduced also differentiates the two cases. The original Hungarian reforms of 1968 were introduced into a domestic economy characterized by a relatively high degree of internal equilibrium (compared to the other CMEA countries) at both the micro- and macroeconomic levels. Moreover, the maintenance of equilibrium was then regarded as a major macroeconomic policy goal (Antal 1985). This allowed the Hungarian reformers to partially link domestic raw materials prices to world-market prices. Because of the absence of major pent-up inflationary pressures, this linkage conveyed relatively accurate information to producing enterprises about the true costs of hard-currency imports. Later, when macroeconomic (and terms-of-trade) conditions worsened during the late 1970s and 1980s, the preservation of internal equilibrium on consumer-goods markets remained a high priority, even at the cost of unpopular price increases.

By contrast, the Polish reform was introduced into an environment characterized by an exceptionally high degree of internal disequilibrium (Herer and Sadowski 1981). During 1979-81 (the three years immediately preceding the reform's introduction) for example, national income fell in real terms by 2.3, 6, and 12%, while nominal incomes grew at yearly rates of 10.2, 12, and 30.3%[3] (retail prices increased yearly by 6.6, 8.9 and 21.2%, that is, at about half the pace necessary to absorb the increases in nominal incomes given the downward trend in real output). In addition to reducing the effectiveness of financial instruments in general, this disequilibrium increased the zloty's overvaluation, exacerbating the difficulties of linking domestic raw-materials prices to world-market prices. It also further reduced enterprise incentives to export to either hard-currency or CMEA markets, since virtually everything the Polish industry produced could be sold on the domestic market during the shortage conditions prevailing in the early 1980s. This contrasts with the relatively greater imperative faced by many Hungarian industrial producers of finding export markets (usually CMEA) for their output, in order to guarantee efficient levels of scale utilization (Inotai 1986).

Terms of trade for the Polish economy during the 1980s have on the balance been more favorable than for the Hungarian economy; in fact, since the introduction of the New Economic Mechanism in 1968, Hungary experienced simultaneous terms-of-trade improvements on both CMEA and Western markets only during 1969-70. In particular, the 1978-84 period saw Hungary's terms of trade with nonsocialist countries decrease by 13.7%; further marked deterioration occurred in 1985-86. By contrast, the Polish economy's terms of trade with nonsocialist countries have displayed no major downturn in the 1980s: deterioration in 1981, 1983, and 1984 was counterbalanced by improvement in 1980, 1982, and 1985. A slight downward trend in the Polish economy's terms of trade with the socialist countries is apparent in the 1980s, while for Hungary, the terms-of-trade decline with the socialist countries that occurred throughout the 1970s (with the sole exception of 1973) was arrested during 1980-82, before starting again in 1983 and continuing until the present.[4]

In sum, terms-of-trade conditions in the 1980s have not been particularly favorable for either country, while in the Hungarian case, a downward trend is visible since the early 1970s. This has put additional pressure upon the foreign-trade mechanism in the two countries, since greater shares of output must be devoted to export in order to obtain a given level of planned imports. It is also an unfavorable statement about the abilities of foreign-trade and industrial policymakers in the two countries to improve the commodity composition of trade.

Finally, although both Hungary and Poland face major problems stemming from high levels of hard-currency indebtedness, the Hungarian situation is much more favorable than the Polish one. Although Hungary's per capita hard-currency debt increase during the 1980s has been higher than Poland's by 10-25% (the 1984 figures were 833 million US dollars and 726 million, respectively),[5] Hungary's per capita hard-currency exports during the 1978-85 period have typically exceeded Poland's by a factor of 2 to 2.5.

Also, Poland's March 1981 request for debt rescheduling dealt the country's creditworthiness on international money markets a blow from which it has yet to recover. (The introduction of martial law in December 1981 further reduced Poland's stature in the eyes of many governments and lending institutions.) Consequently, new bank and government credits during 1981-87 have not been forthcoming in significant quantities, so that approximately 60% of Poland's hard-currency imports during this time had to be financed from the country's meager hard-currency export revenues. These liquidity problems resulted in catastrophic reductions in the volume of hard-currency imports of 31.5 and 24.2% during 1981-82.

Hungary, by contrast, survived its balance-of-payments crisis during 1982 without having to reschedule its hard-currency debts, thanks in part to its admission to the International Monetary Fund and World Bank in that year (Marer 1986b). Consequently, Hungary has been able to finance the vast majority of its hard-currency imports either through loans offered by public and private sources in the exporter's country, or through short-term Euromarket loans. Although hard-currency imports have been subject to administrative controls during most of the 1980s, hard currency in Hungary does not seem to be in such great demand as is the case in Poland. As evidence of this, the black-market zloty-dollar exchange rate in Warsaw has consistently exceeded the official rate by a factor of four during 1983-87, while the black-market forint-dollar rate in Budapest rarely exceeded the official rate by more than 20% during the same period.

In addition to the two countries' hard-currency indebtedness, both Poland and Hungary are in debt to the Soviet Union. Here again, the Hungarian situation would seem more favorable than the Polish situation. In 1986, Poland's indebtedness to the Soviet Union exceeded 6 billion transferable rubles (Zadłużenie 1986). This indebtedness is the result of the balance-of-trade deficits that the Soviet Union permitted Poland to accumulate during the first half of the 1980s, when the volume of Poland's hard-currency imports was decreasing yearly by as much as 40%. The 1986-1990 Five-Year Plan calls for the stabilization and then reduction of this indebtedness, within this five-year period.

The ruble debt burden for the Polish economy is not as serious as the country's hard-currency debt, since its magnitude is approximately equal to the value of one year's exports to the Soviet Union and the repayment of the ruble debt is not governed by commercial criteria to the same extent as the repayment of hard-currency debt. Still, the ruble debt burden should not be dismissed altogether for two reasons. First, it represents another set of claims upon the Polish economy's limited export capacity. Second, and more importantly, the commodity composition of Polish exports to the CMEA (of which exports to the Soviet Union comprised approximately 58% in 1985) seemed to harden during the 1981-84 period. The share of fuels and energy exports (which could almost certainly be sold for hard currency) in total CMEA exports more than doubled (6.3 to 13.0 %) during this time; while the share of electronics and light-industry exports (which are much more difficult to sell for hard currency) in total CMEA exports fell from 61.2 and 9.6% in 1981 to 56.6 and 5.1% 1984. Thus, to the extent that these trends are valid for future exports to the Soviet Union, repaying the ruble debt may come at a rising cost in terms of exports that could be sold for hard currency, and in turn could be used to service Poland's hard-currency debt or to increase hard-currency imports.

Based on discussions with Hungarian economists and policy-makers, it is my impression that the Hungarian ruble debt possesses relatively less operational significance than the Polish ruble debt. In any case, Hungary's ruble debt did not prevent the Soviets from continuing to pay for a share of Hungarian exports in hard currency (Marer 1986b).

IV. FOREIGN TRADE REFORM IN POLAND AND HUNGARY: CHANGES IN INSTITUTIONAL STRUCTURES

Reform of the foreign-trade mechanism's institutional structure is essentially a phenomenon of the 1980s, since the Hungarian foreign-trade reforms of 1968 focused almost exclusively on foreign-trade instruments. By contrast, institutional changes played a major role in the 1981 Polish foreign-trade reform blueprint and the second stage foreign trade reforms, while the 1980s have seen important structural changes made in the Hungarian foreign-trade mechanism as well.

Three main institutional changes in the Polish foreign-trade mechanism were envisioned in the 1981 Polish reform blueprint:

1.   The Foreign Trade Ministry was reorganized in order to increase its control over macrotrade and industrial policy issues, and at the same time to reduce its influence on operational foreign-trade decisions made by FTOs and producing enterprises. This reorganization was regarded as necessary to facilitate the transition from a direct-planning to a primarily financial set of planning instruments. Minor reductions were absorbed in the Ministry's staff and budget.

2.   The FTOs were to be freed of the Foreign Trade Ministry's direct control in order to become more receptive to the needs of producing enterprises, who were now legally authorized to conduct independent foreign-trade activities without the close supervision of the ministry and its agents. The majority of FTOs were transformed into joint-stock companies, with ownership shares being held by the FTOs' major domestic clients, as well as by the ministry. It was hoped that this arrangement would help to better integrate production and trade activities, particularly in terms of improving domestic producers' information about world markets, as well as generating enterprise investments in export-oriented projects. Producing enterprises were to be permitted to select the FTOs with whom they wanted to do business in order to encourage competititon among the FTOs.

3.   The number of producing enterprises with direct-trading rights should be expanded, especially on the export side.

The guiding principles underlying the foreign-trade component of the 1968 Hungarian reforms were roughly similar to those of the Polish case, except that no wholesale changes were made in the legal status of the Hungarian FTOs. Instead, emphasis was placed on increasing their number, increasing the number of producing enterprises with direct-trading rights, promoting integration between the FTOs and producing enterprises, and increasing competition among the FTOs themselves.

As is the case with many other components of the Polish reform, however, there is a wide gap between the spirit of the reform and what has been introduced in practice. Not withstanding the intention of loosening the ministry's tight control over the FTOs and enterprises with direct-trading rights, the environment in which the Polish foreign-trade mechanism has functioned since 1982 (i.e., major reductions in hard-currency imports and national income, as well as all kinds of supply problems, both foreign and domestic) has either forced the ministry to retain tight control over the FTOs and enterprises, or provided a rationale for continued tight control, depending upon one's point of view. The ministry's tightened grip has been facilitated by its formal strengthening vis-à-vis other subcentral organs (i.e., the branch ministries) in 1982 when all the FTOs and the trading activities of enterprises with direct export rights were subordinated to its purview.[6]

The core of the structural reform, transforming the FTOs into joint-stock companies, seems to have had little positive effect and a number of undesireable effects upon the Polish foreign-trade mechanism.[7] The main problem lies in the fact that the Foreign-trade Ministry, as the representative of the National Treasury, is the majority share holder in all the new FTOs/joint-stock companies. This essentially affords the ministry as much leverage over the new FTO's as it did the old. This arrangement has caused a number of undesirable side effects, including the following:

1.   In addition to facing de facto ministerial subordination in the joint-stock companies, producing enterprises were forced to invest their capital in the new FTOs in the form of ownership shares. This caused some cynicism among enterprise managers and reform economists concerning the authorities' true intentions in introducing the "new, improved" FTOs.

2.   The Foreign Trade Ministry's dominant position in the new FTOs can provide a basis for foreign contractors, actual or prospective, to question the legal identity and uniqueness of the FTO's with whom a commercial arrangment is being considered (Rymarczyk 1985). Given the Polish government's lack of financial creditworthiness in the eyes of many Western banks and corporations, the ministry's position could retard the development of much-needed commercial ties with Western firms.

In sum, the reform of the FTOs seems to have changed little, if anything, for the better. The situation for producing enterprises would seem to be a little better, but not much. Although legislation passed September 25, 1981, guaranteed enterprises the right to select the FTO of their choice, in practice, as one observer noted: "so many regulations have been attached to the choice of exporter that this phenomenon virtually never occurs" (Rymarczyk 1985).

In terms of concessions, the number of producing enterprises with direct trading rights has increased significantly since the reform was introduced. As of June 1986, approximately 110 producing enterprises and cooperatives had direct trading rights. Moreover, similar rights had been granted to 172 private individuals, many of whom were involved in the polonia, small joint-venture firms. On paper, this is indeed a major change. In practice, however, matters look a little different. In 1985, for example, only 67 of the 104 non-FTO legal entities (mostly enterprises, cooperatives, and producer organizations created by enterprises and cooperatives) actually took advantage of their direct trading rights. For individuals, the numbers were 169 and 46, respectively. Thus, as incredible as this appears in light of Poland's desperate need for increased contacts with Western firms, know-how, and technology, the vast majority of Polish enterprises and individuals authorized to interact directly with Western firms choose not to do so. There are two major reasons for this: (1) production for the domestic market remains incomparably "easier" than for Western exports; and (2) at least during the first years of the reform, many producing enterprises were handicapped by a lack of experienced and qualified personnel in attempting to increase hard-currency exports to Western markets. In any case, the share in total exports represented by exports from firms and individuals with direct trading rights has not been significant; in 1984, for example, it measured 6.8% (Rymarczyk 1985).

Poland's (re)admission to the International Monetary Fund (and subsequently the World Bank) in May 1986, and the Jaruzelski leadership's call for a second stage of economic reform at the Tenth Party Congress during June/July of that year, seem to have increased the authorities' awareness of the need for further institutional reforms. Consequently, two pro-reform institutional changes were introduced in 1986: (1) an Export Development Bank, whose function is to conduct an active, pro-export credit policy in coordination with the Foreign Trade Ministry, was created; and (2) legislation liberalizing restrictions on large-scale direct foreign investment in Poland became law. Although these changes created a more appropriate institutional basis for interacting with Western financial and trading firms, the institutional component of the Polish foreign trade mechanism remained quite removed from the principles expressed in the 1981 reform blueprint. Consequently, the authorities in 1987 took further steps intended to bridge the gap between theory and practice, including the following:

1. The requirements pertaining to FTO ownership were liberalized, so that the treasury's share of the FTOs can fall below 51% (except for products of "central importance to the national economy") and any state enterprise can purchase shares in FTOs.
2. The Foreign Trade Ministry was again reorganized (becoming the Ministry for International Economic Cooperation) and absorbed further cuts in budget and staffing.

Finally, in light of the response to the 1986 joint-venture law on the part of potential investors (only five ventures had been registered as of January 1988 (Zaproszenie 1988) liberalization of the new law is called for in the draft program of the second stage. Amendments would focus both on simplifying application procedures and on making the financial and tax provisions of the new law more "competitive" with other socialist countries. (Two clauses in particular are candidates for revision: (1) the requirement that the Polish government own 51% of the mixed enterprise's capital, and (2) the obligatory sale of hard-currency export receipts to the Polish treasury.) Liberalization of the 1981 statute pertaining to small-scale (polonia) activities is also anticipated in 1988 ("Program realizacyjny..." 1987).

In sum, however, the Foreign Trade Ministry has retained its tight grip on the vast majority of FTOs, and choice among competing FTOs has been denied for most producing firms. The traditional institutional structures of the Polish foreign-trade mechanism survived the reforms introduced in 1981-82 largely intact. It is too early to tell whether the changes introduced since 1987 will reverse this trend.

Structural reform of the Hungarian foreign-trade mechanism was initiated in 1968, although on a very small scale, with the granting of direct trading rights to a few large enterprises, and by relaxing some of the regulations restricting the integration of FTO and domestic production activities. In the 1980s, institutional changes have concentrated primarily on increasing the number of

FTOs, enterprises with direct foreign-trading rights, and on encouraging competition among the FTOs, and between FTOs and enterprises with direct trading rights.

The number of domestic enterprises possessing some type of direct trading rights had risen to 211 by September 1983 (Marer 1986a, p. 253), and has continued to increase in the interim. (For example, 38 more firms, including the foreign-trade affiliate of the *Skala* department store chain, received foreign trade rights January 1, 1987 (Varga 1987). The number of foreign-trade enterprises has also increased since 1981, and is now above 50. This increase has resulted in some competition between FTOs for domestic sales, for example, that which began to occur in produce trading after the creation of the General Impex FTO in January 1981. Some FTOs (for example, Hungarotex) have become "trading houses:" they have expanded upstream into production-for-export activities, and may accumulate capital for small investment projects as well.

These increases in the number of FTOs have by and large not resulted from the creation of new FTOs by the Foreign Trade Ministry; instead, they tend to be cooperative ventures formed by producing enterprises to handle their import-export needs.[8] In addition, as of 1984 approximately 100 foreign-trade partnerships between FTOs and producing enterprises were in existence (Marer 1986a, p. 253). The pattern of granting direct trading rights displays an interesting sectoral differentiation: as of 1985, approximately 60% of Hungarian machine-producing enterprises have received these rights, while virtually no enterprises in light industry have received them (Marer 1986a, p. 253). By all accounts, Hungarian enterprises take advantage of their trading rights with much greater frequency than their Polish counterparts; this is one of the main reasons behind the Hungarian foreign-trade mechanism's vastly superior per-capita hard-currency export figures.

V.   FOREIGN-TRADE REFORM: CHANGES IN THE FOREIGN-TRADE INSTRUMENTS

In both Poland and Hungary, foreign-trade reforms have sought to do the following:

1. use world prices to rationalize the domestic price system, by unifying exchange rates and linking the domestic prices of imports and import substitutes to world-market prices;
2. effect a transition away from direct-planning instruments towards a system of predominantly financial foreign-trade instruments (to the extent that the CMEA trading mechanism makes this possible); and
3. orient the focus of foreign-trade instruments towards production for export.

The Polish reform blueprint went beyond this, however; it called for the creation of a domestic market for hard currency which, ultimately, would play a major role in exchange-rate policy (Rymarczyk 1985). According to official policy, significantly increasing the degree of the domestic currency's convertibility is a long-term reform goal in both countries. In the Polish case, however, these principles have been honored mostly in the breach. The unification of the commercial and tourist rates in 1982 was combined with the abolition of sector- and enterprise-specific foreign-exchange multipliers to create a de jure unified exchange rate. During the so-called transition period (lasting either until 1985, 1986, or until environmental conditions improve sufficiently, according to various official interpretations) this exchange rate is supposed to be "sub-marginal." that is, it should be set so that 75-85% of planned exports to both currency areas are profitable. Deviations from this standard by more than 5% are supposed to trigger compensating revaluations. Prior to 1987, these principles had not been realized in determining the dollar-zloty exchange rate; indeed, until 1986, exchange-rate policy for convertibile currencies did not even come close to hitting the target.

Beginning from a state of severe inflationary pressure (which contributed to the zloty's perennial overvaluation) in 1982, the zloty in 1982-83 was devalued by 25% against the dollar. During this time period, industrial prices rose by 60% and retail prices by 130% (Rymarczyk 1985). Annual and, in some years, semiannual devaluations followed, and the rate of (overt) inflation came down to around 10-15%, which helped to move the dollar exchange rate closer to a submarginal level. Still, a study commissioned by Warsaw's Foreign Trade Institute of Prices and Markets found that in 1984, around 40% of Poland's hard-currency exports were unprofitable at prevailing exchange rates; moreover, if the profitability of coal exports is ignored (the official zloty prices for coal are estimated to cover about one third of the full social costs of its production) approximately 50% of hard-currency exports became unprofitable.

The zloty's overvaluation was implicitly valued by the authorities, since it dampened imported inflation by artificially reducing the relative prices of imported primary products. This, however, runs counter to another main reform principle: linking the domestic prices of imports to their world-market prices. According to the reform blueprint, deviations of more than 10% (in either direction) in world-market prices are supposed to elicit corresponding corrections in domestic prices for primary products (Boffito in Marer and Siwinski 1987). Until 1987, however, this did not occur. Instead, the domestic prices of primary products have played a catch-up game with world-market prices: successive devaluations have widened the gap between world-market and domestic prices, while the correction principle has been applied in too gradual a fashion to make up the difference between devaluations. The end result has been that the rationalizing effects of world-market prices upon the domestic price system have been largely absent; shortages of imported raw materials continued and provided a justification for their continued central rationing.

Although the zloty's overvaluation makes Polish exports more expensive, and hard-currency imports less expensive, the imperative of achieving hard-currency balance-of-payments surpluses remains unchanged. Consequently, the Foreign Trade Ministry employs a comprehensive price correction mechanism for both imports and exports, as well as export incentives, which attempt in an enterprise-specific manner to counteract the exchange rate's pro-import bias. Not only does this mechanism prevent producers from absorbing the full costs of imports; it also taxes away the difference between the world-market prices obtained for many exports (for example, coal) translated into zlotys through the exchange rate, and their regulated prices on the domestic market (Kleer and Poprzeczko 1987). In effect, this mechanism violates the theoretical unity of the zloty-dollar exchange rate, since different enterprises face different de facto exchange rates for different exports and imports. These measures are accompanied by pressure from above to "export at any price," and by administrative restrictions on hard-currency imports.

In addition to the Foreign Trade Ministry's role, the branch ministries' influence was also significant, particularly in directing enterprises in their purview to increase exports and in ensuring that scarce hard-currency imports are allocated to priority sectors, both formally (i.e., within the framework of operational programs and government orders) and informally. Approximately 80% of imports were centrally allocated through 1984 (Boffito in Marer and Siwinski 1987).

Exchange-rate and pricing policies have, however, undergone some changes since the second stage was announced. The zloty was devalued against the dollar by approximately 40% in nominal terms (around 15% in real terms) during late 1986 and early 1987, while the submarginal exchange-rate policy seems to have been adhered to much more closely during the second half of 1987 than in the past. Further liberalization of import and export prices, as well as reductions in the number of centrally-rationed imports, are slated for 1988 ("Program realizacyjny..." 1987).

The only significant export-promotion activities carried out during the 1982-86 period occurred within the framework of the so-called small industrial restructuring program, administered by the Foreign Trade Ministry. Since central investment priorities continue to favor the completion of the capital-intensive projects begun during the 1970s, the small restructuralization program tried to direct the remainder of investment funds towards small, export-promotion projects. Approximately 50 such projects had been started through 1986, and had absorbed around 55 billion zloty. The share of hard-currency loans in this program is supposed to increase in importance over time. This program was expanded under the supervision of the Export Development Bank in 1987 (Kleer and Poprzeczko 1987) and is slated for further growth in 1988 ("Program realizacyjny..." 1987).

The attempt at establishing the internal hard-currency market has been ineffective, and essentially has consisted of introducing foreign-exchange accounts for exporting enterprises. Hard-currency auctions administered by the Foreign Trade Bank have played an insignificant role in allocating foreign exchange, since less than 1% of the yearly stock of hard currency has been allocated through auctions during 1982-86 (Boffito in Marer and Siwinski

1987), and because, as a rule, enterprises with foreign exchange retention bank accounts are not permitted to participate in the auctions. Enterprises are not permitted to sell their export receipts to other firms, although they are permitted to transfer them as payment for services rendered.[9]

Enterprise foreign-exchange accounts were established in 1982, primarily as a result of pressure applied by large enterprises; the percentage of hard-currency imports financed by these accounts, however, has not risen above 15% of total hard-curency imports, and the percentage of export revenues retained by enterprises has been held to a limit of 20% (Boffito in Marer and Siwinski 1987; Mizsei 1987; Rymarczyk 1985; Slay in Marer and Siwinski 1987). During 1982-86, the percentage of export receipts retained by enterprises was determined by an ad hoc interministerial committee on which the branch ministries were represented. Not surprisingly, the percentage of export receipts which enterprises are permitted to retain has traditionally been determined on a sector- and enterprise-specific basis. Enterprise purchases made with these funds have often been subject to administrative controls. Delays in granting central approval for the use of funds in these accounts have at times been substantial, lasting up to a year for many enterprises in early 1986. These delays were at that time regarded as bringing the system of exchange-retention accounts close to death.

Despite these problems, the currency-retention system is widely regarded in Poland as a major proexport instrument. Because the foreign-exchange accounts provide a useful, if secondary (to the central allocation mechanism) method of obtaining hard currency (good, for example, for obtaining small but essential trifles like spare parts) enterprises seem to want to have a foreign-exchange account, even if once granted permission to open one (or to become joint members of an account already opened by other enterprises), they do not use the funds in the account to the fullest possible extent.[10]

Since the mid-1986 turning point in foreign-trade policy, a number of changes were introduced during 1987 in the enterprise foreign-exchange retention system. Granting exporting enterprises *ownership rights* to the funds in their accounts, in order to reduce the delays experienced in obtaining central approval, may have been the most beneficial change. Restrictions on inter-enterprise hard-currency transfers are to be loosened as well. These changes, however, were accompanied in 1987 by a number of steps backwards as well (Kleer & Poprzeczko, 1987), including the following:

- reducing the percentage of export revenues retained by 20% during 1987;
- requiring enterprises to *purchase* the hard currency in their account for zloty (at the official exchange rate); and
- requiring that these purchases take place within the first three months of the time of deposit. (Otherwise, the enterprise loses the right of purchase.)

The 1988 changes called for increasing the percentage of export receipts retained by enterprises and for unifying the percentages of hard-currency receipts which exporters in different sectors were allowed to retain ("Program realizacyjny..." 1987). It is too early to judge the extent and impact of these changes.

Until now, virtually nothing has been said about reform of the CMEA trading mechanism. This is because almost nothing has changed here. Indeed, the Polish reform has attempted precious little in this area. The Foreign Trade Ministry continues to disaggregate the intergovernmental trade agreements by issuing mandatory import and export targets for the FTOs. These plans are binding both for traditional FTOs (dealing mostly in raw materials and primary products) and the joint-stock association FTOs, who are supposed to be free of the Ministry's direct supervision (Rymarczyk 1985). Formally, the FTOs are not, in most cases, supposed to issue production orders to enterprises in order to fulfill the plan for CMEA exports. In practice, however, little seems to have changed in this area. Although the reform did envision the introduction of competitive bidding procedures in import allocation, they have been applied only in hard currency imports allocation, not for CMEA imports, and on an insignificant scale (Zarzycki 1985).

The one innovation in CMEA foreign-trade instruments introduced by the reforms was the creation in 1985 and subsequent expansion of enterprise *transferable-ruble* retention accounts. Although of much smaller potential importance than the hard-currency accounts (since transferable rubles do not allow their possessor to make claims upon other CMEA countries' currency or products) significance has been ascribed to the ruble accounts for two reasons: (1) they help to finance inter-enterprise cooperation agreements between Polish firms and enterprises from other CMEA countries (Kleer and Poprzeczko 1987); and (2) they provide CMEA exporters with "prestige" equal to that accorded to hard currency exporters, who have their own foreign exchange accounts.

In sum, although the proposals contained in the reform blueprint called for fundamental changes in Polish foreign trade instruments, few if any of these changes have been realized in practice. Instead, while financial regulators have increased in importance since 1982, many holdovers from the traditional direct-planning instruments remain. On the other hand, since the second stage began, a more active exchange-rate policy has been followed, greater effort has been made to link the domestic prices of primary products with their world-market prices, and steps have been taken to reinvigorate the enterprise hard-currency retention system. A great deal remains to be done, however.

The 1980s have seen a number of changes in Hungarian foreign-trade instruments. Unlike the Polish case, in which January 1, 1982 heralded the introduction of a host of reform measures, reforms of Hungarian foreign-trade instruments have been introduced in a gradual manner since 1968. An acceleration in the introduction of the reform measures is apparent, however, since the Kadar leadership returned the Hungarian economy to the "reform path" in the late 1970s.

Although the reform measures introduced in 1968 largely bypassed foreign-trade, they did establish closer links between domestic and world-market prices for primary products. And although a system of multiple exchange rates (called foreign-trade multipliers) was employed until 1976, exporters usually received the selling price for the goods shipped abroad, thus reducing the buffers between domestic and foreign customers. Also, the price-correction mechanism for imports was reduced in scope, although import competition never really took on significant dimensions. While the 1970s saw regression in terms of increased divergence between domestic and world-market prices, which resulted in the growing subsidization of hard-currency imports, an "active" exchange-rate policy was pursued, in which average exchange rates, that is, those determined by the cost of acquiring a unit of foreign exchange, were present in both CMEA and hard currency trade. Although approximately half of planned exports are unprofitable under this regime, the forint-dollar exchange rate since 1973 has been revalued relatively frequently, in accordance with this criterion (Kozma 1981, p. 212, Marer 1981, p. 169.)[11] And while enterprise foreign-exchange retention accounts were not established, according to one specialist writing on the Hungarian foreign-trade mechanism of the 1968-79 period:

> The basic idea and practice are that, if an enterprise has the import license and the forints, the National Bank automatically grants it the necessary foreign exchange ... obtaining the license is almost automatic in many cases (Marer 1981, pp. 166, 175).

Nonetheless, the 1970s saw an increasing divergence between the principles embodied in the 1968 reforms and the composition of actual foreign-trade instruments. In addition to the anti-export effect of the average exchange rate, increases in enterprise earnings caused by rising export prices were subject to taxation. These export disincentives required pro-export countermeasures, which included export refunds to compensate the most efficient exporters (whose profits on low-cost exports were siphoned off to the state budget through the average exchange rate), as well as tax rebates for exporters in general (Kozma 1981, p. 210). Just as subsidies for hard-currency imports increased sharply after 1972, export rebates also increased then. These policies were continued, with minor corrections, until 1980.

The turnaround in economic policy came in 1979, with major reductions in import subsidies, as well as subsidies for consumer goods, which resulted in the major price increases of July 1, 1979. The competitive pricing system, introduced in the manufacturing sector in 1980, linked enterprise prices and profits on the domestic and CMEA markets to hard-currency exports and imports, and wage mangerial-bonus preferences became more closely tied to hard-currency exports (Crane 1986, p. 442; Marer 1986b, p. 316). The tourist and commercial exchange rates were formally unified in 1981, although product- and enterprise-specific taxes and subsidies still created exaggerated de facto variations between enterprises. A 20% tax on hard-currency imports was in effect from

September 1982 through July 1, 1984. These changes were indicative not only of the rationalization of foreign-trade instruments, but of their increased importance relative to other regulators. At the same time, these changes have been accompanied by increased administrative controls on hard-currency imports, primarily via enterprise import licenses, and by increased informal pressures from the subcentral authorities to increase hard-currency exports (Crane 1986, p. 442).[12] A large-scale export promotion program has been administered by the Foreign Trade Bank since the mid-1970s. Hard-currency loans for export oriented projects have come to play an important role in this program since Hungary joined the World Bank in 1982.

Like the Polish reforms of the 1980s, the changes introduced in Hungarian foreign-trade instruments have been directed almost solely at hard-currency trade and have bypassed the CMEA trading mechanism. Although in most cases enterprises are not formally required to fulfill a CMEA production order, informal pressures from above play a major role here, as do taxes and subsidies intended to keep production for CMEA export roughly as profitable as production for hard-currency export and/or the domestic market (Marer 1986a, p. 246). In any case, the task of planning CMEA export volume is made easier by the fact that many manufacturing enterprises are dependent upon the CMEA market in order to achieve efficient levels of output.

VI.   THE POLISH AND HUNGARIAN FOREIGN-TRADE MECHANISMS: CONCLUSIONS

The above discussion of reforms introduced in the Polish and Hungarian foreign-trade mechanisms contains a certain paradox: the Polish reform blueprint is in many respects more radical than the principles embodied in the Hungarian foreign-trade reforms. In some areas, the Polish foreign-trade reform as implemented is more advanced than the Hungarian as well—the enterprise hard-currency retention system and official exchange-rate policy (the Polish submarginal versus the Hungarian average exchange-rate regime). Such comparisons, however, overlook the question of what is being compared. We are interested in changes in the foreign-trade *mechanism,* that is, changes in the behavior of traders and producers in the *real* sphere, while only the mechanism's systemic and/or policy components (i.e., elements of the *control* sphere) are directly affected by reforms. In many respects, the impact of the Polish reforms has been limited to the control sphere (and even here, the gap between theory and practice is often substantial), while reforms of the Hungarian foreign-trade mechanism have had a more organic connection with the behavior of the producing and trading enterprises. The gradual nature of the Hungarian foreign-trade reforms, as well as the fact that they have been introduced in much more favorable environmental conditions, would seem to be the most important factors in explaining these differences.

In sum, the Polish foreign-trade mechanism as of 1986-87 remained largely unreformed. The traditional institutional structures linking the FTOs to the Foreign Trade Ministry remained largely intact. The pervasive shortage conditions which have dominated the environment in which foreign-trade decision making has taken place since 1982 have reinforced traditional institutional structures and exacerbated the difficulties associated with the application of financial foreign-trade instruments. (The reorientation in foreign-trade policy away from trade with the West towards CMEA trade also played a role here.) Exchange rates, foreign-trade prices, hard-currency retention accounts, and other financial regulators have been prevented from performing the functions ascribed to them in the reform blueprint. Instead, the central allocation of imports and foreign exchange, enterprise participation in operational programs and government orders, and informal pressure from above have been the dominant instruments. Indeed, foreign trade during 1982-86 seems to be one of the least-reformed sectors of the Polish economy. The extent to which the changes which have appeared since mid-1986 are indicative of a more committed proreform attitude on the part of the authorities remains an open question.

If sustained progress is made in securing internal and external equilibrium, and if Poland's membership in the IMF and World Bank results in a much-needed infusion of hard currency (some pretty big "ifs") then "greater determination" on the part of the authorities could lead to the abandonment of direct planning instruments, as well as significant progress in implementing the far-reaching changes proposed in the reform blueprints (both the first and second stage). No doubt this is the optimistic scenario which Polish officials are advancing to representatives of the IMF and World Bank who hold the key to future hard-currency infusions.

In my judgment, however, the smoke which has been generated since the Tenth Party Congress has yet to be matched by fire of equal magnitude. Of the reform steps which have been taken since mid-1986, only one, the more active exchange-rate policy, seems to have made much of an impact upon the Polish foreign-trade mechanism. Attempts at shoring up the enterprise hard-currency retention system seem ineffectual, and the goal of establishing an internal market for convertible currencies seems as distant as ever. The establishment of the Export Development Bank and the new law on joint ventures, although positive developments in and of themselves, still leave Poland a less-desirable site for large-scale foreign investment than Hungary, Yugoslavia, or China, and do not really resolve the country's credibility problems in the eyes of Western commercial institutions.

Even the more active exchange-rate policy, itself a step in the right direction, is symptomatic of what is perhaps the major weakness of the entire Polish reform effort: the lack of public support for reforms based on progress towards restoring equilibrium as was demonstrated by the results of the referenda held in November 1987. Despite the abolition of the industrial branch ministries in October 1987, the creation of two *wspolnota* (economy-wide trusts) for the mining and energy sectors indicate the staying power of the traditional lobbies, which have consistently frustrated attempts at rationalizing investment and industrial policy. Repeated devaluations of the zloty in this context can only lead to unpopular price increases, sold to the public in the name of economic reform, that fail to bring about long-overdue structural changes. The long-run social consequences of this policy must certainly be disasterous, if they are not so already.

By comparison, the Hungarian foreign-trade mechanism is healthier than the Polish mechanism. Perhaps most importantly, it is freer of direct-planning instruments, since relatively more flexible, market-oriented behavioral patterns on the part of producing enteprises and FTOs have been able to evolve over a 20-year period (1968-87) in an environment relatively free of shortage conditions. Nonetheless, the preservation of the traditional CMEA trading mechanism, central pressures (both formal and informal) on enterprises to increase hard-currency exports, and the control of hard-currency imports through import licences, imply the presence of some direct-planning instruments. Still, as far as hard-currency trade flows are concerned, the extent of these practices is fairly limited. Crane (1986, p. 444) found that, during 1982, Hungarian enterprises generally refrained from unprofitable hard-currency exports, and that pressures to increase these exports did not usually result in ratchet-type phenomena. This contrasted sharply with the pre-1982 Polish foreign-trade mechanism, and certainly with much of the post-1982 mechanism as well.

The Hungarian foreign-trade mechanism, however, has also undergone a certain systemic regression during the mid-1980s. After posting increasing surpluses in hard-currency trade during 1981-84, the hard-currency trade surplus came in way below plan in 1985 and disappeared altogether in 1986. This has resulted in part from the sustained terms-of-trade deterioration which Hungary has experienced since the late 1970s, and in part from the cumulative effect of slow growth in investment and hard-currency imports. These performance problems raise the question of whether the relatively favorable external conditions, which have continued to differentiate the Hungarian mechanism from the Polish mechanism, can last, and whether Poland's problems today might not be Hungary's tomorrow.

ACKNOWLEDGMENTS

I would like to express my gratitude to the International Research and Exchanges Board, the Fulbright Foundation, Indiana University's Polish Studies Center, and Loyola Marymount University's Liberal Arts Division for providing the funding which made the research for this chapter possible.

NOTES

1.   Unless otherwise specified, all data are derived or taken from the official Polish and Hungarian statistical yearbooks.

2.   This absolute numerical preponderance of Polish (relative to Hungarian) enterprises and cooperatives involved in foreign trade activities masks the fact

that a much higher percentage of Hungarian firms are involved in foreign trade activities.

3.   Retail-price inflation was used here as a measure of price increases.

4.   The Hungarian terms-of-trade data for 1968-78 are derived from Kozma (1981), p. 216. His calculations are based on the selection of the preceding year as the base year. Hungarian data for 1978-84 are from Marer (1986b), p. 314; here, 1978 is taken as the base year. For the Polish data, the preceding year is taken as the base year.

5.   The data presented here are derived from Marer (1986b), p. 320, Bernát et al. (1986), p. 41, and official Polish sources.

6.   During the 1970s, only one third of the FTOs were subordinated to the Foreign Trade Ministry. The others were responsible to branch ministries and trusts, Crane (1986), p. 438.

7.   Not all the FTOs were transformed into joint-stock companies. As of June 1986, in addition to 38 joint-stock FTOs, 12 traditional FTOs were still active, as were 13 foreign-trade "associations" (which seem to be relatives of the joint-stock FTOs), 2 FTOs organized as cooperatives, as well as 15 other intermediate-level trading organizations acting as intermediaries between the producing enterprises which founded them on the one hand and foreign actors on the other. (These data, as well as the information about the number of direct-trading rights granted by the Foreign Trade Ministry presented subsequently, are found in the 1986 Polish Foreign Trade Statistical Yearbook, pp. 82-83 and pp. 320-336).

8.   An example here would be the cooperative FTO Trade-Coop, which was created in 1987 by, among others, two other FTOs, in order to act as a trading house for producing cooperatives (Lindner 1987).

9.   There are indications, however, that an informal inter-enterprise *credit market* has developed through the hard-currency accounts. According to some observers, the growing number of inter-enterprise hard-currency transfers are evidence of an informal hard-currency financing mechanism in which exporters lend their foreign-exchange receipts to other firms. In 1985, for example, the number of these transfers increased by 56-58% (Lipinski 1986, p. 4). Combined with the fact that interest has been paid on funds in the enterprise hard-currency accounts since 1984, this implies that an informal (but tangible) opportunity cost of spending these funds on hard-currency imports does exist, which reduces the need for administrative restrictions upon the disposition of these funds.

10.   There was, however, a trend during 1982-85 toward increased utilization by exporters of the funds in their foreign-exchange accounts to finance hard-currency exports: the percentage of funds held idle during the course of the year dropped from 69 to 10% during this time. Of course, this tendency also reflected a more liberal attitude toward the funds on the part of the central authorities.

11.   The forint-ruble exchange rate was not revalued until January 1, 1976, when the foreign-trade multipliers were abolished.

12.   The extent to which administrative restrictions reduced hard-currency imports in the 1980s is not clear. While various restrictions have been in force since 1980, Crane found that many of the enterprises he surveyed in 1982 were issued hard-currency import quotas which could be drawn down without the supervision of an FTO. He also found that managers were often able to obtain

hard-currency imports through bargaining with subcentral officials. The outcome of the negotiations depended upon the following: (1) the supply of hard currency at the given moment in time, and (2) whether domestic or CMEA substitutes are available (Crane 1986, pp. 440, 442).

REFERENCES

Antal, L. *Gazdasagiranyitasi es penzugyi rendszerunk a reform utjan* (Our Managerial and Financial System on the Reform Path). Budapest: Kozgazdasagi es Jogi Konyvkiado, 1985.

Baczynski, J. "Samotny mały bankier" (Poor Little Banker). *Polityka* 7 (May 17, 1986): p. 15.

Baka, W. *Polska reforma gospodarcza* (The Polish Economic Reform). Warsaw: Państwowe Wydawnictwo Ekonomiczne, 1982.

Bako, E. "Five Years with the World Bank." *Hungarian Exporter* 37 (April 1987): pp. 3-4.

Balassa, B. "Reforming the New Economic Mechanism in Hungary." *Journal of Comparative Economics* 7 (1983): pp. 253-276.

Bartoszewicz, T. "Co dalej z ROD-ami?" (What Next with the Foreign Exchange Accounts?). *Rynki Zagraniczne* 3 (1986): p. 15.

Bernát, T., G. Bora, I. Kalász, A. Kollarik, and M. Matheika. *Magyarorszag gazdasagfoldrajza* (An Economic Geography of Hungary). Budapest: Kossuth Konyvkiado, 1986.

Blazyca, G. "The Polish Economy under Martial Law: A Dissenting View." *Soviet Studies* 37 (July 1985): pp. 428-436.

Botos, K. "Socialist Countries in the International Capital Market in the 1970s and 1980s." Paper presented at Tenth US-Hungarian Roundtable Conference, Budapest, December 1986.

Chadzynski, M. "Przymus eksportu: Rozmowa z ministrem Stanisławem Długoszem" (The Export Imperative: An Interview with Minister Stanislaw Dlugosz). *Życie Warszawy* 7 (February 14-15, 1987): p. 3.

Crane, K. "Foreign-Trade Decisionmaking under Balance of Payments Pressure: Poland versus Hungary." In *East European Economies: Slow Growth in the 1980s*, vol. 3. Washington DC: U.S. Government Printing Office, 1986.

Fallenbuchl, Z. "The Polish Economy Under Martial Law." *Soviet Studies* 36 (October 1984): pp. 513-527.

Gomulka, S., and J. Rostowski. "The Reformed Polish Economic System 1982-83." *Soviet Studies* 36 (July 1984): pp. 386-405.

Hare, P. "The Beginnings of Institutional Reform in Hungary." *Soviet Studies* 36 (July 1983): pp. 313-330.

Herer, P., and W. Sadowski. "Nawis Inflacyjny" (The Inflationary Overhang). *Życie gospodarcze* 32 (August 9, 1981).

Inotai, A. (ed.). *The Hungarian Enterprises in the Context of Intra-CMEA Relations*. Budapest: Hungarian Scientific Council for World Economy, 1986.

Jermakowicz, W. "Gra o instrumenty" (A Game of Instruments). *Przeglad techniczny* 44 (November 2, 1983): pp. 16-17.

Jermakowicz, W., and R. Krawczyk. *Reforma gospodarcza jako innowacja społeczna* (Economic Reform as a Social Innovation). Warsaw: Mlodziezowa Agencja Wydawnicza, 1985.

Jung, A. "Exporting, Refinancing, Restructuring." *Eastern European Economics* (Summer 1986): pp. 40-50.

Kierunki reformy gospodarczej (Directions of Economic Reform). Warsaw: Książka i Wiedza, 1981.

Kleer, J., and J. Poprzeczko. "Dobry towar za dobrą cenę" (A Good Product at a Good Price: An Interview with Andrzej Wójcik, Minister of Foreigntrade). *Polityka* 4 (January 24, 1987): p. 3.

Konsultacyjna Rada Gospodarcza. "Gospodarka w latach 1981-85" (The Economy in the Years 1981-85). Warsaw, 1986.

Kornai, J. "The Hungarian Reform Process: Visions, Hope, and Reality." *Journal of Economic Literature* 24 (December 1986): pp. 1687-1737.

————. *Economics of Shortage.* Amsterdam/New York/Oxford: North Holland, 1980.

————. *Anti-Equilibrium: On Economic Systems Theory and the Tasks of Research.* Amsterdam/London: North Holland, 1971.

Kozma, F. "The Role of the Exchange Rate in Hungary's Adjustment to External Economic Disturbances." In *Hungary: A Decade of Economic Reform*, edited by Hare, Radice and Swain. London: Allen & Unwin, 1981.

Kozminski, A. "Marzenie o twardej złotowce" (Dreaming about a Hard Zloty). Interview by M. Rostocki in *Polityka* 5, Import-Export section (February 1, 1986): pp. 13, 15.

————. *Gospodarka na punkcie zwrotnym* (The Economy at the Turning Point). Warsaw: Państwowe Wydawnictwo Ekonomiczne, 1985.

Lindner, A. "Trade-Coop." *Hungarian Exporter* (May 1987): p. 24.

Lipinski, S. "W dewizowym krzywym kole" (In the Crooked Circle of Foreign Exchange). *Życie gospodarcze* 24 (April 6, 1986): pp. 1-4.

Loch, E. "Tesknota za konsekwencja" (A Hankering for Consistency). *Polityka* 24 (June 14, 1986): p. 5.

Majewski, J. *Węgiel na rynku światowym* (Coal on the World Market). Warsaw: Państwowe Wydawnictwo Ekonomiczne, 1983.

Marer, P. "Economic Reform in Hungary: From Central Planning to Regulated Market." In *East European Economies: Slow Growth in the 1980s*, vol. 3. Washington DC: U.S. Government Printing Office, 1986a.

————. "Hungary's Balance of Payments Crisis and Response, 1979-84." In *East European Economies: Slow Growth in the 1980s*, vol. 3. Washington DC: U.S. Government Printing Office, 1986b.

————. "The Mechanism and Performance of Hungarys Foreign-trade, 1968-79." In *Hungary: A Decade of Economic Reform*, edited by Hare, Radice, & Swain. London: Allen & Unwin, 1981.

Marer, P., and W. Siwinski (eds.). *Creditworthiness and Reform in Poland: Western and Polish Perspectives.* Bloomington, IN: Indiana University Press, 1987.

Mizsei, K. "A valutazisszateritesi rendszer-eszkoz a gazdasag intezmenyi nyitottsaganak kialakitasahoz" (The Currency-Retention System: Towards the Gradual Establishment of the Economy's Institutional Openness). Budapest: Institute for World Economics, 1987.

_____. "A valutavisszaterites lengyel rendszer" (The Polish Currency-Retention System). Budapest: Institute for World Economics, 1986.

Parkola, A., and R. Rapacki. "Dziś i jutro reformy w handlu zagranicznym" (The Foreign-Trade Reform Today and Tomorrow). *Przegląd techniczny* 45 (November 11, 1982): pp. 24-26.

Pełnomocnik rządu ds. reformy gospodarczej *Raport o realizacji reformy gospodarczej w 1984 roku* (Report on the Implementation of the Economic Reform in 1984). Warsaw: Rzeczpospolita (August 1985).

Plesinski, K. "O społkach z kapitałem zagranicznym" (On Joint Ventures). *Życie gospodarcze* 18 (May 4, 1986): p. 2.

Plowiec, U. *The Functioning of Poland's Foreign-trade: Experience and Prospects.* Warsaw: Institute of Prices Business Trends, 1984.

_____. "Reforma gospodarcza a proeksportowa orientacja gospodarki" (Economic Reform and Pro-Export Orientation of the Economy). *Gospodarka planowa* 1 (1983).

"Poland Emerges from Economic Crisis...." *IMF Survey* (February 23, 1987): pp. 59-61.

"Program realizacyjny drugiego etapu reformy gospodarczej (projekt)" (The Draft Program for Implementing the Second Stage of the Economic Reform). Warsaw: *Rzeczpospolita* (October, 1987).

Rymarczyk, J. "Proba diagnozy" (An Attempt at Diagnosis). *Życie gospodarcze* (August 18, 1985): p. 8.

Schweitzer, I. "The Hungarian Alternative to Soviet-Type Planning." *Acta Oeconomica* 23 (3-4, 1981).

Sebok, E. "Joint Ventures Operating in Hungary." *Hungarian Exporter* 3 (March, 1987): pp. 5-8.

Szamuely, L. *A Magyar Kozgazdasagi Gondolat Fejlodese 1954-78* (The Development of Hungarian Economic Thought, 1954-1978). Budapest: Kozgazdasagi es Jogi Konyvkiado, 1986.

Tabaczynski, E. "Export Oriented Changes in Polish Industry." *Eastern European Economics* (Spring 1987): pp. 86-92.

Trzeciakowski, W. "The Possibility of a Solution to the Polish Debt." *Forschungsberichte*, Vienna Institute for Comparative Economic Studies, 1987.

_____. "Up-To-Date Rules of Joint Ventures in Hungary." *Public Finance* 28 (January 1986).

Varga, A. "Nem kiteleznek velunk, hanem loyalisak velunk szemben" (Loyalty, Not Special Treatment). *Figyelo* (January 22, 1987): p. 9.

"Z zagranicznym kapitałem" (With Foreign Capital). *Życie gospodarcze* 11 (March 16, 1986): p. 11.

"Zadłużenie zagraniczne Polski i drogi jego przezwyciężenia: Skrót raportu Instytutu Koniunktur i Cen Handlu Zagranicznego oraz Instytutu Gospodarki Narodowej" (Poland's External Indebtedness and the Way to

Overcoming It: An Excerpt of the Report Prepared by the Institute of Prices and Markets in Foreign-trade and the National Economic Institute). *Życie gospodarcze* 40 (October 5, 1986): pp. 10-12.

"Zaproszenie dla obcego kapitalu" (An Invitation to Foreign Capital). *Życie gospodarcze* 1 (January 3, 1988): p. 16.

Zarzycki, Z. "Tanio kupić" (Buy Cheap). *Życie gospodarcze* 49 (December 1, 1985): p. 12.

SOVIET REFORMS AND EASTERN EUROPE:
IMPLICATIONS FOR POLAND

David Mason

I. INTRODUCTION[1]

The political and economic changes unleashed by Mikhail
Gorbachev have changed the face of the Soviet Union and effected
a fundamental transformation of the regimes in Eastern Europe
as well. There is an intimate connection between the Soviet and
East European reform programs. Some of the Soviet reforms are
inspired by similar reforms in Eastern Europe, and some are being
pressed on the Eastern European regimes, often in the face of
reluctance or even outright hostility by the leaders of those
countries. Where the Soviet-style reforms are implemented, there
will be wrenching changes in the ways these societies are organized
and run. In the economic sphere, these changes include a reduction
in the role of central planning, decentralization of decision
making, an expanded role for market mechanisms, and more
opportunity for private initiative in services, production, and

agriculture. The associated political changes include greater "openness" in the media (with reduced censorship), competitive and secret elections for state and party bodies, expanded opportunities for independent interest groups, and an enhanced political role for workers in state enterprises (through "self-management" and employee selection of managers and directors). Many of these ideas have been advocated by reformers and dissidents within Eastern Europe, and efforts to apply them in the past have sometimes led to severe repression (e.g., Poland in 1981) or Soviet intervention (e.g., Czechoslovakia in 1968). The chances for such reforms to succeed now are much greater, with a Soviet leadership that is supportive rather than skeptical and fearful.

But even in the absence of substantial domestic reforms in Eastern Europe, the "new thinking" in the Soviet Union promises dramatic, perhaps even revolutionary, changes in the nature of Soviet-East European relations. Gorbachev and his colleagues on the Politburo have called on the East European leaders to abandon old ways and have begun to redefine the relationship between Moscow and the capitals of Eastern Europe. "Socialist internationalism," the standard formula that was used, for example, to justify the Soviet interventions in Czechoslovakia and Afghanistan and which formed the core of the Brezhnev Doctrine of limited sovereignty, is now being downplayed. If the Soviets mean what they say, and if the East European leaders take them at their word, Eastern Europe will move even further down the road of polycentrism. Furthermore, change and reform in Eastern Europe is likely to rebound to the Soviet Union, further accelerating the reform process in that country. Before 1989, it seemed that the reform process had to be kept within certain limits, defined by the cardinal principles of the leading role of the party and commitment to the political and military alliances of the Soviet bloc. Even these principles, however, were challenged in Poland and Hungary, and crumbled throughout the region. Moscow faces a task that is both difficult and dangerous: how to promote reform in Eastern Europe without jeopardizing stability.

These issues are particularly acute for Poland which, more than any other country in the bloc, has been subject to periodic cycles of revolt, reform, and repression. The changing rules in the Soviet Union served to legitimize the reform process in Poland and to strengthen the position of the reformist elements in the Polish

United Workers' Party. Most of the economic and political reforms being implemented by the Gorbachev leadership have already been tried in Poland, making Poland a role model of sorts for the Soviets. The emergence of a noncommunist government in Poland provides the Kremlin with a test case of multiparty democracy in Eastern Europe. If Poland succeeds in its experiment while maintaining a semblance of stability, the experiment will spread to other East European states, probably even to the Soviet Union.

Indeed, within the Soviet Union, the interrelated reform processes of glasnost, perestroika, democratization, and "new thinking" in foreign policy are changing the face of the Soviet system. There are numerous skeptics who have wondered "whether real reform is viable at all in the Soviet Union" (Kusin 1987) or who doubt that Gorbachev can win the "race with time" (Goldman 1987). But it is becoming increasingly clear that Gorbachev's intentions are serious, that the reforms are real and not cosmetic, and that, in the short run at least, the changes are far-reaching and significant. There is obviously opposition to the reforms, both in the leadership and in the bureaucracy, but more and more of the central leadership positions are filled with Gorbachev's people, and the major reformers (e.g., Zaslavskaya, Aganbegyan) have been given more visibility and more influence. The question is no longer whether the reforms are real, but whether the regime can carry them through to completion and, even more importantly, manage the destabilizing consequences. Gorbachev himself recognizes the challenge. At the June 1987 Central Committee plenum, he said that the reforms were "aimed at achieving a qualitatively new level of Socialist society. History has not left us much time to face this task" (*Tass* June 26, 1987). Even if he succeeds, though, the planned changes will unleash grievances and conflicts that the Soviet system is not well equipped to handle.

II. SOVIET INTERESTS IN EASTERN EUROPEAN REFORM

The fact of genuine political and economic reform in the Soviet Union is itself both interesting and important; it is even more remarkable that the Soviets are also encouraging glasnost and reform in Eastern Europe. Gorbachev and the Soviet leadership have admitted that the Stalinist model of economic and political development no longer works in the more complex social and economic environment of contemporary Soviet society. In pushing such reforms in Eastern Europe, the Soviets are also admitting that the Soviet model has not always been appropriate for their East European client states. The Soviets have a number of reasons for fostering reform in Eastern Europe: to revive the faltering economies of the region, upon which the Soviets depend heavily for trade; to insure the political stability of these regimes at a time of disruptive change; to test some of the Soviet reforms in the East European contexts; and to confirm the ideological legitimacy of the Soviet system and the applicability of that system to other countries.

The most important stimulus is the economic one. Soviet plans for *perestroika* are based on a more technologically oriented economy and envisage rapid growth of investment in new equipment, especially in engineering and electronics. But this is not to be based entirely on imports of Western technology. Rather, the Soviets hope to accelerate imports of high quality machinery (and consumer goods) from Eastern Europe.[2] The Soviets already conduct over half of their trade with CMEA countries, and this percentage has been increasing in the last few years. So to a large extent the success of the Soviet economic reform depends on increased productivity, and especially of increases in the *quality* of production, in Eastern Europe. Soviet economists have admitted that "the problems of the economic slowdown exist in all socialist countries in one form or another."[3] The Gorbachev leadership apparently feels that the path to renewed growth and increased quality is through the kinds of decentralizing and market oriented reforms that the Soviets are themselves pursuing.

The relationship here, though, is a symbiotic one: the Soviets hope the East Europeans will follow their model; but they also hope to borrow from the experiences of the more progressive members of the socialist community. The Soviets expressed particular interest in Hungary's market-oriented economic reforms and studied its multicandidate electoral reforms before testing that experiment in the Soviet parliamentary elections of 1989.[4] The new Soviet project to allow joint ventures with Western firms follows earlier experiments in this area by Bulgaria, Czechoslovakia, Hungary, and Poland. In terms of glasnost, the Soviets are now opening up areas for discussion that have long been treated in the media of other East European countries (especially Yugoslavia, Poland, and Hungary).

The problem for Eastern Europe, even more so than for the Soviet Union, is that economic reforms are likely to be destabilizing, and to undermine the fragile legitimacy of those governments. Any major reforms will take time to lock in and to produce results, and in the meantime, there may well have to be some belt-tightening. But the legitimacy of most of the East European regimes increasingly has come to rest on socio-economic performance, so economic stagnation may well jeopardize that legitimacy. "Democratization" is meant to remedy this dilemma, by attempting to enlist popular participation in and commitment to the reforms, and to inject a measure of political legitimacy at a time of economic retrenchment. It can also help to shake up and dislodge those in the party, bureaucratic, and economic structures who feel threatened by the reforms and therefore oppose them.

During their own struggles over reform, the last thing the Soviets need is further Solidarity-type disruptions in Eastern Europe. Moscow could try to avoid this either by imposing stricter regimentation and wielding the threat of intervention, or by encouraging autonomy and domestic relaxation. Gorbachev has basically said that the first of these options is no longer valid, so the only alternative has been the latter. At any rate, the Gorbachev-style economic reforms require the support of the population and, in Eastern Europe at least, such support is unlikely to be won without some *quid pro quo*. A measure of political relaxation has been the *quid* in this case.

III. THE POLISH CASE

Poland has been the premier beneficiary of change in the Soviet Union and, along with Hungary, is setting the pace for political reform in the communist world. In April 1989, after eight weeks of "round-table" negotiations between Solidarity and the regime, the parties signed an agreement providing for unprecedented changes. Solidarity was legalized; the opposition guaranteed a bloc of seats in the existing parliament, the Sejm; and a second chamber of the legislature, the Senate, was reconstituted and elected in free and open elections the following June. Solidarity's bloc of candidates swept the Senate and won almost all of the seats available to them in the Sejm. So for the first time in the communist world, a legal opposition came into being, and it immediately won control of one chamber of the national legislature.

The Polish United Workers' Party had guaranteed a majority position for itself and its two allied parties in the new Sejm. But after the election, these two parties refused to ally themselves with the communist party, making it impossible for the latter to form a government. By default, the formation of a government fell to the Solidarity-led opposition, which in August constituted the first noncommunist government in Eastern Europe since World War II.

Poland had always been an anomaly in the Soviet bloc and since 1981 was even more so: a regime that had crushed Solidarity and imposed martial law, yet which tolerated a flourishing underground press and left at large its most outspoken political opponents. Poland also had the freest press in the communist world (with the possible exception of Yugoslavia), thus presenting a kind of benchmark for glasnost in the Soviet bloc. Consequently, the Jaruzelski regime was the most vocal supporter of the Gorbachev reforms in the Soviet Union, which in turn served to legitimize the limited autonomy and liberalization that the Poles had managed to secure, even before the round-table agreements. In a strange twist over time, the Poles had changed from the *bete noire* of the Soviet bloc under Brezhnev to the favorite sons of Gorbachev.

Even before the path-breaking events of 1989, the Polish press had covered the Soviet reforms more extensively than any of the other East European countries, publishing in full Gorbachev's major speeches and CPSU resolutions. They developed Polish translations for the three key Soviet terms describing the reforms: *przebudowa* for perestroika, *jawnosc* for glasnost, and *przyspieszenie* for *uskorienie*. The Polish media also reported on the release of Soviet dissidents, the disturbances in Armenia, Azerbaijan, and Georgia, and other previously unmentionable events. At first this coverage was almost entirely *descriptive*, with little commentary on these events or discussion of how they might affect Poland.

After the January 1987 CPSU plenum, however, and even more so after the June plenum later that year, both coverage and commentary increased dramatically. An index of this increased coverage is the number of entries under the category "domestic politics and economics of the USSR" in the Polish monthly periodical index, *Bibliografia Zawartosci i Czasopism.* During 1986, there were usually two or three entries in this category each month. In February 1987, after the January plenum, there were fourteen, eleven of which addressed change, reform, openness, or restructuring in the Soviet Union. It is also interesting, and perhaps of symbolic importance, that the overall category heading in the bibliography was changed in January from "Communist and Socialist Construction (*budownictwo*)" of the USSR and the Peoples Democracies to "Domestic Politics and Economics" of the USSR and the Socialist Countries.

After the June 1987 CPSU plenum, coverage became even more extensive. In the weekly *Polityka,* for example, there were major, often front page, interpretive articles on the June plenum and Soviet reform (subtitled "the greatest changes since the time of NEP"), on the "blank spots" in the history of Polish-Soviet relations, and on the revised historiography of the Stalinist era. There were also long interviews with Anatoly Rybakov (author of the controversial novel *Children of the Arbat*) and with Polish foreign minister Orzechowski (the article entitled "The Polish Style"), which included extensive discourse on Soviet-Polish relations.

Poland, more than any of the other countries of the region, illustrates the symbiotic nature of the reform process in relations with Moscow. Soviet leaders openly discussed their interest in the Polish reforms, and the Poles capitalized on the Soviet reforms to push ahead with their own. When Polish party leader Jaruzelski met with Gorbachev in Moscow in April 1987, he noted that:

> The Polish public is following the course of restructuring in the USSR with avid interest and attention and wishes its Soviet comrades success in this historic undertaking, which also provides Poland with an inspiring example of how a policy of socialist renewal is implemented (*Pravda* April 22, 1987, p. 1).

Polish officials described developments in Poland and the Soviet Union as a process of "mutual influencing."[5] The Poles took a certain pride in the fact that the Soviets studied their reforms, and even adopted some elements of it. An article on the Soviet reforms in *Polityka* mentioned that the new Soviet law on enterprises was based in part on the experience of the socialist countries, including Poland, and that a number of elements of the new Soviet law were based on the Polish law on enterprises: "In Moscow it is no secret that during his recent visit to Warsaw premier Ryzhkov was interested in the details of the Polish economic reform and that Zbigniew Messner [the Polish premier] gave him the text of our law on enterprises" (*Polityka* July 11, 1987, p. 11).

In a 1987 interview with Western reporters, the first in two years and itself an indication of the growing glasnost in Poland, Jaruzelski praised Gorbachev effusively, and said that the Soviet economic reforms made it easier for him to promote radical economic change in Poland. He also said that for the first time in 40 years [!], the Soviet leader was more popular in Poland than the U.S. president (*Wall Street Journal* July 30, 1987, p. 14).

The Poles had a decentralizing economic reform on the books since 1982, but had little success in implementing it, partly due to bureaucratic inertia and partly to conservative opposition. Gorbachev's reforms, and his railings against bureaucratic resistance in the Soviet Union, had the effect of encouraging the reformers and muting their opponents in Poland. It was much more difficult for conservatives in Poland to argue that the reforms violated communist orthodoxy when the homeland of communist orthodoxy was pursuing the same kinds of reforms. The Soviets on occasion even directly encouraged the liberals in Poland. A 1986 article in the Soviet party monthly, *Kommunist,* on the Polish party congress asserted that "the party...cannot arbitrarily, without considering the situation, set tasks which are correct from the point of view of Marxist-Leninist theory, but which are impracticable in the given concrete circumstances."[6] When Gorbachev visited Warsaw in July 1988, he pressured the Polish leadership to accelerate the pace of reform.

The Polish regime took the Soviets at their word and moved ahead with reform on a number of fronts, in terms of the economy, of glasnost, and of democratization. The 1982 economic reform, which provided for enterprise autonomy, self-financing, and self-management (in Polish, "the three S's") stagnated, with little real progress in any of the three areas. To try to get things moving, Jaruzelski announced, in 1986, the second stage of the reform, and reconstituted the Commission on Economic Reform (first established in 1980) to supervise its implementation. While the details of this second stage were slow in forthcoming, Jaruzelski said that the new economic policies would "eliminate" the present "centralistic model that hasn't passed the test of time" and would rely heavily on market mechanisms (*Wall Street Journal* July 30, 1987, p. 14). Opposition to this second stage was evident at the end of 1986, when a revised version of the plan watered down much of the original. There was a storm of protest, however, including from members of the Commission, and the revised version was withdrawn. Wladyslaw Baka, head of the Polish National Bank, later said, "there is no doubt that the process Gorbachev has initiated in the Soviet Union has been a very strong support for the proreform sector in Poland." [7]

Impetus for the reforms was slowed somewhat by the inability of the regime to attain a sufficiently strong endorsement for the reforms in a referendum in November 1987. Nevertheless, the regime initiated a series of scaled-down but sizeable price increases in an attempt to rationalize the price structure in 1988. Many of these decisions made sense in strictly economic terms, but ran into the usual political problems in terms of the impact on workers and the standard of living. For example, the government raised procurement prices for agricultural goods by 48%, hoping to insure a more plentiful and reliable supply of foodstuffs to the market. The consequence, however, was substantial increases in retail food prices as well, always an explosive issue in Poland.

In the summer of 1988, the government attempted to make real some of the reform provisions by closing down 21 unprofitable enterprises and warning that 140 others were being considered for closure. One of these was the Gdansk shipyards, where Solidarity was born in 1980 and where union activism remains strong. Both of these decisions contributed to the disaffection that led to a new round of strikes in August. These strikes were terminated only after the regime had agreed to negotiate with Solidarity. This led to the opening of the round-table discussions in February 1989.

Just as Soviet perestroika stimulated economic reform in Poland, Soviet glasnost encouraged Polish *jawnosc*, even before the 1989 changes. *Dr. Zhivago*, which was finally published in the Soviet Union, was also serialized in Poland. A new daily television news show in Warsaw, factual and without commentary, was so popular that its ratings equaled some of the Western-made shows. The anchor of the program had been a member of Solidarity. Censorship was relaxed, and after the amnesty of political prisoners in 1986, the regime generally stopped jailing those arrested for publishing samizdat. In line with Soviet practice, the Polish regime ceased jamming Voice of America and Radio Free Europe. By 1988, even opposition figures were given favorable exposure in the official media. The most dramatic example of this was the November 1988 live televised debate between Lech Walesa and Alfred Miodowicz, the leader of the official trade union alliance.

As in the Soviet Union, a number of banned films and plays were released, and the regime began allowing, even encouraging, nonparty members to take leadership positions in the cultural field. In 1987 the regime approved publication of a privately owned monthly magazine with an independent political stance, *Res Publica*. Its editor, Marcin Krol, said, "censorship isn't the problem it used to be. Since Gorbachev, it's obviously changed" (*Wall Street Journal* July 23, 1987). The limits on press freedom were pushed back even further with the 1989 round-table agreements, which allowed Solidarity both to publish a newspaper and to air television and radio programs.

As in the Soviet Union, some of the most delicate issues in Poland concern history, and especially Polish-Soviet relations. The two countries have begun to address some of these issues, and in 1987 agreed to establish a joint commission to look at the "blank spaces" in the history of Soviet-Polish relations. In the words of the Polish co-chair, the commission "will help to open closed pages in our history."[8] Most Poles are familiar with these issues, which include the 1920 war between Russia and Poland, the Comintern's dissolution of the Polish Communist Party in 1938, the 1939 Molotov-Ribbentrop Pact which divided Poland between Germany and the Soviet Union, the Soviet army's failure to support the Warsaw uprising against the Germans in 1944, and the most delicate and inflammatory issue of all, the wartime death or disappearance of some 15,000 captured Polish army officers in Soviet territory (many of them discovered in mass graves in the Katyn Forest).

The potentially explosive nature of these issues caused the joint commission to move slowly, and as of early 1989 there had been no public report on their findings. There were, however, hints of a Soviet reassessment of the Katyn incident, and, perhaps encouraged by these stories, the Polish government finally broke ranks on this issue and boldly declared in March 1989 that Soviet forces were responsible for the massacre. On another sensitive issue, the literary weekly *Życie Literackie* published a ten-part series on the Molotov-Ribbentrop pact and the Soviet occupation of Poland, which included the publication for the first time of the secret protocol of the pact, while acknowledging that the Soviets do not recognize the legitimacy of the document.[9]

In the realm of political reform, the Poles suddenly moved to the forefront of democratization in Eastern Europe with the signature of the round-table agreements in April 1989 and the parliamentary elections two months later. The April agreements included provisions on social policy, economic reform, and trade union pluralism (which legalized Solidarity), but the most important were those concerning political reforms. The agreement called for "radical reform of the state" and for "political pluralism" including the right to freely form political and social organizations. It also recognized the right of a political opposition to legal activity. An institutionalized role for the opposition was provided in a restructured national legislature, with 35% of the seats reserved for "nonparty" candidates in the Sejm, and freely contested elections for all 100 seats in the reconstituted Senate. The Senate had the right to veto legislation passed by the Sejm (*Trybuna Ludu*, April 7, 1989). Lech Walesa was not exaggerating when he said at the signing of this historic pact, "this is the beginning of democracy and a free Poland."

Solidarity's legal reemergence raises the question of the opposition's attitude toward Gorbachev and his reforms. Normally in Poland there was a sharp contrast in the way the regime professed to view Moscow and the way the opposition did. But in another of the paradoxes of the changes occurring in the region, the *unofficial* attitude toward the Soviet Union became rather similar to the *official* one. After initially being both pessimistic and skeptical of the Soviet reforms, the general line of argument expressed by Solidarity leaders and by dissident figures like Jacek Kuron and Adam Michnik, was that the Soviet reforms would help the Polish opposition by pressuring the Polish authorities to keep up with Gorbachev's reformism. As the Soviets conceded more, the

Polish authorities could afford to be more conciliatory, but they would only do so under pressure from the population and the opposition.[10]

But, the opposition argued, it was important that pressure from the population did not boil over and jeopardize what Gorbachev was trying to do in his country. As Walesa said in his November 1988 television debate with Miodowicz, the Soviet Union is "really implementing things that Solidarity fought for and is still fighting for. Therefore we should not obstruct perestroika."[11] Walesa, Michnik and others have recognized that there is a power struggle in the Soviet Union, and that a revolt in Poland could tip the balance in favor of the conservatives in the Kremlin. As Michnik put it, "one does not have to make revolution when there are chances for evolution. If the changes taking place at present in Poland continue, there is a real chance that totally new relationships will be established in Eastern Europe."[12]

Michnik made those remarks in May 1988, before the strikes of August and the dramatic events of 1989. The changes in Poland are occurring at a pace few people expected. There is still a long way to go before Poland emerges from its extended crisis, but the possibilities now seem greater than ever before, largely because of the presence of Gorbachev. With the emergence of a Solidarity-led government in Poland, we see the beginnings of pluralism, the erosion of the party's monopoly of power, and a major blow to communist authoritarian rule.

IV. CONCLUSIONS:
THE TRANSFORMATION OF EASTERN EUROPE

The changes occurring in the Soviet Union are momentous. There should no longer be any doubt that these changes are real and serious. This is not to say that they could not be reversed, but the longer the reforms continue and the more deeply they become entrenched, the more difficult it will become to reverse the process. If the process does continue, it portends a dramatic transformation of the socialist system in Europe.

In the East European capitals, there was a kind of wait and see attitude in the early years of the Gorbachev reforms. After all, these regimes, with far less internal support and legitimacy than the

Soviet one, had a great deal to lose by adopting these potentially destabilizing changes. At the least, such reforms could accelerate the departure from office of the old guard, which in most cases included the party leaders. At the most, decentralizing the economy and "opening" the society could lead to rising expectations and the potential ferment that often accompanies such a phenomenon. By early 1987, however, it was becoming clear that Gorbachev was going to be around for a while. Sensing the shift in the winds, the East European regimes increasingly began to accept, and then to acclaim the Soviet reforms and to begin some of their own.

After 1987, the process of reform in the Soviet Union and Eastern Europe accelerated to an almost unbelievable extent. Indeed, the changes in countries such as Hungary and Poland can no longer be considered "reforms." They are not revising the old system, but establishing completely new ones. With each new series of developments in Eastern Europe, the old "limits" to reform disappear. In 1988 most Westerners, at least, assumed that the minimal necessary requirements for a communist party state were maintenance of the "leading role of the party" (a provision in the constitutions of each of these states) and continued membership in the Warsaw Pact. With the formation of a noncommunist government in Warsaw and the dissolution of the Hungarian Socialist Workers' Party in mid-1989, the former limit was broached. Since that time, statements by Gorbachev and other Kremlin spokesmen have suggested that even Warsaw Pact membership is no longer required.

With the disappearance of these last two limits to change in Eastern Europe, and the Kremlin's acquiescence and even encouragement of these changes, one should expect even more startling developments in the region. The sudden emergence of a reformist leadership in East Germany, previously considered the most resistant to Gorbachev-style reforms, suggests that the reform process may soon spread to Czechoslovakia, Bulgaria, and perhaps eventually even to Romania. The reform process will continue to be symbiotic: change in Eastern Europe will influence further change in the Soviet Union, which will in turn rebound to Eastern Europe again.

Perhaps the main limit to change in Eastern Europe is now a practical one rather than ideological: the ability of these governments to maintain sufficient stability to avoid revolt, rebellion, or economic collapse. The changes in the region have raised popular expectations for economic improvement and political liberalization. The second of these may be easier to achieve than the first, however. If expectations are not fulfilled in some degree, there is likely to be a reemergence of social and political unrest. If this were widespread, it could well spill over into the Soviet Union, and affect, in particular, the already incendiary situation in the Baltic Republics. Political or economic chaos in Eastern Europe could, therefore, mean an end to the reform process in the Soviet Union. And without a reform leadership in Moscow, the changes in Eastern Europe are jeopardized.

Poland will play a central role in the newly emerging Europe. As in the past, the changes in Poland and the Soviet Union will continue to be interrelated. The Kremlin has looked on with equanimity, even approval, as the regime first sat down with Solidarity at the round-table negotiations, then allowed contested elections to the legislature, and then stepped aside to allow the opposition to form a government. From the Soviet point of view, the changes in Poland are more important, and more sensitive than those in Hungary, simply because of Poland's vastly greater strategic and economic importance. The changes in Poland are also probably more relevant as a model for potential reform in the Soviet Union. Poland is a Slavic nation, the largest and most populous state in Eastern Europe, and a country with a history of rebellion and unrest. If Poland can successfully manage the transition to democracy and a market-oriented economy, there is hope that the Soviet Union could do the same. If Poland fails, so will the Soviet Union.

NOTES

1. This text was updated in early 1989 and does not reflect the fall of the communist governments beside Poland's in the autumn of that year.

2. See Gorlin (1986), p. 326.

3. Professor Leonid Abalkin, Director of the Institute of Economics of the Soviet Academy of Sciences; cited in Radio Free Europe Research (hereafter RFER), Yugoslav Situation Report no. 3, May 4, 1987.

4. For example, during Yegor Ligachev's 1987 press conference in Hungary. *Pravda*, April 26, 1987.

5. Mieczysław Rakowski cited in RFER, Polish Situation Report/3, March 12, 1987.

6. *Kommunist*, September 1986; cited in Dawisha and Valdez (1987), pp. 12-13.

7. Quoted in the *Washington Post*, April 7, 1987.

8. *Pravda*, May 22, 1987, p. 4.

9. RFER Background Report no. 69, April 22, 1988.

10. See, for example, the interview with Jacek Kuron in *Harpers*, July 1987, pp. 26-27; and with Adam Michnik in the *Washington Post*, May 22, 1987.

11. RFER, Polish Situation Report/19, December 16, 1988, p. 4.

12. In an interview with the Paris daily *Liberation* (May 2, 1988); quoted in RFER, Polish Situation Report/7, May 6, 1988, p. 34.

REFERENCES

Dawisha, K., and J. Valdez. "Socialist Internationalism in Eastern Europe." *Problems of Communism* 36 (March-April 1987): pp. 1-14.

Goldman, M. "Perestroika Comes to the Soviet Union." *Harvard International Review* (November 1987): pp. 3-5, 45.

"Gorbachev: The View from Warsaw." *Harpers* (July 1987): p. 27.

Gorlin, A. "The Soviet Economy." *Current History* 85 (October 1986).

Kusin, V. "What Gorbachev's Reforms Mean for Eastern Europe." RFER *Background Report* 10 (February 5, 1987).

SOVIET REFORMS AND EAST EUROPEAN RESPONSES

Josef C. Brada

I. INTRODUCTION

The promulgation of a program of radical reform of the Soviet economic system by Mikhail Gorbachev in June 1987 signaled a major change in the attitude of the Soviet leadership toward the viability and the desirability of the orthodox system of central planning. Whether that attitude can be sustained in the long run depends on the ability of the reform to achieve the improvements in Soviet economic performance that the party demands. The reform's ability to meet these expectations will, of course, depend as much on Gorbachev's ability to implement reform measures in the face of bureaucratic obstructionism and worker apathy as on the soundness of the reform's economic logic. In Eastern Europe, particularly in the short run, before the ultimate fate of reform in the Soviet Union is determined, East European leaders will be forced to respond to this major policy change. Evidence from similar events in the past, the New Course of the 1950s, de-Stalinization, and the formation of industrial associations in the 1960s and 1970s, suggest that East European responses will not be uniform nor will they be implemented or run their course at the same pace. In those countries, such as Hungary, where the pace of reform traditionally has been viewed as being slowed by the need to avoid raising Soviet concerns, the new Soviet attitude would seem to create the possibility for more rapid and far-reaching reform. For countries such as Czechoslovakia, where meaningful reform measures have been long suppressed, the new winds from the East are more likely to have long-term political consequences as current leaderships are replaced by new ones. Events in the Soviet Union will influence the political and economic attitudes of those likely to rise to the top in the succession process. At the same time, whether or not reform can succeed in Eastern Europe in the long run will also have second-round effects on the reform movement in the Soviet Union: either by providing favorable results that will sustain the Soviet reform through inevitable reverses or by hampering the efforts of Soviet reformers by providing their opponents with anti-reform arguments based on foreign experience.

In this essay, I will examine the likely consequences of the Soviet reform measures for three East European countries, Czechoslovakia, Hungary, and Poland. Among the three there is sufficient diversity of economic circumstance and economic reform experience to permit some generalization. At the same time the three countries vary appreciably in their relationship with, attitudes toward, and dependence on the Soviet Union.

II.   CZECHOSLOVAKIA

Surely the last expectation that the Czechs and Slovaks witnessing the 1968 Soviet-led Warsaw Pact invasion of Czechoslovakia could have had was that 20 years later the visit of a Soviet head of state would give rise to popular expectations of Soviet-induced economic reform and political liberalization in Czechoslovakia. Nevertheless, Mikhail Gorbachev's visit to Czechoslovakia fueled speculation not only there, but also among western observers, that Gorbachev would act decisively and expeditiously to spread perestroika and glasnost to Czechoslovakia.

My assumption is that if Gorbachev wished to pressure the Czechoslovak leadership to undertake radical economic reforms, then he must have been convinced that the objective factors, both economic and political, that make economic reform an urgent necessity in the Soviet Union were equally present in Czechoslovakia; the chances for successful reform in Czechoslovakia must be at least as good as they are in the USSR, and the likely benefits to the Soviet Union of a successful reform in Czechoslovakia must outweigh the potential costs of a failed reform. Moreover, if Czechoslovak leaders were to acquiesce to reform, they needed to share these assessments.

A. The Need for Economic Reform in the USSR and in Czechoslovakia

The economic pressures for reform in the Soviet Union are almost entirely internal; over the past fifteen years the foreign trade sector and external events in general have had a benign influence on Soviet economic performance. The principal manifestations of the failure of the economic system in the Soviet Union is the steady decline in the rate of growth of output since the early 1960s. In part this is attributed to the exhaustion of the so-called extensive factors of growth, meaning increases in productive inputs. Gorbachev has chosen to attempt restoring growth by increasing investment in modern machinery and equipment; if productivity increases as well, then the growth in output should be sufficient to both cover the higher level of investment and provide for the increased consumption needed to sustain labor morale.

The case for economic reform in the Soviet Union is thus compelling in that the economic mechanism is seen as the cause of the economic crisis. Other cures, including the Kosygin reforms of the 1960s, the formation of associations, and the importation of Western technology and capital, have proven unsuccessful. Combined with the need to break the vicious cycle of slower growth of output leading to slower growth of capital and the imminent decline of oil prices, these past failures to restore the economy's dynamism provide a powerful impetus for radical economic reform.

Simultaneously, the political factors are favorable to reform; these factors can be viewed as a "revolution from above" that not only changes the economic system but also alters social relations and causes personnel changes in the middle levels of the government and the party. The new leadership is free to criticize the policies of the past, and, indeed, such criticism, accompanied by personnel changes in the bureaucracy, strengthens Gorbachev's position by creating a class of supporters whose welfare and success is tied to his own and whose ideals and aspirations closely reflect his own.

In 1988, in Czechoslovakia neither the economic nor the political forces favor reform so strongly as in the Soviet Union. While it is true that many of the defects that characterize Soviet economic performance can also be seen in Czechoslovakia, it is more difficult to ascribe them to the shortcomings of the system, or, at least, it is easier to defend the system by pointing to mitigating circumstances. A large part of Czechoslovakia's economic problems can be ascribed to the foreign trade sector and to the policies adopted to maintain external equilibrium.[1] The same upsurge in raw materials and energy prices that benefited the Soviet economy imposed severe losses on Czechoslovakia. Between 1970 and 1982 Czechoslovak terms of trade declined by nearly 25%. At the same time, recession in Western Europe and financial difficulties among a number of Czechoslovakia's Third World trading partners reduced possibilities for increasing exports. These external shocks were exacerbated by errors in macroeconomic policy; in 1976-80 the investment to net material product (NMP) ratio reached historic highs. As a result of this investment binge the failure to complete investment projects became a major drag on economic performance. The 1981-85 period thus was a consolidation phase in which deflationary policies were employed to restore internal and external equilibrium. The volume of investment was slashed and imports, particularly from the West, were restrained, thus enabling the authorities to reduce the backlog of incomplete investment projects and to reduce foreign indebtedness. NMP grew at only 9% over the five-year period, starting with a decline in 1981 but increasing in the later years. As a result of this consolidation, the growth of NMP has been in the 2.5-3.5% per year range since 1983, suggesting that the quantitative, if not the qualitative, ills that plagued the economy at the turn of the decade have been, and may continue to be, held at bay without a radical economic reform.

In addition to a less compelling economic rationale for economic reform in Czechoslovakia, there was also greater political resistance to the idea, particularly among the higher echelons of the party. In the Soviet Union, Gorbachev and the reformers surrounding him first assumed power and then introduced reform, in part because reform measures were a way for them to strengthen their political position and weaken that of their opponents. In Czechoslovakia, the top leadership had been in power for 20 years and a reform could do nothing but weaken their position. The raison d'être for the existing Czechoslovak leadership was the purification of the economy and of society of the effects of the 1968 reform. Thus, the leadership did not debate the philosophical question whether the only difference between Dubček and Gorbachev is, as the popular saying has it, "only twenty years." They could already see in Gorbachev's reform proposals that there really was nothing more than 20 years separating Ota Šik, the father of the 1968 reform, and Tatyana Zaslavskaya. That is, there was very little difference between the 1968 Czechoslovak reform and the measures outlined by Gorbachev at the June 1987 Plenum. Table 1 shows the similarities between these two reforms; they are striking and can be ignored neither by the Czechoslovak people nor by the leadership. Not only would such a reform fly counter to 20 years of the leadership's rhetoric, but it would also stimulate the highly dangerous connection between economic reform and the types of social and political ferment that accompanied the 1968 period.[2]

Any effort at reform in Czechoslovakia would require the participation of reform-minded members of the party and of society. Since these individuals were not then in positions of power, an economic reform would represent not a revolution "from above" as in the Soviet case, but rather one "from below," which would at best reduce the power of the ruling elite and at worst exacerbate political tensions among them. In Czechoslovakia such tensions had a unique aspect since, due to the federal nature of the state, the existence of a Czech and a Slovak Communist Party imbued changes in power within the party at the national level with many of the characteristics of a two-party political system. Thus, a change in power between pro- and anti-reformers carried with it the potential for much greater and thus potentially more destabilizing changes in the political power of the Czech and Slovak parties.

Table 1.   Comparison of Gorbachev's Reform Proposal and
the Czechoslovak Reform of 1968

Czechoslovak Reform	*Gorbachev's Proposal*

Central Planning

Detailed physical plans replaced by broad monetary aggregates: Macroeconomic policy implemented through credits and government purchases.	Detailed physical plans replaced by "stable normatives." Enterprises draw up own plans based on control figures, state orders, contracts and limits on key imports.

Enterprise Management

Enterprises run by management boards made up of workers' and customers' representatives. Boards select managers.	Workers' councils to be elected; managers and foremen to be elected by workers.

Enterprise Finance

Enterprises to maximize profits which may be used to boost pay or finance investment. Subsidies eliminated. Unprofitable enterprises will be closed. Bank credits finance operations and investments.	Enterprises maximize profits, which finance investment, and modernization (except for major projects). Workers' incomes influenced by profit. Enterprises on full self-accounting and self-financing. Bankruptcy possible for unprofitable firms.

Enterprise Operations

Enterprises free to determine input and output mix. Enterprises given greater freedom to contract with scope for choice in suppliers and customers.	Enterprises draw up own detailed plans for input and output on basis of contracts and State Orders. Greater scope for choice in purchase of inputs. Direct trade between enterprises envisioned.

Prices

Wholesale prices adjusted to reflect capital and labor inputs. Some flexibility envisioned. Retail prices adjust much more slowly.	Wholesale prices revised to better reflect production costs and to allow for price flexibility in contracting for purchase of some manufactured goods. Flexibility for above-plan contract prices; price ceilings. Retail price changes unclear.

Private Enterprise

Private and cooperative enterprise permitted in service sector.	Small scale private activity in catering and services permitted.

B. The Possibility for a Successful Economic Reform in Czechoslovakia

Even if the 1988 leadership were to have succumbed to Soviet pressure and attempted to implement a meaningful reform of the economy along the lines of Soviet reform, there are serious doubts whether such a reform could have succeeded. The first set of obstacles can be gleaned from the experiences of reform efforts in other socialist countries. These experiences show that reform is a difficult process. The conception of reform measures is by no means simple, and the admonitions of Soviet politicians and economists that the reforms of one socialist country cannot be grafted on to the mechanism of another are as true for Czechoslovakia as they are for the Soviet Union. Consequently, Czechoslovak economists and politicians must develop an understanding of the shortcomings of the present economic mechanism, reach agreement on which aspects are amenable to improvement through reform, and form a consensus on the broad outlines of a reform. Whether this conception would be a correct one is by no means clear. Moreover, the broad outlines of a reform must be given life through the drafting and enactment of legislation, decrees, and regulations needed to create the appropriate organizations and to guide their day-to-day activities. The Hungarian experience with both the 1968 reform as well as with the current wave of reforms indicates that this is a terribly difficult and time-consuming task.

Against this background it is important to bear in mind that Czechoslovakia had a poor record of implementing reform and that current reform thinking and experimentation may not be adequate to support a rapid implementation of reform measures. The first Czechoslovak effort at reform occurred in 1958, when investment decisions were decentralized to the enterprise level and enterprises were encouraged to maximize profits. The reform resulted in excessive investment and in confusion that culminated in the Czechoslovak recession of 1961-62.[3] The 1968 reform, many of whose features were gradually introduced in 1966 and 1967, clearly did not have a fair test in terms of its economic effects, but its political consequences were catastrophic.

Thus, thinking about economic reform in Czechoslovakia in 1988 had a good deal of cautionary experience on which to rely, but very little in a positive vein. Reform experimentation was characterized by ambiguity of intentions, slow implementation, signs of resistance at lower levels, and uncertainty among the leadership. The essence of these experiments was a decentralization which would leave the center concentrating on medium-term and structural strategy and enterprises on day-to-day operations. Plans to try these experiments in selected enterprises were announced for the 1986-90 five year plan period, but there was little evidence of implementation. Only if (and the *if* was strongly stressed by the leadership) these experiments proved successful would they be extended to the entire economy in the next decade. It seems reasonable to conclude that there was no meaningful reform that had the support of a sufficiently broad group of economists and politicians. Their efforts were intended more to show that the Czechoslovak leadership understood the direction in which the winds from the Kremlin were blowing and to have something to put on the table for Gorbachev's inspection than as a serious inquiry into the feasibility of a well-defined reform model.

Even if a well-conceived reform model had existed in Czechoslovakia, and even if it could have been translated into the requisite laws and regulations in a short period of time, there were additional obstacles to its success. One was Czechoslovakia's extensive trade dependence on the CMEA. In a small economy a major objective of reform must be to align domestic and world prices in order to foster the rational allocation of resources and greater specialization. Czechoslovakia, however, was so oriented to the Soviet market, both as an outlet for its exports and as the source of its imports, the reliance on world market signals was infeasible due to the low volume of Czechoslovak trade with nonsocialist countries. Reliance on world prices would also have been counterproductive since it would have interfered with Czechoslovak efforts to align the economy to the needs of the Soviet Union.

More important, reform required a serious commitment from the leadership. If the leadership does not have a stake in the success of the reform then, as is the case in Bulgaria and Poland, we have only the form but not the substance of a new economic mechanism. As in the Bulgarian case, one set of institutional changes may follow another with little time for implementation and, as in the Polish case, major economic and financial imbalances may simply prevent decentralization and market forces from functioning in the face of inflation and the breakdown of normal producer-consumer relations. In 1988 such an interest in reform was not yet evident in Czechoslovakia.

C. Is Economic Reform Worth the Risk?
The View from the Kremlin

In view of the resistance and delays that Gorbachev's reform efforts are facing in the Soviet Union, there is no one better aware than he that implementing a reform is a time-consuming, difficult and, possibly, an ultimately unsuccessful effort. Consequently, before he chose to pressure the leadership in Prague to follow the Soviet reform efforts, he was likely to weigh the potential costs and benefits carefully. To understand these it is necessary to first recognize that reform of the economic mechanism is but one of the strategies being used to reverse the long-term decline in the growth rate of the Soviet economy. The other strategy involves an increase in investment directed primarily toward "leading edge" sectors such as machine tools, production automation, electronics, chemicals, and energy.

Technological progress is to be spurred by retooling existing plants with more sophisticated machinery and by introducing new production technologies. Since these ambitious demands for new machinery and technology cannot be met by the domestic machine-tool sector, the Soviets had also chosen to strengthen CMEA integration. Gorbachev called for the closer coordination of five-year plans of the member countries, for joint efforts in research and development, and for long-term bilateral specialization agreements between the Soviet Union and the East European countries.

These developments were then viewed with satisfaction in Prague, since Czechoslovakia had been a long-standing and staunch supporter of CMEA integration. Indeed, the Czechoslovak leadership viewed CMEA integration and Gorbachev's economic strategy as an opportunity to modernize Czechoslovak industry and to place Czechoslovakia at the technological apex of CMEA. This was because Czechoslovakia had long followed an industrial policy aimed at developing nuclear energy, electronics, cybernetics, instrumentation, machine building, and chemicals with a view to serving the needs of the Soviet market, often in cooperation with

Soviet ministries, research institutes, and enterprises. With the possible exception of Bulgaria, Czechoslovakia's economy was more closely integrated into the Soviet economy than that of any other East European nation. Gorbachev's economic strategy focused precisely on those areas where Czechoslovak industrial policy had been seeking to create productive capacities, and thus it represented an important opportunity for Czechoslovakia to develop exports in these sectors. Conversely, of course, despite the size difference between the two economies, Czechoslovakia's exports of machinery and equipment were a significant component of Soviet investment plans.

An economic reform that could revitalize Czechoslovak industry and raise its technological level would obviously be a boost to the Soviet Union. Such benefits, however, are long term, since a reform is unlikely to make rapid improvements in technology, and, given the Hungarian experience, may not occur in heavy industry, the sector that is of greatest interest to the Soviet Union. The Soviets need better machinery during the current five-year plan if Gorbachev's strategy is to prove successful. Thus, their economic strategy imposes on their policy toward Czechoslovakia greater considerations for the short run. Here, the policy that Gorbachev generally urged upon his CMEA allies, to promote greater discipline, to speed modernization, and to show greater vigor in pursuing CMEA integration, was much more palatable to the Czechoslovak leadership.

A failed reform that created chaos in the Czechoslovak economy would be very costly to the Soviet Union. It would obviously strengthen anti-reform elements within the Soviet Union. To the extent that Czechoslovakia became less able to meet its export commitments to the Soviet Union, the strategy of modernizing and retooling Soviet industry would be imperiled; by how much is uncertain, but, given the general tightness of the current Soviet five-year plan, any setback could be a decisive one. If the Czechoslovak reform were to lead to political chaos, Czechoslovakia would become a liability to the Soviet Union politically as well. Gorbachev has followed an aggressive policy of détente, in part to increase Soviet-Western trade prospects and in part to reduce the defense burden on the Soviet economy. Should the Soviet Union be forced to intervene in Czechoslovakia again, these overtures to the West would be severely compromised.

D. The Long-Term View

I have argued here that so long as the existing leadership remained in power in Czechoslovakia there was neither a powerful incentive for the Soviet Union to press reform upon the country, nor any likelihood that the leadership would take up the issue of reform with any great vigor. The resignation of Gustav Husak as General Secretary of the Party and his replacement by Miloš Jakeš could not provide the type of leadership change that would lead to reform since Jakeš' appointment changed neither the ideological orientation of, nor the division of power among, the remaining leaders. Once the current leadership was forced to leave the scene, possibilities for reform would come to the fore with new leaders. It is in this succession that the prospects for economic reform in Czechoslovakia will be determined. Since such a succession process already began by the end of the 1980s, we, and the Czechs and Slovaks, will know more about the pace and success of reform in the Soviet Union, and it is this knowledge that will shape developments in Czechoslovakia.

III. HUNGARY

In Hungary talk of reform dominates economic and political discussions. Nevertheless, without a change in political leadership, Hungary could not probe the outer limits of Gorbachev's vision of reformed socialism due to the country's economic and political situation and to the role that past and potential reforms have played and can play in improving that situation.

A. Recent Reforms

Despite setbacks and difficulties facing reformers, waves of reform continue to wash over the Hungarian economic landscape. In the late 1970s, a price reform lowering consumer goods subsidies, but also reducing enterprise taxes, and making prices more reflective of those achieved in foreign trade was implemented, as were a number of tax, foreign trade and organizational measures, the most significant of which, and surely the most imitated, was the consolidation of branch industrial ministries into a single

Ministry of Industry.[4] In the early 1980s, despite some setbacks for reformers, further changes were introduced. In 1982, small private and cooperative enterprises were legalized. These could operate both outside the socialized sector, utilizing their own means of production, or within the socialized sector, using the facilities of state owned enterprises under contractual arrangements.[5] A new wage system evolved, one that linked wages to enterprise performance. Partly at the behest of the International Monetary Fund (IMF), enterprise subsidies were reduced. Worker self-management was strengthened in 1985, with workers and workers' councils given the right to select managers; simultaneously, enterprise autonomy was increased. On the financial front, bankruptcy became a possibility and a banking reform had the National Bank serving as a central bank, while lending to enterprises devolved to five new commercial banks.

Despite these reform measures, one sensed both a reluctance to pursue reform as vigorously as in the past, the suspicion that reforms increasingly appeared to deal with issues peripheral to Hungary's fundamental economic problems and that they were intended more to affect the style rather than the substance of economic processes. This loss in the vigor of reform measures may have stemmed from the fact that while reform measures may have achieved notable successes in the early years of the New Economic Mechanism (NEM), particularly in eliminating disequilibria in a number of consumer goods markets, by the late 1970s and early 1980s reforms may have become economically disfunctional. The evidence for this lies in an examination of Hungary's macroeconomic performance, in the formulation and implementation of policy, and in the way in which the reforms transform macroeconomic outcomes in the lives of Hungarian workers and consumers.

B.   Economic Outcomes

Table 2 presents the basic data on Hungary's macroeconomic performance for the past decade. Economic growth has slowed sharply from the early 1970s largely due to domestic deflation that was intended to reequilibrate the hard-currency balance of payments by reducing imports. Investment has borne the brunt of the deflation, falling every year since 1979. The resources freed up

Table 2. Hungarian Economic Performance, 1977-1986
(in % per year)

Growth of Real:	1977	1978	1979	1980	1981	1982	1983	1984	1985	1986
Net Material Product:	7.1	4.0	1.2	-0.9	2.5	2.6	0.3	2.5	-1.4	0.5
Gross Investment:	12.1	4.8	0.7	-5.8	-4.3	-1.6	-3.4	-3.7	-3.6	0.0
Incomes:	4.9	2.9	-0.2	0.4	2.9	0.9	1.1	1.1	1.9	

Source: United Nations Economic Commission for Europe. *Economic Survey of Europe in 1986-1987* (New York: United Nations, 1987).

by reducing investment were apportioned in part to protect the standard of living and in part to reduce Hungary's external debt. Neither of these objectives has been achieved with notable success. Living standards have stagnated at best, and the picture is even less encouraging than that suggested by the data in Table 2 if one accepts the possibility that the official measure of inflation may understate the real rate by as much as 2 to 3 percentage points. Moreover, this sacrifice on the part of Hungarian workers has yielded little improvement on the foreign front. The reduction in net convertible currency debt for the 1980-85 period was less than half a billion dollars and in gross terms the debt rose to $11.76 billion by the end of 1985. Because a large part of the hard-currency surplus achieved during the 1980-85 period was achieved by reducing imports, Hungary's debt-service ratio now stands at 49%.

Hungary's macroeconomic performance reflects the operation of a vicious deflationary spiral. Cuts in domestic absorption have short-term effects but cannot generate a long-term hard-currency surplus, and consequently lead policy makers to impose more deflation, which shrinks all economic activity, including exports, even more, thus further reducing living standards. The current policy stance for the remainder of the 1980s calls for more deflation and a further fall in living standards while, in addition, raising the possibility of significant unemployment.

C.   Interactions between the Macroeconomy and the Reform

How reforms are viewed by politicians depends to a large extent on how such reforms appear to be able to resolve economic and political problems. Workers and consumers evaluate reforms not so much in terms of abstract economic outcomes but rather in terms of the way in which such outcomes are translated into their experiences as workers and consumers. On both counts Hungarian reform measures are open to criticism.

From the standpoint of politicians, reform measures have hampered both the implementation and the formulation of macroeconomic policy, largely because the reliance on indirect central direction coupled with case-by-case exceptions for individual enterprises and sectors leaves the authorities with little leverage to achieve their macroeconomic objectives. Exports to hard-currency markets have stagnated largely because the decision to undertake such exports has devolved to the producer. Indirect tools for stimulating hard-currency exports have been both ineffective and misapplied.[6]

Industrial restructuring, a key objective of the authorities, has also been difficult to achieve under the reform. Under Hungarian conditions of enterprise-center bargaining, deflation does not kill off weak and inefficient producers. Rather, the weak receive subsidies at the expense of the strong, and both languish indefinitely.[7] This stretches out the length of the period of credit austerity required to achieve a restructuring and clearly hampers the development of progressive sectors. Moreover, so long as declining sectors continue in existence through deflationary periods, they will again flourish or at least emerge as competitors for resources when the deflationary period is over. The decision to eliminate branch ministries in favor of one Ministry of Industry, made for the laudable (but probably unrealized) objective of freeing enterprises from central interference, also expanded the scope of "departmentalism," the tendency of a ministry to protect inefficient firms at the expense of profitable ones. With one ministry overseeing all firms, intersectoral, in addition to intrasectoral, movements of resources are encouraged. This of course hampers structural adjustment more than does the reallocation of profits from successful firms to unsuccessful ones within one sector of industry as was the case under the old system of branch ministries. Finally, structural change requires long-term considerations of profitability and market conditions. Whether such considerations can be made in an environment where the rules of the game are constantly being altered by new reforms is doubtful since rational investment decisions need to be based on expectations of profits earned over the life of the investment.

The reforms also hamper the fight against inflation. To base workers' wages on enterprise performance is logical at the microeconomic level since such a direct relationship between results and rewards provides appropriate incentives for high productivity. The implications of such a mechanism for the labor market, however, are problematic, since a firm would not ordinarily raise wages unless it sought to attract more workers or unless it needed to retain workers leaving for higher paying jobs elsewhere. There is no reason to believe that all profitable firms fall into either of these categories, particularly under a system where worker inputs into managerial decisions are being strengthened and pressures for employment expansion are consequently weakening. As a result, the reformed wage system creates a secular upward drift in wages as well as a, possibly unjustified, dispersion of wages between profitable and unprofitable firms.[8]

These negative aspects of the existing mechanism are recognized by both pro- and anti-reform elements. The pro-reform argument is that these faults are due to the compromises imposed on the implementation of reform measures. The action needed to unleash the "hidden reserves" and resolve the macroeconomic impasse is a deeper, more comprehensive reform. This argument has given rise to a sophisticated Hungarian literature on the design and functioning of the economic mechanism. In contrast, the debate over macroeconomic policy has neither attracted the same intellectual following nor approached the level of sophistication as the reform debate. The focus on reforms implies macroeconomic policy has been slighted, if not effectively ignored, and is consequently viewed by politicians and economists as less important than reform. Whether or not more energy needs to be expended on developing a macroeconomic policy as imaginative and bold as Hungarian proposals for reform is a question that should not have to be asked. Government guidance of economic activity by indirect and aggregate economic levers such as monetary and fiscal policy is the basic premise of the Hungarian reform. Nonetheless, no compelling work has been produced by Hungarian economists demonstrating that monetary and fiscal aggregates can actually be controlled by the government or that changes in these aggregates have the impact on enterprises and households attributed to them. These instruments to target linkages are prerequisites for the effective functioning of a reformed economy.

Workers' perceptions of the effects of reform in the current situation are unlikely to be any more favorable than those of the leadership. Macroeconomic deflation and price hikes impose obvious costs on workers and consumers, but the design of the economic system also influences how the public views the magnitude and equity of these costs. In this regard the reform measures have a number of undesirable features. By making workers' incomes dependent on the economic performance of their enterprises while simultaneously increasing the possibility of lower wages, unemployment, and bankruptcy because of the government's deflationary policy, the reform sharply increases risks faced by workers without being able to provide any compensating benefits. The size of the pie is fixed, but workers are now forced to scramble to retain their share. Moreover, enterprises, and workers who must increasingly bear managerial responsibility, are being asked to accept greater independence and to undertake riskier strategies at a time when enterprise success and survival are most problematic. To many Hungarian workers it must be evident that, through no fault of their own, their enterprises are not economically viable; their wages are likely to fall and their jobs may disappear. Increased responsibility and self-determination are not viable means for improving their lot in the current period of investment cutbacks; rather, such changes are the means of imposing on these workers the social costs of past mistakes made by others.

Under present conditions, the reform translates efforts to strengthen incentives during a period of austerity into an increasingly unequal distribution of income. As Table 2 shows, incomes have stagnated. A booming second economy and opportunities for certain workers to increase income in the socialist sector through enterprise contract work and greater wage differentiation according to enterprise performance, have widened income differentials. If consumer goods production and incomes were increasing, such trends might be tolerable because consumers could relate the increasingly unequal distribution of income to incentives that increase the supply of goods. If consumers merely see the low-priced goods and services of the socialized sector replaced by the same quantity of high-priced privately produced goods, the resulting incomes of private producers will not be seen in the same favorable light. By appearing to foster among the population an increasingly open competition for shares of a fixed national income, the government runs the risk that the reform will be viewed as a repudiation of social justice by the leadership.

The growing dispersion of incomes is exacerbated by the effects of inflation in two ways. First, there are goods, such as housing, that are distributed bureaucratically and in such a way as to favor upper income groups.[9] Continuing inflation raises the implicit prices of such goods and, therefore, increases apace the benefits to the subsidized recipients. In addition, it appears that, contrary to popular expectations, the effects of the second economy and of the marketization of the economic system through reform have not diminished the differentials caused by such nonmarket allocations; rather they appear to have strengthened them.

Workers can respond to these unfavorable outcomes of the reform process in two ways, neither of which bodes well for social harmony or political stability. On the one hand they can come to view economic outcomes, such as their wages and jobs, as random events beyond their control. This will engender alienation, feelings of social and economic powerlessness, risk-avoidance, and apathy. Alternatively, workers can react militantly, either to reject the freedoms and responsibilities proffered by the reforms or to seek social institutions that will give them the political power commensurate with their new economic responsibilities.

D.   Is Poland the Future of Hungary?

Clearly the economic and social scene in Hungary has been bleak for the past decade, and in quantitative terms the situation is approaching that which precipitated the Polish crisis. There are also some qualitative similarities. First, there are tensions over income distribution. In both countries workers and consumers are forced to compete for their share of fixed or shrinking incomes and consumer goods. Second, the authorities do not have the ability to exercise control over the economic variables that are the keys to reversing the economic situation.

The retirement of Janos Kadar, his replacement by Karoly Grosz and the elevation of reformers to important policymaking posts must be seen as positive developments. Nevertheless, it is unlikely that the new leadership can throw off its ties to the past in the way that Gorbachev has cast aside the Brezhnev era. Indeed, a good deal of the new leadership's legitimacy rests precisely on maintaining continuity with Kadar's political legacy. To what extent it will be possible to hew to Kadar's policy of domestic political tolerance while moving away from his cautious attitude toward economic reform remains to be seen. Perhaps the most likely course for the new regime will be to continue both threads of Kadar's policy, with relatively minor shifts toward more economic reform and some reduction of political tolerance for dissenters.

There are also important differences between Hungary and Poland as well. Comisso and Marer (1986), for example, point to the collegial decision making process of the Hungarian Socialist Workers' Party (HSWP), and the reluctance of party officials to use outside groups to influence decision making.[10] While this is an important difference between Hungary and Poland, where such efforts to mobilize public support were made, it is worth noting that collegiality is easier to impose when party power is growing. However, if the party's power or legitimacy is diminishing, then party leaders, like Hungarian workers, must strive to retain their share of a shrinking pie. Further reform is likely to reduce such power, or at least the perception of power, among those used to wielding it in a particular way. Legitimacy, too, may be a victim of events. It has been based either on the ability to deliver economic performance, or, failing that, at least giving the appearance of making an effort to provide it by being at the forefront of economic reform in the socialist camp. When the economic performance is not forthcoming and when the reforms are matched by other countries, particularly by the Soviet Union, then little is left. To date there appear to be no mass organizations that do anything more than reflect party, rather than member, interests. But, when workers are forced to take interest in, and responsibility for, enterprise performance, then the desire to utilize mass organizations to articulate group interests intensifies. Economic self-interest will induce workers to utilize political channels to influence the macroeconomic environment within which enterprise performance is determined.

Most critically, gradual reform can no longer be used as a panacea. It cannot cure Hungary's macroeconomic problems, nor can it have a significant impact on the Hungarian economy unless macroeconomic problems are resolved. Moreover, those policies that can resolve Hungary's macroeconomic woes are not likely to come out of the incrementalist consensual decision making process that Comisso and Marer describe. Hungarian leaders may believe that they are pursuing a policy of Thatcherism that will eventually lead to a leaner, more dynamic, and more prosperous economy. In reality their macroeconomic policies as well as the reform measures being introduced are inadequate to the task, and Hungary's policies reflect the stop-go policies followed by Britain for much of the postwar period. The structural stagnation and economic decline that Britain suffered for following these policies may be the best outcome that can be hoped for in the case of Hungary.

IV. POLAND

To understand the role that reforms can play in Poland's recovery from its current economic and political situation, it is necessary to have an understanding of the sources of that crisis. There is a popular view that the crisis is attributable to Poland's economic system. From that premise it follows that reform of the system is, if not a complete solution to Poland's difficulties, as some would claim, then at least a prerequisite for recovery.[11] The alternative view, which is partially spelled out in my discussion above of the difficulties facing Hungary, is that the crisis was a combination of poor macroeconomic policy, a loss of control over economic aggregates (particularly investment and incomes) and an effort to solve economic problems by forcing the population to bear the burden of bad policy decisions without providing for popular input into the policy. These difficulties were caused by party-government and intra-party strife as well as by the breakdown of the "social fabric," as workers recognize the duplicity and cynicism behind economic policy.[12] The question to be addressed is whether, given the complex nature of the causes of the crisis and the severe dislocation of Polish society and of the economy, economic reforms can be expected to play an important role in aiding the Polish economy's recovery.

A.   The Polish Reforms

The Polish reform of February 1982 resembled the Hungarian NEM, partly because of the Poles' admiration for and belief in the efficacy of the NEM, partly because they perceived parallels between Hungary's emergence from 1956 and Poland's need to emerge from its own crisis, and partly because the NEM appeared to be the only logical way to reform.[13] The architects of the Polish reform hoped that it would stimulate economic growth and promote social and political stability by reviving individual and enterprise initiative and by involving workers in the management of enterprises. Further, they believed it would facilitate a major restructuring of the Polish economy without the need for excessive central management.

At the microeconomic level, the major reform measure was the introduction of the 3-S program: self-direction, self-finance, and self-management. Enterprises were to be free to decide their input and output levels, influenced only by government purchases, taxes, and subsidies in addition to market signals. Self-financing implied that enterprise profits would influence both workers' wages and investment possibilities. Self-management established workers' rights to influence major enterprise decisions directly or, in enterprises with more than 300 workers, through a workers' council.

After a major price increase in 1982, price flexibility was to provide microefficiency while financial discipline would be imposed on enterprises by tight credit policies and by the threat of bankruptcy. Macroeconomic plans were to become more indicative rather than directive and the government's objectives were to be achieved increasingly through indirect levers and less through direct controls. Under the conditions prevailing in Poland in 1982, it was not expected that all reform measures could be introduced in full force at the outset. Implementation would, in part, depend on the progress made in economic and social normalization. Thus, for example, the Tenth Party Congress called for going on to the second stage of the reform where equilibrium would be achieved, prices would be realigned, self-financing strictly observed, subsidies curbed, and work discipline strengthened. Such a list of further objectives does not speak well for results already achieved.

The reform package contained some elements of dubious value under the best of circumstances. Under the chaotic conditions prevailing in the Polish economy of the 1980s, many reform measures are nugatory at best and counterproductive at worst. Self-direction has not progressed very far, largely because the center continues to ration critical commodities and imports while other commodities are simply not available in sufficient quantities to meet the demand at existing prices. Similarly, self-financing has not been an important factor in enterprise operations since, as in Hungary, profits are redistributed from profitable to unprofitable firms. Moreover, it is doubtful that state enterprises can be expected to operate on a hard budget constraint so long as the government continues to fuel inflation through its own deficits.[14] Nor have credit policies proven useful. Some enterprises hardly need to invest because of excess capacity while others have an interest-inelastic demand for funds. In any case, with prices of many consumer goods and important raw materials frozen, it would be counterproductive to take self-financing provisions seriously. Many of the firms that would go bankrupt are producing the goods in greatest demand and of greatest use to the economy.

As in the case of Hungary, microeconomic measures are being deployed to deal with what is essentially a macroeconomic problem. There is no doubt that improved rationality in the allocation of resources would contribute to a better functioning of the Polish economy. It would be foolhardy, however, to believe that any program of partial measures toward marketization could in fact achieve a better allocation of resources. Both experience and economic theory suggest precisely the opposite. The experience of market economies that have suffered through double-digit inflation, as in Poland today, suggests that in such circumstances markets generate a great deal of disfunctional behavior: hoarding, disinvestment, the breakdown of financial discipline over firms, and financial disintermediation. The notion that partial marketization of the economy, however extensive, should improve economic rationality is counter to the findings of the theory of the second best which suggests that if some prices remain distorted, then eliminating distortions in other prices will in fact worsen the allocation of resources.

B.   Economic Objectives of the Reform

A useful way to think about the desirability of reform in Poland is to consider the economic objectives that Polish policy makers are seeking and to explore the extent to which these objectives can be met by means of a market-oriented reform.

The primary object in Poland must be to restore the economy to its full production level and thus to improve the efficiency with which inputs are utilized. The first, and most important, aspect of this issue is that productive resources remain un- or underutilized and the economy therefore produces well inside its production possibility frontier. Capital is unutilized because factories cannot be operated at full capacity (or at all) due to shortages of imported or domestically produced inputs. Labor is underutilized because the need to maintain full employment prevents redundant employees from being fired. So long as inflation continues apace and so long as the supply of inputs, particularly imported ones, remains uncertain, enterprises will have a very inelastic demand for inputs. Therefore, an effort to allocate inputs by means of the market would lead to sharp inflationary pressures without, in the case of imported inputs, leading to any appreciable increase in supply. A more effective response would be to centrally allocate imported and perhaps other key inputs to break as many domestic-supply bottlenecks as possible. In this way, inflationary pressures would be reduced both by avoiding cost-push inflation and by increasing domestic output.

Instead of addressing this form of allocative efficiency, which does represent a means of tapping "hidden reserves," the reform instead focuses primarily on the efficient allocation of resources among competing uses. This is an issue that is relevant only to an economy where resources are fully utilized but one without meaning for an economy with 20-30% excess capacity. Nevertheless, some Polish economists argue that unless "real" bankruptcy and unemployment can be brought about, mainly by strengthening the reform, then the economic crisis will not be resolved. Such a policy again casts the reform as a deflationary tool. Admittedly, some inputs would be shifted from bankrupt firms to profitable ones, and unemployment would reduce the wage bill, but it is unlikely that any consequent gains in efficiency could offset the lost output of the bankrupt firms and their unemployed labor force.

It is argued by proponents of reform that innovation and increased exports can be promoted by a more vigorous application of marketization. The Hungarian experience suggests otherwise. Increasing the pace of innovation requires being able to direct resources to priority sectors and creating enterprise-level incentives for innovation. But a system that has tied wages to net enterprise production and that maintains double-digit inflation has no positive incentives to offer innovators. Similarly a disequilibrium exchange rate, often set at the level of the firm, provides little incentive for increasing efforts to export since the profitability of export activities will invariably be limited by adjustments in the exchange rate.

In sum, reform measures are not suited to restoring the economy to a full employment level of production unless inflationary pressures are first brought under control. The large monetary overhang (not eliminated by the 1982 price increases), the existing rules for wage formation, and the government's deficits are the primary sources of inflation. None of these problems are addressed by the reform measures. The market is a powerful and rational economic mechanism. At the same time it is a fragile one, likely to produce unexpected and undesirable outcomes in the wrong environment. Whether Poland's leaders can address the macroeconomic issues, a prerequisite for any reform to bear beneficial results, is a question of whether they have the political will and power to do so.

C.   The Politics of Polish Macroeconomic Policy

A number of political analysts have drawn parallels between the military regimes of Latin America and the Jaruzelski government. This parallel can be fruitfully extended to macroeconomic policy formation. Like many Latin American countries, Poland is burdened by problems of external liquidity and crushing foreign debts. More important, the Polish government, like its Latin American counterparts, is running large budget deficits that are largely the result of subsidies to support the operation of inefficient industries and the consumption of industrial workers. The result of this is inflation. In Latin America, neither military nor civilian regimes have had the will or the power to eliminate the government deficit and, thus, to halt inflation. They fear a politically active, organized, and volatile urban work force that is able to bargain for nominal wage increases often in excess of the rate of inflation. Consequently, inflation is both uncontrolled and unable to lower the excessive real wage costs of the industrial sector and the government bureaucracy.

That the Polish economy labored under a similar set of circumstances was evident to earlier regimes, but their efforts to deal with the issue by means of increases in the price of food failed, largely through the resistance of industrial workers. In this regard it is instructive to recall that Solidarity's economic program was largely Peronist. Workers, with good justification, sought co-responsibility neither for the state of the economy nor for austerity; rather they sought to protect their relative position in the wage hierarchy.[15] In this they have largely succeeded. Despite the increase in prices of 1982 and the inflation of the 1980s, the relative position of industrial workers in the income hierarchy appears not to have changed. For example, all wages in 1987 were planned to increase by 15.7%, but in the socialist sector they were to increase by 30%. With prices of many consumer staples controlled and industrial prices tied to costs, the government's budget has been in deficit since 1980, adding fuel to the inflation. Moreover, despite the run-up in prices, there remains a large monetary overhang that has not been eliminated. It has been conservatively estimated that it would take an increase in prices of 30-50% over and above the "normal" rate of inflation to eliminate this overhang.

The results of the recent referendum on the pace of the reform indicate that workers are no more willing now than they were earlier to accept price increases sufficient to approach a level of macroeconomic equilibrium necessary for the functioning of a reformed economy. Consequently, the future of reform in Poland rests on the possibility that a more gradual rate of inflation can eliminate the monetary overhang, restore some measure of equilibrium, and pave the way for the operation of a reformed economic system. In one sense, the Jaruzelski regime has an important advantage over its predecessors: inflation, which was unacceptable in the past, is now an accepted fact of economic life. Thus, the question is simply whether or not a "slower" rate of inflation can reestablish macroeconomic equilibrium; if so, then the Polish reform movement can be revived—if not, reform will be meaningless.

The experience of Latin America suggests that Poland will not be able to inflate its way to equilibrium. An economic obstacle is the price system: a cost-plus system for industrial goods coupled with a fixed-price system for many strategic goods, especially imports. Government subsidies, and therefore deficits, will continue, generating high rates of inflation as a result of new money creation. It is not enough for the government to limit increases in real consumption, which appears more easily achieved than limiting real wages. Limits on consumption, but not on wages, merely exacerbate the monetary overhang and undermine the feasibility of reform. Moreover, by continuing with a policy of long-term inflation, the government runs two risks. The first is that it will generate inflationary expectations that will fundamentally alter attitudes toward saving, work, and asset holding. Second, to the extent that the reform has given enterprises the incentives and opportunity to react to their environment, under continued high rates of inflation these responses can become irrational and disfunctional. As a result the prospects for an effective reform must be seen as slim at best.

V. CONCLUSION

The situations of the three countries analyzed are at once similar and different. The similarity lies in the fact that all three have a historic opportunity to reform their economic system and in all three the need for extensive reform exists. Moreover, in all three countries the Communist party represented the greatest stumbling block to reform, but for very different reasons. In Czechoslovakia, the party's lack of legitimacy and its self-imposed ties to the post-1968 repression served as a political obstacle to any meaningful reform. Indeed, it could be argued that reform and the continuation in power, if not of the Communist party itself, then at least of its upper- and middle-level members, were totally incompatible. In Hungary and Poland on the other hand the party was willing, even eager, to reform. However, the economic situation in these countries was such that economic reforms conceived within a framework acceptable to the party, that is a framework of predominant social ownership, could not improve the economic situation. Indeed, as I have argued here, such reforms would, in fact, have created greater resistance to the reform program and eroded the legitimacy of the Communist party. Thus neither reform nor refusal to reform could help the Communist parties in these countries to improve economic performance or to increase their legitimacy.

Zvi Gitelman has written that "the arrival of Mikhail Gorbachev as the Soviet leader and his talk of radical reform at the Twenty-Seventh Party Congress may create a more favorable external environment for reform than at any time in the past two decades." [16] This is admittedly true, but as I have argued here, Gorbachev's seeds of reform are likely to fall on barren ground. Evidently revolution has been easier to spread than reform.

ACKNOWLEDGMENTS

This paper extends and updates Brada (1987, 1988) and it benefited from discussions following presentations at the Wilson Center Conference on Economic Dilemmas of Eastern Europe, the Wichita State University Conference on New Dimensions of the International Economy and Its Impact on Poland, and the Eleventh Hungarian-American Economists' Round Table. I am indebted to Jan Svejnar, Paul Marer, Robert Campbell, Ed A. Hewett, and David Kemme for comments and suggestions and to Ellen Comisso for a particularly helpful and detailed critique of a previous draft. I also acknowledge the financial support of the National Council for Soviet and East European Research.

NOTES

1. See, for example, Dýba and Kupka (1984) and Šujan (1982).
2. One might try to pass this similarity off by arguing that there is, after all, only one way in which to reform a planned economy, but this is simply not so. See Boot (1987).
3. See Brada (1971).
4. See Hare (1983) and Comisso and Marer (1986).
5. Varga (1988) describes such ventures and their consequences.
6. Balassa (1986) and (1988).
7. The record government deficit in 1986 comes in large part from subsidies to inefficient sectors that are suffering from the effects of deflationary policies.
8. The high marginal tax rates for large wage increases are a tacit recognition of this problem.

9. Daniel (1985) deals with the case of housing.
10. Comisso and Marer (1986), pp. 258-271.
11. This view has been put forward by Fallenbuchl (1984) and Hunter (1986).
12. These points are argued in Montias (1982) and Poznanski (1986).
13. Gitelman (1987).
14. The firing of Stanislaw Niekarz from the Ministry of Finance is a reflection of dissatisfaction over the deficits although the deficits are clearly beyond the control of the Ministry.
15. Blazyca (1985). The distinction between relative wages and real wages is, of course, critical.
16. Gitelman (1987), p. 147.

REFERENCES

Balassa, B. "The 'New Growth Path' in Hungary." *The Hungarian Economy in the 1980s: Reforming the System and Adjusting to External Shocks*, edited by J.C. Brada and I. Dobozi. Greenwich, CT: JAI Press, 1988.

_____. "Adjustment Policies in Socialist and Private Market Economics." *Journal of Comparative Economics* 10 (June 1986): pp. 138-159.

Blazyca, G. "The Polish Economy under Martial Law—A Dissenting View." *Soviet Studies* 37 (July 1985): pp. 428-436.

Boot, P. "Incentive Systems and Unemployment: The East European Experience." *Comparative Economic Studies* 29 (Spring 1987): pp. 37-62.

Brada, J.C. "Is Hungary the Future of Poland or is Poland the Future of Hungary?" *Eastern European Politics and Societies* 2 (Fall 1988): pp. 466-483.

_____. "Sartor Resartus? Gorbachev and Prospects for Economic Reform in Czechoslovakia." *Harvard International Review* 10 (November 1987): pp. 18-21.

_____. "The Czechoslovak Economic Recession, 1962-1965: Comment." *Soviet Studies* 23 (January 1971): pp. 402-405.

Comisso, E., and P. Marer. "The Economics and Politics of Reform in Hungary." *Power, Purpose, and Collective Choice*, edited by E. Comisso and L. D'Andrea Tyson. Ithaca and London: Cornell University Press, 1986.

Daniel, Z. "The Effect of Housing Allocation of Social Inequality in Hungary." *Journal of Comparative Economics* 9 (December 1985): pp. 391-409.

Dýba, K., and V. Kupka. "Prízpu beni československé economiky vnejším narazum." *Politická ekonomie* 32 (1984): pp. 43-55. [Published in English translation in *Soviet and Eastern European Foreign Trade* 23 (Spring 1987): pp. 6-30.]

Fallenbuchl, Z. "The Polish Economy Under Martial Law." *Soviet Studies* 36 (October 1984).

Gitelman, Z. "Is Hungary the Future of Poland?" *Eastern European Politics and Societies* 1 (Winter 1987): pp. 135-159.

Gomulka, S., and J. Rostowski. "The Reformed Polish Economic System 1982-1983." *Soviet Studies* 36 (July 1984): pp. 386-405.

Hare, P.G. "The Beginnings of Institutional Reform in Hungary." *Soviet Studies* 35 (July 1983): pp. 313-330.

Hunter, R. "The Management Perspective on Poland's Economic Crisis and Recent Attempts at Reform." *The Polish Review* 31 (1986): pp. 299-313.

Montias, J.M. "Poland: Roots of the Economic Crisis." *ACES Bulletin* 24 (Fall 1982): pp. 1-20.

Poznanski, K. "Economic Adjustment and Political Forces: Poland since 1970." *International Organization* 40 (Spring 1986): pp. 455-488.

Šujan, I. "Analyza podielov jednotlivých faktorov na spomaleni tempa rastu československej ekonomiky v rokoch 1975-1980 (simulacná analyza s pouzitim ekonomitréckeho modelú)." *Politicka ekonomie* 30 (1982): pp. 595-610. [Published in English translation in *Soviet and Eastern European Foreign Trade* 23 (Spring 1987): pp. 31-53.]

Varga, G. "The Role of Small Ventures in the Hungarian Economy." In *The Hungarian Economy in the 1980's: Reforming the System and Adjusting to External Shocks,* edited by J.C. Brada and I. Dobozi. Greenwich, CT: JAI Press, 1988.

POLAND'S REFORM, RENEWAL, AND RECOVERY:

OPTIONS FOR U.S. POLICY

Jean F. Boone and John P. Hardt

I. OVERVIEW

The economic collapse experienced by Poland in 1979-81, originating in the overaccumulation of debt and resulting in a precipitous fall in output (25% in 1981-82), was unprecedented among both socialist and Western economies. Yet Poland's economic potential as measured by resource endowment, labor skills, and capital formation would suggest that the country could achieve a much higher level of output under a favorable policy environment. By 1987, Poland had not demonstrated the willingness or ability to translate this potential into progress by putting new policies effectively into practice. Since 1986, a confluence of developments has led to changes in the environment which provide opportunities previously unavailable for Poland's economic reform, political renewal, and reentry into the world economy. This chapter considers the evolution of the Polish program for economic reform and renewal, the consensus that began to emerge in 1986-1987 for implementation of reform, and the opportunities for interaction among the various influential actors that could contribute to Polish recovery.

These major actors—the Polish state (as represented by Jaruzelski), Polish society (whose influential spokesmen include Cardinal Glemp, Lech Walesa, and the Sejm), the international financial community (the International Monetary Fund, World Bank, Paris Club, and Western commercial banks), the United States, and the Soviet Union—all agree on the need for Poland's reform and recovery and on the general blueprint for moving toward these goals. Notably, the blueprint for economic and social renewal that was accepted in principle in 1980-81 but never fully implemented was revived in 1986, and its incomplete application was acknowledged. Using this program as a starting point, a potentially more far-reaching "second stage of reform" was to be implemented in 1989-90, as a follow-up to the "round-table" negotiations between the government and opposition forces in April 1989.

The objectives of the Polish program—economic reform, social renewal, and national recovery—are shared in principle by the major actors inside and outside Poland. While the Polish state has first and primary responsibility for ensuring forward movement toward these goals, the contributions that each of the other actors can offer to the process may be critical to its prospects for success. If all the interested actors pursue a policy of providing specific contributions in return for fulfillment by the Polish leadership of its stated intentions (a process of conditionality), the blueprint may be implemented and produce positive results. Of course, none of the external forces, though they may be important in facilitating improvement, can serve as a guarantor of success. Only a demonstrated commitment to change within Poland can initiate the process and ensure its effective implementation.

The elements in an interactive process of conditionality and contributions might include the following, beginning with and dependent upon actions taken by the Polish state:

1. *Polish state:* implementation of a new plan (based on intensive, decentralized growth), reform of the economic mechanism, expansion of "pluralism," and implementation of an export strategy directed to the West which will improve debt management and hard-currency earnings.

2. *Polish society:* responsiveness to genuine opportunities for participation, through active involvement in worker and management organizations; the Sejm; and other participatory bodies.

3. *International financial community:* implementation of a policy of managing debt through growth, involving improvement in Poland's repayment conditions based on Polish acceptance of strict conditionality requirements on performance.

4. *United States:* completion of the diplomatic step-by-step process (removal of barriers) and initiation of a new stage of relations based on conditional, constructive reengagement. Congressional initiatives by Congressmen Rostenkowski, Fascell, and Hamilton, and Senator Kennedy, and the substantive visit of Vice President Bush to Poland in the fall of 1987 marked the beginning of a new phase in the U.S. policy of step-by-step reengagement with Poland.

5. *Soviet Union:* encouragement and facilitation of Polish economic reform and restructuring that, in the short run, may mean reduced deliveries to the USSR and longer-term debt management conditions.

What is clear about Poland's economic development is its past record—the poorest of any socialist economy in recent years. What is not clear, however, is the current policy commitment and what results it could achieve. The uniqueness of Poland's dynamics suggests that the major actors can contribute to either gridlock or to fulfillment of a strategy for significant progress. Therefore, the unique consensus among all key actors influencing Polish developments could take on considerable cumulative weight, if it results in a coordinated consensus policy that offers promise of improvement in Poland's economic prospects and escape from the traps of indebtedness and stagnation.

II. THE POLISH BLUEPRINT:
A BASIS FOR CONSENSUS

The crisis that erupted in Poland in 1980-81 and led to the prolonged economic and political stagnation that still persists had its roots in the policies of the 1970s. Although the factors contributing to the crisis have been well documented and described elsewhere, a brief review of the situation which gave rise to the Polish "blueprint" of 1980-81 and the fate of the blueprint since that time serves to highlight the importance of establishing a new consensus for reform and change.[1]

A.   Historical Perspective: The Evolution of the Blueprint

In the early 1970s there appeared to be a form of social contract between the Polish state and the governed—the centrally controlled system was not challenged in return for substantial improvement in living conditions. Since increased food prices had been the spark setting off demonstrations in 1970, leading to the removal of Gomulka, Gierek's predecessor, the supply of key consumer goods at constant prices, especially meat, was subsequently assured by the government. To the extent that this simplistic formulation of the social contract was maintained in the 1970s, it was ruptured by the turn of the decade.[2]

In July 1980, faced with a rapidly expanding external debt, Polish planners sought to reduce expenditures by indirectly raising the price of meat and holding down increases in wages. While these actions had an understandable economic purpose—reducing costly state subsidies—they ignited the tensions which had been building in Poland, leading to strikes, the founding of Solidarity, and the fall of the Gierek government. With these developments, the Communist Party's control and, perhaps more importantly, its claim to any legitimacy as the representative of the working people was thrown into serious question.

To address the economic and political crisis, a program for comprehensive reform, restructuring of the economy, and national dialogue was adopted by the Polish Party at the Ninth Extraordinary Party Congress in July 1981. Legislation mandating the program's implementation was approved by the Sejm over the period 1981-83. This blueprint for economic reform included elements of decentralization, price flexibility, greater enterprise autonomy, self-financing, and support of private sector activities in agriculture and services. As Paul Marer observed, however, even though the Polish leadership is on record as having approved reform and has repeatedly restated its commitment to the 1981 program, "reality is fundamentally different than the blueprint."[3]

During 1983-84, some stabilizing elements of the approved blueprint were put into place, leading to an end to economic decline and modest revival of growth, reduced inflation, and small trade surpluses, although these were not sufficient to keep pace with the country's debt-servicing requirements. To a large degree, significant reductions in investment, combined with a stringent austerity program made politically manageable by the imposition of martial law, allowed Poland to produce these results. Some analysts have noted that the inconsistent and piecemeal implementation of reforms, offset by the continuation of contradictory practices of the past, limited the reforms' effectiveness. In particular, Marer and Siwinski commented that "the kind of adjustments that have been implemented in Poland under martial law indicate that its leaders opted for short-term solutions of the 'expenditure reducing' type rather than the 'expenditure switching' kind."[4]

While some of the economic aspects of the blueprint were pursued in a limited and gradual way, the imposition of martial law and the suppression of Solidarity repudiated the consensus behind the reform program and the idea of national dialogue. The imposition of martial law also led to Poland's isolation internationally. Western support for and participation in Poland's development, support which had played a major role (through extensions of credit, preferential tariffs, active exchanges, and political interaction) in the growth strategy of the 1970s, was withdrawn. Sanctions imposed by the United States and Western Europe after martial law were made still more stringent following the Polish government's outlawing of Solidarity in 1982. As a result, from 1982 until 1986, Polish relations with the United States and with the West in general were strained and distant, rising and falling slightly depending upon internal developments in Poland.[5]

In the same time period, the Soviet Union was more benignly disengaged. To some extent, it provided spare parts and investment for export industries unable to compete in Western markets or to operate without Western spare parts, for example, textiles, coal, steel, and construction equipment. Some suggest that the Soviet Union began at this time to establish a degree of direct territorial control over some Polish enterprises using their exclusive market and investments as tools of negotiation.[6]

B.   1986-87: Emergence of a Consensus

During 1986, Poland's isolation began to slowly diminish as a number of events coalesced into new momentum for change. In this period, the various actors influencing developments in Poland—the Polish state, Polish society, the international financial community, the USSR and the United States—each took steps reaffirming the need for Poland to implement its blueprint but explicitly or implicitly acknowledged that renewal rhetoric had not yet been translated into action.

On May 29, 1986, the IMF, by majority vote, approved Poland's application to rejoin the organization, membership that included reentry to the World Bank as well. By regaining a degree of acceptance by the international financial institutions (five years after its initial application), Poland hoped to restore confidence among its creditors and obtain access to new credits. Still, it may be noted that it is unusual for the IMF and World Bank to accept into membership a country with such a serious debt burden, and it presented the institutions with unique problems. Thus, the initial level of support provided by the IMF and World Bank may well have been low, but the potential availability of significant resources under external economic conditionality (IMF credits would be available only under a standby program) provided an incentive to reform that had been missing in the past.

As the international financial community moved toward reengagement with Poland, an important shift in the Party's view of reform was indicated in General Jaruzelski's speech at the Tenth Congress of the Polish United Workers' Party (PZPR) in June 1986. In contrast to the past when party and government officials contended that the 1981 reform program had been fully implemented, Jaruzelski admitted at the Congress that reform had not, in fact, been consistently or effectively put into practice. After critically assessing the shortcomings in the economy, the Polish leader placed his full support behind the reform program and called for a general review of the nation's economic structures that "should support economic reform, reveal loopholes and shoals, and release various brakes." Encouraged, perhaps, by the example of Gorbachev's openness (glasnost) and frank criticism of his economy at the Twenty-Seventh CPSU Congress, Jaruzelski did not attempt to dodge the dilemmas of Polish economic development:

... either we reach the balance more quickly while accepting consequences related to it—a radical reduction of subsidies, the rationalization of prices, the strict observance of the self-financing principle, the strict regime of saving and labor discipline; receiving in exchange a good market, increased motivation to work, and therefore quicker growth in national income— or, by not accepting these rigors we will live longer with the burden of market shortages, the producer's advantage over the consumer, a permanent threat of speculation, weakened work incentive and reduced prospects for rapid development.[7]

The renewed commitment to reform at the highest levels of the Polish party was also expressed in studies prepared by government institutions—the Foreign Trade Ministry and PRON (Patriotic Movement for National Revival), institutions which had not been advocates of substantial economic change before.[8] Following up on Jaruzelski's call for a review of the economy, a Commission for the Economic Reform was created and charged with developing a reform program. In its "Theses for the Second Stage of the Economic Reform," published in April 1987, the Commission acknowledged that only "temporary solutions" had been implemented following the adoption of the 1981 blueprint and that the "second stage" would in fact represent the "faster implementation of these plans and changes in the functioning of the economy which are included in the 'Directions' adopted in 1981."[9]

In addition, there appeared to be renewed efforts in 1986 to expand the dialogue between the Party and the population and to build a consensus for reform. During martial law, the broad-based Polish opposition forced the Polish state and the Soviet Union to accept the fact that the clock could not be turned back to the 1950s in the state's relations with society, as essentially occurred in Czechoslovakia under Husak. Severely weakened in the economic and political crisis of 1980-81, the Polish Communist Party had been unable to recapture its authority; according to official statistics, total Party membership declined by one-third from July 1980 to May 1986.[10] Thus, it can be argued that the inability of the Polish state to remove a large-scale, well-supported opposition made resumption of national dialogue possible.

The nearly complete amnesty of political prisoners in September 1986 and the creation of the State Consultative Council suggested some accommodation to the continuing existence of opposition forces. Furthermore, the Sejm seemed to become a more active forum for debate in 1986-87, taking the unprecedented action of reversing two government proposals submitted in November 1986 which were said to weaken the decentralizing goals of reform. The church, too, became a more vocal advocate of democratization, particularly since the visit of the pope to Poland in the summer of 1987. As the independent Catholic weekly *Tygodnik Powszechny* concluded, the pope's message was one of activism against injustices: "During the first visit he woke us up, during the second he consoled us, and now he wants much more—he demands!"[11]

For those advocating reform and restructuring in Poland, developments in the USSR and the appearance of support by the top Soviet leadership for implementation of Poland's reform blueprint were other factors of great importance. At the Twenty-Seventh Soviet Party Congress, Gorbachev proclaimed the need for "radical reform" of the Soviet economy and in his first two years in power announced a number of important economic initiatives relevant to the Polish blueprint:

1.   Legalization of some forms of individual private enterprise and granting of a larger role for cooperative, family, and contract labor.

2.   Reform of the foreign trade structure allowing certain enterprises and ministries to have direct relations with foreign firms and legalizing equity joint ventures.

3.   Reform of the structure of planning and management involving significant reduction in the size and authority of the central planning bodies and increased autonomy in management for the enterprises.

The endorsement by the Soviet leadership of a program of reform and the encouragement of debate among economists on far-reaching issues such as unemployment, subsidies, and price reform aided Polish reformers in at least an indirect way: it precluded opponents of reforms in Poland from using fear of Soviet opposition as an argument for blocking progress. Moreover, the leaders of these countries publicly identified a major opponent of effective change as the ministerial bureaucracy in both Moscow and Warsaw.

Finally, the United States, beginning in November 1986, with a meeting between U.S. Assistant Secretary of State Rozanne Ridgway and Polish Deputy Foreign Minister Jan Kinast, initiated a process of step-by-step reengagement with Poland, following five years of disengagement based on U.S. sanctions. With indications of a revived commitment on the part of the Polish leadership to renewal and economic reform, and specific Polish actions which met the stated preconditions, the U.S. lifted its remaining sanctions in March 1987. A series of official U.S.-Polish meetings throughout 1987 began gradually to reestablish the diplomatic framework of bilateral relations, providing a crucial element in the developing consensus for Polish reform and opening the way for a more active U.S. role in encouraging change.

C. Implementation of the Blueprint:
A Process of Conditionality and Contributions

With the range of developments in 1986-87—reentry to the IMF/World Bank, renewed effort by the Polish state to advance economic reform and national dialogue, reinforcement of reform initiatives by Soviet domestic policies, and reengagement by the United States—a new environment was created for resolving Poland's crisis. By early fall 1987, the first stage may be seen as drawing to a close, as the barriers to a process of normalization were largely removed. Going further toward reengagement and recovery—entering the second stage—now requires the full implementation by the Polish state of the economic-reform objectives around which the new consensus has been built. Based on the "second stage of reform" blueprint and the discussion generated through its circulation during 1987, an implementation program of economic and political reform was submitted to the Sejm in October 1987. In principle, the United States, the international financial institutions, Polish society, and the Soviet Union support progress toward the shared goals of economic reform, social renewal, and national recovery—goals which are interrelated and mutually reinforcing.

What, specifically, is possible in terms of contributions to Poland's recovery from external actors? If the new program of restructuring, reform, export strategy, and socialist pluralism is actually put into practice in Poland, a longer-term process of reengagement might be set into motion, leading to favorable action on debt management and credit by the international financial institutions and Poland's creditors. This could be followed by the joint implementation of constructive reengagement programs— bilateral and multilateral programs that would foster constructive change and full normalization. But first, a credible and detailed program for implementation of the wide-ranging reforms agreed to in principle must be set into motion.

D.   Entering the Second Stage of Reform: The Critical Role of the Polish State

1.   Economic Reform

Managing debt with growth rather than austerity is a possibility now if Poland implements its plans for restructuring, reform, and increased exports. The debt servicing burden has approached 90%,[12] requiring, if fully paid, nine out of every ten dollars earned in hard currency to go toward paying interest and capital to creditors—an unsustainable level. If however, Poland can achieve and maintain a current account balance, the international financial and trading community might respond with positive, coordinated debt management policies that allow for the reduction of debt-service payments to a sustainable level, such as 30%.[13] Clearly, a strategy that allows for debt management through growth, rather than austerity, would bring economic recovery more closely within Poland's grasp. But entering into a comprehensive debt management program requires achieving a current account balance; increasing exports requires reform of the economic mechanism and institutions, and restructuring of the economy toward export industries.

Can Poland accomplish this? Jaruzelski has stated his intent to move forward, "The reform does not need applause but success of application." [14] The new economic reform package may contain the programs that fulfill his intent. According to the assessment of the World Bank, improvement in efficiency, investment, and creditworthiness is feasible, if Polish policy is based on increasing exports and a commitment to reaching a current account balance by 1991.[15] The internal and external adjustments that would be necessary to achieve these goals include the following:

1. Decentralization, involving not only mechanisms for self-management and self-financing, but the redefinition of the central administrative structure and institutional changes. Increased efficiency and responsiveness will depend on a real redistribution of authority and responsibility and the limitation of the role of branch ministries and other bodies that have traditionally influenced allocation and pricing decisions.

2. Implementation of price reforms and elimination of subsidies is required to establish market signals and create incentives for improved performance. However, the elimination of subsidies should be pursued carefully and selectively, with attention to the impact on consumers, whose continuing support for the objectives of the reform is crucial.

3. A new investment plan is needed since the current plan is based on the old principle of extensive, centrally controlled, East-oriented growth. It has been noted that reluctance to abandon old investment projects has continued to lead to greater than planned outlays of investment and lengthening of gestation periods. Most importantly, investment in outdated, unfinished projects often is unresponsive to economic and financial criteria.

4. Annual import plans should be linked to annual investment plans so that imports will be targeted to the most efficient and promising investment projects, particularly those which have potential for modernizing the domestic economy and expanding Poland's export capability.

5. A shift in the share of output exported (sufficient to achieve a current account balance) can be accomplished but requires improvement in the capacity of the economy to respond to opportunities, the elimination of domestic shortages, and adequate incentives for export.[16]

2. Socialist Renewal

Implementing plans for economic growth will also require the implementation of "some degree of pluralism," that is, broad democratization and participation of managers, workers, peasants, and society as a whole in an active process of government and managing the economy. By demonstrating a willingness to share power and the benefits of recovery, the Polish state might expect a healing of antagonism, a positive environment for productivity—a new social contract. Again, there is rhetorical evidence of Jaruzelski's intent:

> We will consistently implement the principle that whoever is the best is one of us, regardless of Party membership. In accordance with the Tenth Congress resolution, we favor a broad appointment of non-Party people to managerial and responsible posts ... As we've learned in the past, even the most beautiful and well constructed decisions and intentions, if they do not command the support of society, they fail.[17]

Translating these words into effective deeds and contributions to social confidence and support requires actions beyond the amnesty of political prisoners and the creation of the Consultative Council. The following actions are needed:

1.   Broadening of democratic participation in the economy and government of Poland is essential to win the support of society for economic reform.

2.   Given the strength of opposition forces in Polish society, reform cannot move forward without broad-based societal support—past crises following price increases provide evidence. Thus the state must find ways to engage the opposition and achieve real national reconciliation.

3.   "Increased pluralism" must be realized through the institutionalization of the rights of individuals, workers, managers, peasants, and parliament to make decisions and possess real authority. Only by granting these rights can the state expect Polish society to share responsibility for the implementation of difficult changes.

While the referendum carried out by the government in December 1987 may be significant as a symbolic recognition of the vital role of society in accepting and responding to reform, it is not a sufficient mechanism of participation; fully institutionalized forms of participation may be required for achieving real national reconciliation on which reform and recovery can be built. The opposition of Solidarity to the referendum and the disinterest of many in voting reflects the continuing perception that the government is interested only in a superficial endorsement of its decisions, not the active involvement of society in selecting among alternatives. Participation or acceptance of decision making might be extended through new mechanisms, such as cooperatives in services and agriculture, and through action to address environmental and health concerns. Two important caveats, however, with respect to expanded participation should be kept in mind:

1.   Participation in economic decisions that provides a basis for consensus, acceptance of mutual obligations, and equitable sacrifices is necessary; but micromanagement of the enterprise by workers' consensual decisions could be chaotic.

2.   Polish citizens are not like the Japanese or British in their traditional acceptance of the benefits of exports. Too often in the past, exports and inequitable austerity have been part of the Polish citizens' experience.

Politically, Poland has become unique in East Europe. In other East European countries, adjustment to macroeconomic crises or destabilization may be imposed by the party leadership and upheld by the central planning system, but in Poland forced compliance does not now appear feasible. The Polish authorities and Polish society can each precipitate gridlock but neither can effect change unilaterally. Therefore, the creation of genuine pluralism, as called for by the state and elements of Polish society, may represent the only way to attain effective consensus and full implementation of the second stage of economic reform. Furthermore, creation of institutionalized and assured bases for pluralism is an essential precondition for a positive assessment by the international financial community of the attainability of economic revitalization.

3.   National Recovery

Looking at the broader context, the implementation of Polish plans for economic reform and increased pluralism is essential for enhancing the independence of the sovereign Polish state. By reengaging with the Western market and governments and developing a firm base of domestic support, the Polish state could be more independent in its dealings with all external actors that critically influence its policy. Jaruzelski has expressed this hope,

"The rule of the people—when everyone may feel and become master in his own house, when he finds a place and the means for effective influence over the state and development of his own place of work, town and village, voivodship, and country—is becoming a fact."[18] While successful implementation of reforms leading to economic recovery may improve Poland's standing as a nation, such a recovery may be constrained if Poland does not assert its independence and avoid commitments that contradict its objectives of restructuring the economy and increasing exports to the West.

Having accepted in principle the need for far-reaching economic reform, social renewal, and national recovery, the Polish state must begin to tackle the challenge of implementing its blueprint in cooperation with Polish society. As one observer has noted, this is Poland's "principal, and perennial dilemma: the difficulty of applying solutions that nearly everyone agrees are correct to problems nearly everyone agrees require solutions."[19] Yet in an interactive process of conditionality and contributions involving all influential actors, the Polish state may have the opportunity to make the "impossible" possible in the wake of roundtable agreements and elections.

III. THE EXTERNAL ACTORS:
CONTRIBUTIONS AND CONDITIONS

Each of the external actors in Polish developments—the international financial institutions; the creditor governments, particularly the United States; and the Soviet Union—has an interest in successful Polish recovery and each has some means to contribute to that success. Under conditionality that ensures effective use of its contributions, each actor may pursue a specific program which, in concert with the actions of others, could make a critical difference in the implementation of reform and renewal, and the prospects for achieving recovery.

A.   The International Financial Community

A comprehensive, long-term package for debt management might provide an alternative to an austerity policy that places the burden of debt servicing on Polish society through further declines in the standard of living and further restrictions on new investment and imports, and a continuing policy of debt arrears which would lead to Poland's further isolation internationally. Such a growth-oriented debt management strategy could include a variety of elements—an IMF standby program, World Bank programs, Paris Club rescheduling, and new money from commercial banks—with each step building on the successful establishment of preceding steps, and responding to specific achievements of the Polish authorities in implementing reforms.

The *World Bank* may be first to move forward with a program if a credible plan for reform and export strategy is approved in Poland and becomes government policy. Such a bank program would focus first on project loans, directed to activities where they can have a direct, positive impact on Poland's balance of payments. Investment in spare parts, intermediate goods, and raw materials needed to increase exports—"de-bottlenecking" investment—could be closely linked to specific enterprises and sectors with the greatest export potential, for example, food processing, gas production, and lignite production. Rather than supporting investment in new plants, these projects would emphasize improving the efficiency and export potential of existing plants. According to observers, World Bank loans of this nature would likely be extended on a fifteen-year repayment schedule, with a three-year grace period. A second phase of lending, branching out into restructuring of investment and balance of payments support, could follow in the 1990s, if Poland remains current on its payments and has reached agreement on rescheduling with its government and commercial bank creditors.

A *stabilization program under the IMF* would be important for establishing greater confidence among Poland's creditors and the World Bank in policy reforms in Poland and responsiveness to conditionality. It would serve as a fundamental element in establishing a debt management strategy linked to growth, necessary to relieve some of the pressure of Poland's rising debt service burden. If Poland adheres to required conditionality, an IMF standby arrangement might be accompanied by a restructuring of the debt beyond the normal repayment period of ten years (up to twelve to twenty years), as well as new credits for investment.

(Informed observers estimate that about $350 million might be made available.)

An IMF precedent in restructuring Poland's debt could also affect the *approach of the Paris Club* governments in their rescheduling negotiations. Such parallel action by the Paris Club would multiply the benefits to Poland in terms of reduced immediate debt burden and widen the prospects for escaping the indebtedness trap. Going still further, creative debt management strategies might be considered as well, including for the government creditors the conversion of debt into local currency projects, building on the precedent of the U.S. Public Law 480, and for the commercial creditors, debt-equity swaps and debt-commodity swaps. Although discussions in the Paris Club on rescheduling Poland's debt were stalled during most of 1987, the commercial banks moved forward anyway, agreeing in July 1987 to a fifteen-year rescheduling of half the debt, with the other half awaiting comparable action by the Paris Club and the implementation of an IMF standby program. An initial agreement with the Paris Club was reached in November 1987 to reschedule payments due between 1986 and 1988 for ten years. While the United States—the most disengaged participant in the international financial constituency—is critical for initiating a conditional process, the leading role may subsequently shift to the Federal Republic of Germany as the largest holder of government and commercial debt.

B.   Gorbachev's Policy and Soviet Programs

The endorsement by Gorbachev of a program of reform and the encouragement of debate among economists on far-reaching issues such as unemployment, subsidies, and price reform has aided Polish reformers to the extent that opponents of reform can no longer use fear of Soviet opposition to generally block progress. Nevertheless, Soviet economic relations with Poland may, in practice, be inhibiting the implementation of reforms. Soviet encouragement of joint Soviet-Polish enterprises raises the possibility of increased Polish dependence on the USSR and increased flow of domestically needed resources and output to the East. Furthermore, by promoting continued Polish investment in industries that serve Soviet needs (for example, coal and steel), the trade relationship with the USSR makes deep restructuring of the Polish economy and orientation toward export industries more difficult.

Given these concerns, Western governments and financial institutions would likely look for assurances that increases in Poland's production and financial resources were not flowing to the Soviet Union to the detriment of achieving stated restructuring goals. Western flexibility on Polish debt would need to be met with a comparable degree of accommodation on the part of Eastern partners.

C. Advancing the Step-by-Step Approach: Options for U.S. Policy

The role of the United States in this interaction of policy forces may at first glance seem relatively minor and U.S. policy instruments relatively weak. The funds available to the U.S. government for foreign assistance are severely limited, given the restraints posed by the huge budget deficit; furthermore, Poland's debt to the United States and to U.S. banks has been said to be too small to stimulate new debt management schemes.[20] But the potential impact of even small amounts of assistance, carefully targeted, should not be underestimated.[21] To the extent that assistance relieves a bottleneck in the economy or releases scarce hard currency for imports needed to expand exports, it can have a multiplier effect on Poland's productive capacity. Furthermore, bilateral interaction, even on a small scale, could help to increase the morale of Polish society and confidence in the prospect of effective change by providing a connection with the West that might promise not only new economic resources, but a credible alternative source of assurance outside both the Polish regime and the Soviet Union. Through a variety of limited efforts responding to Polish actions and signalling U.S. support, a momentum might be generated that would expand the scope of support by other actors as well, and thus the overall possibilities for improvement in Poland's economic conditions. In this regard, it might be noted that the money market often reacts much more quickly to small changes in the environment than political-economic assessments would seem to justify.[22]

As an influential participant in the IMF, the World Bank, and the Paris Club, the United States can have a critical impact on whether, and how, a coordinated, interactive response to Polish reforms takes place. Therefore, as the Polish government demonstrates a commitment to put its rhetoric into practice and move forward, the U.S. could play a key role in setting the "money trail" in motion and moving beyond diplomatic normalization to full reengagement in bilateral relations with Poland, with the net benefit of probable reduced U.S. losses of unpaid Polish debt and increased leverage in encouraging beneficial changes in Poland. President Bush's support of the round-table results and his July 1989 visit to Poland underlines U.S. support of new Polish resolve.

As described in the chart below, the United States undertook, beginning in late 1986, a step-by-step process of diplomatic exchange with Poland, culminating with the exchange of ambassadors announced in September 1987. The transition of U.S. policy from stage one—diplomatic normalization—to stage two, constructive reengagement began in 1987, as evidenced first by then Vice President Bush's trip to Poland and actions undertaken by Congress. House Ways and Means Committee Chairman Dan Rostenkowski, who played an important role in furthering U.S.-Polish relations in 1987, stated in his report to the Speaker of the House:

> We are close to finishing the process of normalization of our diplomatic relations with Poland ... Now is an especially propitious time to explore the next steps in substantive improvement that we might find in our mutual interest. Some modest U.S. programs that might benefit the Polish citizenry and serve interests we share have been advanced in provisions added to H.R. 3, the 1987 Trade Bill, during Senate debate. I largely support the generous purposes of these provisions and will work in the Conference Committee to bring them to enactment.[23]

During his October 1987 visit to Poland, the vice president, while stressing the need for internal reforms in Poland as a precondition for deepening U.S.-Polish relations, announced that agreement had been reached on exchanging ambassadors, marking the final step in diplomatic normalization. Taking the next step forward toward substantive reengagement, Mr. Bush stated that the United States would support Poland's debt rescheduling in the Paris Club, indicating an important shift in policy.

If the United States should choose to move beyond the diplomatic elements of reengagement to a more active agenda of supporting debt management and genuine pluralism, as seems to be indicated by these events, a number of forums could provide opportunities for leadership and involvement:

1.   If negotiations in the IMF for a standby program go forward, the United States could play a significant role in shaping the terms and scope of the agreement, should it decide to fully exercise U.S. influence in support of the IMF process.

2.   With an IMF program in place, the United States might move forward with new initiatives for dealing with the government debt. One approach, building on the precedent of P.L. 480, might be to convert some debt to support local currency projects in Poland that the United States considers in its interest, in essence using U.S. leverage over Polish funds to benefit Polish society in specific ways. Examples of projects might be found in proposals for cooperative water projects in rural areas, support for private agriculture, or educational and scientific exchange. An initiative of this kind might be followed by other Paris Club creditors with the result of further reducing some of Poland's immediate debt burden. Here the Federal Republic of Germany is the logical candidate.

3.   With respect to Poland's debt to commercial banks, the U.S. government, in an active debt management approach, might address the regulatory issue of requiring banks to hold assets that total 50% of Polish debt. The banks contend that this requirement limits efforts to pursue innovative debt strategies such as debt-to-equity swaps, which might allow them to get more of the debt back than waiting for full repayment.

4.   Action has been initiated by Congress to provide small amounts of new funding for a variety of projects in Poland. The "American Aid to Poland Act of 1987"[24] provided $10 million for the church-sponsored Polish Agricultural Foundation to support water projects on Polish private farms; $2 million for medical supplies and hospital equipment; $1 million for implementation of the U.S.-Polish Science and Technology Agreement; and $1 million for support of Solidarity, which Solidarity leaders have stated will be used for medical supplies.[25] The legislation also authorized the donation of surplus agricultural commodities to

voluntary organizations and cooperatives in Poland which may use the proceeds from their sales for U.S.-approved local currency projects.

5.   In the wake of the re-legalization of Solidarity, the U.S. may consider granting Poland preferential tariff status under the Generalized System of Preferences (GSP) and access to Overseas Private Investment Corporation (OPIC) investment guarantees.

Although these means of action are available to the United States, the U.S. also has the option of doing less, reverting to the policy of disengagement that led the U.S. to abstain in the IMF/World Bank entrance votes and to refrain from participation in the Paris Club rescheduling talks. Without a substantive response from the Polish government to implement economic and political reform, there would likely be little substantive action by the United States. The Sisyphean process, where step-by-step improvement begins, only to be reversed again, has been set in motion many times in the past.

Taken together, though, the prospect of contributions from each major actor could provide the impetus and incentive for the Polish state to move forward. While each actor's potential for support may seem small and insufficient when considered alone, a number of factors could act as multipliers on the effectiveness of a coordinated, conditional effort. First, if new funds are supplied only for highly sensitive, critical investments with potential for removing bottlenecks, the economic benefits may be proportionately larger than the dollar amount of credit might suggest. Second, modest improvement in Poland's performance, particularly improved debt servicing, could lead to increased availability of external financing given the evidence of behavior of financial markets with respect to Eastern Europe. Finally, a new degree of involvement and authority of well-qualified political economists in determining policy in Poland (for example, Sadowski, Trzeciakowski, and working groups involved in discussions with the World Bank and IMF) may promise greater sophistication in devising and implementing economically effective and politically viable programs. It remains to be seen whether these factors which could maximize the impact of reform and policy changes will in fact be fully utilized. Paradoxically, Poland's future seems to hold out more difficult challenges but also greater promise than that of any other country in Eastern Europe.

Table 1.   The Agenda of U.S.-Polish Step-by-Step Reengagement

Stage 1:   Removal of Barriers

11/86	Meeting between U.S. Assistant Secretary of State Rozanne Ridgway and Polish Foreign Ministry official Jan Kinast in Vienna
2/87	U.S. Deputy Secretary of State Whitehead visited Poland, met with Jaruzelski
3/87	U.S. sanctions lifted; Delegation from Poland's Sejm visited Washington
4/87	Deputy Assistant Secretary of Commerce Frank Vargo went to Warsaw; Congressional delegation led by House Foreign Affairs Committee Chairman Fascell visited Poland
5/87	CSCE official visited Warsaw; Sen. Kennedy visited Warsaw, Gdansk
6/87	Second round of negotiations on U.S.-Polish S & T Agreement was held
	Polish parliamentary delegation visited Washington
	U.S.-Polish Chamber of Commerce meeting held in Poland
	Poznan Trade Fair opened with Rep. Rostenkowski representing the U.S. and with U.S. firms participating
7/87	Polish Minister of Environment visits Washington for signing of cooperation agreement with EPA
9/87	Vice President Bush visited Poland, agreement reached on exchange of ambassadors; Science and Technology Agreement signed

Stage 2:   Charting a New Course

Fall 1987	Submission of Polish government's economic and political reform programs to the Sejm
	IMF Article IV Consultation on Poland
	Issuance of World Bank study of Poland's economy

Stage 3:   Joint Implementation of Constructive Reengagement Programs

1987-88	Rescheduling of Polish debt by Paris Club and commercial banks
	World Bank consideration of sectoral and/or project loans for Poland
	Rockefeller/Ford Foundation program to develop Polish private agriculture—first project relating to swine production
	Support of water projects in Poland using $10 million already appropriated for private agriculture fund
	Support of science and technology exchange; Marie-Sklodowska Curie fund might be supplemented with zloty funds converted from debt
	Support of agricultural programs under Section 416 making surplus commodities available for donation or exchange
	Support of educational, medical, and cultural exchange such as Judiac studies program, Project Hope, The Children's Hospital in Krakow
	Debt-for-nature swap involving U.S. conservation organizations
	Western aircraft for LOT through innovative financing

IV. THE UNIQUENESS OF POLAND AND PROSPECTS FOR CHANGE

In both political and economic terms, Poland holds a special place in Eastern Europe and is unique as a member of the Soviet-led alliances, the Warsaw Pact, and CMEA. Located in the heart of Europe, Poland has historically played a key geopolitical role, its borders changing repeatedly as claims have been laid on its territory and sovereignty by Russia, the Soviet Union, Germany, and other countries. In the historic balance of power in Europe, Poland occupies a pivotal position between Germany, Russia, and the Soviet Union, its control often being critical to the maintenance of power in Europe. In the historical memory of Europe, Poland has always seemed to be at the center of European struggles. Since its incorporation into the East European "bloc" in the postwar years, Poland has remained unique in the strength of its links to Western Europe and has a long history of orientation toward Western institutions.[26]

Poland has always had a unique degree of pluralism:

1. Institutions outside the central authority—especially the Catholic Church—have provided independent sources of education, media, cultural tradition; the church has been a special bulwark of Polish tradition in periods of occupation.
2. Polish agriculture regained a large private or individual sector after 1956, despite earlier efforts to collectivize, and private enterprise provides a significant portion of services throughout the economy.
3. Since Solidarity, there is relatively more independence in Polish society than elsewhere in East Europe, with some moderate worker participation in management.
4. Wide-ranging debates in the moderately controlled press have continued, even under martial law.
5. Military rule has superseded party dominance—the first example of military control in a Warsaw Pact country.
6. The Sejm has become an important forum with some influence on policy and a channel of popular participation in policy.

If the Polish second stage of reform is successful, pluralism in Poland could be more extensive than anywhere else in the socialist world. But the unique characteristics of Poland suggest that the alternatives for its future lie either in progress or decline and that continued reliance on "muddling through" may no longer be an option. Unlike the other communist countries of Eastern Europe, Poland has not possessed the political stability necessary for the state to impose unpopular economic adjustment measures on the population in times of crisis. As a result, until the government-opposition round-table negotiation in 1989, attempts to resolve its economic problems and debt crisis had led consistently to political stalemate, with the Polish regime unable to force the implementation of economic reforms but unwilling to permit the degree of political pluralism necessary to gain societal support.

Kazimierz Poznanski, in an analysis of this uniquely Polish phenomenon, concludes:

> The lesson from Poland's recent past is that the current system does not provide a forum for negotiating conflicting interests, whether those interests are inside the party or outside it. The lack of such political procedures does not hamper the effective functioning of most countries with effectively suppressed group interests—most of the East European countries and the Soviet Union in particular. Yet the extent of the conflicting interests in Poland—the actual rejection of communist ideology by a majority of workers and their commitment to Catholicism instead—and the fact that the PUWP is a deeply divided party still in search of some kind of identity make Poland's economic crisis a unique case (Poznanski 1986).

While Poznanski views the unique degree of pluralism existing in Poland as a constraint on recovery, it might instead be considered as an opportunity. Because of the strength of competing interests, the development of pluralism may be both necessary and possible. The events in Poland in 1989—re-legalization of Solidarity and implementation of significant political reforms—suggest the Polish government has recognized this. If genuine participatory mechanisms are successfully implemented, they could provide the basis for establishing confidence and support for the Polish state's economic reform initiatives, first within Polish society itself, then in the international community. Thus, such steps toward institutionalized pluralism could have an exponential impact in a positive direction on conditions in Poland.

By the same token, failure by the Polish state to establish a means of breaking the stalemate with society could build exponentially in a negative direction, spurring increasing cynicism, confrontation, and isolation. In such a situation, the growth of debt would become insurmountable, possibly entailing formal renunciation and default. The possibilities of recovery would severely diminish. Thus, actions taken by Poland in the short term to begin implementation of the initiatives that the regime has in essence endorsed, are critical for setting in motion a positive train of action that could chart the course toward significant debt-service reduction, new credits, and opportunities for new investment.

It is difficult to predict whether the necessary leadership decisions in Warsaw and Washington will or should be made to enter into a new stage of bilateral relations beyond diplomatic normalization. The spirit of change has been expressed in Poland and ratified in Moscow, and the substance of political reform has emerged from the round-table negotiations of 1989. These developments offer promise for establishing mechanisms and institutions that assure the second stage of reform will be translated into effective change. Such mechanisms would include:

1. A new economic plan redirecting priorities, establishing functional, new planning and management forms and establishing an export orientation to the world market.
2. Institutionalization of the rights of workers, peasants, and managers to assure their ability to participate in and contribute to a political-economic consensus.

These institutionalized and assured bases for political pluralism are essential preconditions for a positive assessment by the international financial community and the United States of the attainability of economic revitalization. But if the common interests of both societies can be served in charting and setting out on this new course, the outcome would likely be beneficial to both partners. The benefits to the United States would be both economic and strategic:

1. A Polish economic recovery under a coordinated debt management framework would increase the probability and predictability of future debt repayment.
2. The creation of institutionalized mechanisms of participation and pluralism would be encouraged as a necessary condition for obtaining the support of Polish society for reform, and hence, the support of Western financial institutions and creditors for support of debt management.
3. Economic recovery and the implementation of socialist pluralism would contribute to Poland's independence as a sovereign state and would reduce the prospects of serious economic and political destabilization in Poland that could have negative implications for U.S. interests in Europe and that would increase the burden borne by the Polish people.

Moreover, the costs of failing to develop a new basis for constructive reengagement would be equally high. If the course is charted for implementation of effective reform and socialist pluralism, a variety of U.S.-Polish bilateral programs of mutual interest may be pursued with vigor, building bridges in bilateral commerce, education, culture, and politics. The traditional affinity of the United States and Poland may in this new context allow for a greater scope of mutually reinforcing efforts than at any time in the past.

Still, the entrance to the second stage of relations remains very problematic. Winning the confidence and support of society, overcoming traditional ministerial resistance, and minimizing the constraints of relations between socialist and capitalist systems remain daunting challenges. Thus, while there may now be a means of escaping from the indebtedness trap—a window of opportunity for Polish recovery—the prospects for translating opportunity into achievement depend on demonstrated changes in Poland and concerted response from the international community.

ACKNOWLEDGMENTS

This paper represents the views of the authors and not necessarily those of the Congressional Research Service or the Library of Congress.

NOTES

1.   For a more detailed discussion of the roots of the crisis see U.S. Congress, House Committee on Foreign Affairs, Subcommittee on Europe and the Middle East, *Poland's Renewal and U.S. Options: A Report prepared by the Congressional Research Service*, 100th Congress, 1st Session, March 7, 1987.

2.   The use of the term social contract in this context can be subject to various interpretations; for discussion of this issue, see Comisso and Tyson (1986).

3.   Marer and Siwinski (1986), p. 26. A comprehensive discussion of the recent history and prospects for reform in Poland can be found in the book which grew out of this conference, Marer and Siwinski (1988).

4.   Ibid., 10.

5.   See House Committee on Foreign Affairs, *Poland's Renewal and U.S. Options*, for a summary of U.S.-Polish relations from 1982-1986.

6.   See Staniszkis (1987).

7.   Jaruzelski, W. (1986).

8.   "Poland's Foreign Debt Problem ..." (1986) and "PRON Report on Economic Reform" (1986).

9.   "Theses for the Second Stage ..." (1987).

10.   Radio Free Europe (1986).

11.   *Tygodnik Powszechny* (1987).

12.   The World Bank (1987).

13.   An historical parallel illustrates the problem in managing the debt through austerity. In 1922-26 there was a Polish financial crisis involving hyperinflation and severe depreciation of the zloty against foreign currencies. The first approach, the Grabski Plan, initiated in 1924, resolved the hyperinflation through increased taxes, sharply reduced government expenditures, and loans floated in the United States and Italy. The tempoprary stabilization gave way to renewed concern of return of hyperinflation and depreciation of the zloty in 1925-26; a renewed crisis contributed to the unsettled political envirionment that facilitated the military coup in May 1926 by General Jozef Pilsudski. See Leland B. Yeager and Associates (1981).

14.   Jaruzelski (1987).

15.   This conclusion—that a current account balance by 1991 is obtainable— is reinforced by Poland's improved export performance in the first half of 1987, up 14.1% over the same period last year to $3.3 billion, resulting in a $780 million surplus. *Business Eastern Europe*, August 24, 1987.

16.   See the World Bank (1987).

17.   Jaruzelski (1987), G5.

18.   Ibid., G4.

19.   Brumberg (1987).

20.   Poland's debt to the U.S. Government was $2.3 billion and its unguaranteed debt to U.S. banks was only about $500 million. As was noted at a 1987 conference, "Poland is much less a threat to the world monetary system or the banks than it was. No precedents on debt renegotiation will be established in the Polish case, for fear that the larger international debtors will follow suit." See Johnson (1987).

21.   Carefully targeted, small amounts of funding may in fact be more effective in promoting productive policies; the policy of "uncritical preference" of the 1970s under which large credits were extended without conditions may be considered to have contributed to the economic crisis. See U.S. Congress, House Committee on Foreign Affairs (1987).

22.   See Gaydeczka (1987).

23.   Rostenkowski (1987). In the U.S. step-by-step reengagement with Poland, Members of Congress have played an active and supportive role in the process through meetings in Washington and in Poland and through legislation.

24.   See the *Congressional Record* (1987). The "American Aid to Poland Act" was passed by the Senate as an amendment to the omnibus trade bill, S 1420.

25.   Walesa (1987).

26.   For further discussion of Poland's uniqueness, see U.S. Congress, House Committee on Foreign Affairs (1987).

REFERENCES

Brumberg, A. "A New Deal in Poland?" *The New York Review* 33 (January 15, 1987): p. 36.

Business Eastern Europe 16 (August 24, 1987): p. 272.

Congressional Record, 100th Cong., 1st sess. (July 15, 1987), S9996-S10001.

Comisso, E., and L. D'Andrea Tyson (eds.). *Power, Purpose, and Collective Choice: Economic Strategy in Socialist States.* Ithaca, NY: Cornell University Press, 1986.

Gaydeczka, P. "Eastern Europe and Yugoslavia in the 1980s: Market Perceptions and Economic Performance." Paper presented at the Conference on Economic Dilemmas of Eastern Europe in the Late 1980s: Reform, Trade and Finance, East European Program, Wilson Center, Washington, DC, September 24-25, 1987.

Jaruzelski, W. Address to the Second PRON Congress in Warsaw, May 8, 1987. *Trybuna Ludu* (May 8-9, 1987). Translated in FBIS Daily Report, Eastern Europe, (May 12, 1987), G3.

_____. Political Report delivered to the 10th PZPR Congress, Warsaw (June 29, 1986). Translated in FBIS Daily Report, Eastern Europe (July 1, 1986), G16.

Johnson, A.R., Chair. *United States Policy Toward Poland: A Conference Report.* Santa Monica, CA: RAND, April 1987.

Marer, P., and W. Siwinski. *Summary Report and Analysis of the Conference on the Polish Economy and Debt: Can Poland's Creditworthiness be Reestablished?* Washington, DC: The Wilson Center, The Smithsonian Institution, January 31, 1986.

Marer, P., and W. Siwinski (eds.). *Creditworthiness and Reform in Poland.* Bloomington, IN: Indiana University Press, 1988.

"Poland's Foreign Debt Problem and Ways of Resolving It: Report of The Foreign Trade Ministry's Institute of Business Trends and Prices (IKG HZ) and [the Planning Commission's] National Economy Institute (IGN)." *Rzeczpospolita* 222 (Sept. 23, 1986). Translated in the Polish News Bulletin of the British and American Embassies, Warsaw, Economic Review, No. 78-86.

Poznanski, K. "Economic Adjustment and Political Forces: Poland Since 1970." *International Organization* 40 (Spring 1986): p. 488.

"PRON Report on Economic Reform." *Odrodzenie* 24 (June 14, 1986). Translated in the Polish News Bulletin of the British and American Embassies, Warsaw, Economic Review, June 27, 1986.

Radio Free Europe, Situation Report 11 (July 22, 1986).

Rostenkowski, D. "Time is Right for Improving Relations with Poland." *Congressional Record,* 100th Cong., 1st sess. (September 9, 1987), H3472-3473.

Staniszkis, J. "The Dynamics of Dependency." Paper presented at colloquium of the East European Program, the Wilson Center, Washington, D.C., August 27, 1987.

"Theses for the Second Stage of Economic Reforms (Summary with Comments)" *Contemporary Poland,* Special edition (June-July 1987): pp. 2-3.

Tygodnik Powszechny, June 21, 1987. Translated in FBIS. "Pope John Paul II's Challenge to Jaruzelski." Media Analysis, July 29, 1987.

U.S. Congress, House Committee on Foreign Affairs, Subcommittee on Europe and the Middle East. *Poland's Renewal and U.S. Options: A Report prepared by the Congressional Research Service,* 100th Congress, 1st Session, March 7, 1987.

Walesa, L. "Letter to the United States Congress, August 11, 1987." *Solidarność News* 96 (August 31, 1987): pp. 1-2.

World Bank. *Poland: Reform, Adjustment and Growth.* Washington, DC: The World Bank, October 1987. Report No. 6736-POL, Volume 1, 62.

Yeager, L.B. and Associates. *Experiences with Stopping Inflation.* Washington, DC: American Enterprise Institute, 1981.

Index